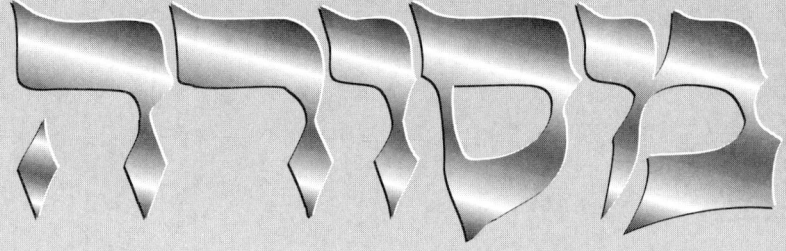

ArtScroll Series®

Rabbi Nosson Scherman / Rabbi Meir Zlotowitz
General Editors

Published by

Mesorah Publications, ltd

חכמת חיים

RABBI YOSEF CHAIM
SONNENFELD
on the Parashah

Compiled by
Rabbi Shlomo Zalman Sonnenfeld

Translated by
Rabbi Yaakov Blinder

FIRST EDITION
First Impression ... October 2002

Published and Distributed by
MESORAH PUBLICATIONS, LTD.
4401 Second Avenue / Brooklyn, N.Y 11232

Distributed in Europe by
LEHMANNS
Unit E, Viking Industrial Park
Rolling Mill Road
Jarow, Tyne & Wear, NE32 3DP
England

Distributed in Australia and New Zealand by
GOLDS WORLD OF JUDAICA
3-13 William Street
Balaclava, Melbourne 3183
Victoria, Australia

Distributed in Israel by
SIFRIATI / A. GITLER — BOOKS
6 Hayarkon Street
Bnei Brak 51127

Distributed in South Africa by
KOLLEL BOOKSHOP
Shop 8A Norwood Hypermarket
Norwood 2196, Johannesburg, South Africa

Typography by CompuScribe at ArtScroll Studios, Ltd.

Printed in the United States of America by Noble Book Press Corp.
Bound by Sefercraft, Quality Bookbinders, Ltd., Brooklyn N.Y. 11232

☙ Table of Contents

ספר בראשית
BEREISHIS / GENESIS

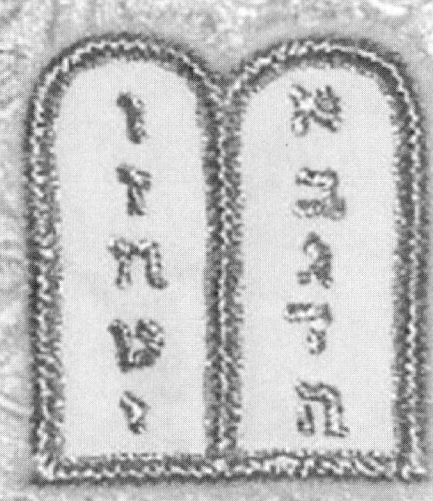

פרשת בראשית
PARASHAS BEREISHIS

◈§ The One Day

וַיְהִי־עֶרֶב וַיְהִי־בֹקֶר יוֹם אֶחָד — *And there was evening and there was morning, one day* (1:5).

*A*ll the other six days of creation are referred to with ordinal numbers: *second*, *third*, *fourth*, etc. Why, in this instance, is the first day called "one day" rather than "first day"?

Rashi addresses this question and answers that the first day was unique in that it was the only day during creation in which God was the sole being, for the angels came into existence on the second day. In this sense, the first day was "a day of oneness," and is therefore referred to as the "one day."

Rav Yosef Chaim suggested another answer to this question as well. As Rashi tells us later (2:4), all the creations of the world were brought into existence on the first day; on the subsequent days, they were placed in their proper position. Thus, it was only on the first day that God created anything *ex nihilo* — out of nothing. It is for this reason that this day is called "one day," for it was "one" — unique in the manner of creation that took place on it.

◆§ The Great Divide

וַיִּקְרָא אֱלֹקִים לָרָקִיעַ שָׁמָיִם וַיְהִי־עֶרֶב וַיְהִי־בֹקֶר יוֹם שֵׁנִי — *God called the firmament "Heaven." And there was evening and there was morning, a second day* (1: 8).

The Midrash notes that unlike each of the other six days of creation, the phrase "And there was evening" is not preceded by the statement that "God saw that what He created (on that day) was good." Why, asks the Midrash, did God not express His approval for what was created on the second day?

The answer given by Rabbi Chanina in the Midrash is that on the second day, division (or *divisiveness*, for both words are represented by the same Hebrew word, מַחְלוֹקֶת) came into being, as the Torah states, "God made the firmament, and it *divided* between the waters which were beneath the firmament and the waters which were above the firmament" (1:7). God did not want to ascribe the tribute of "goodness" to any day that involved division, for divisiveness is the very antithesis of peace and goodness.

The Midrash's explanation raises a difficulty, however. On the first day of creation the Torah tells us that "God divided between the light and the darkness" (1:4). The idea of "division," then, is mentioned on the first day as well, yet God did not hesitate to declare on that day, "God saw that it was good" (ibid.)! What, then, is the difference between the "division" that took place on the first day and that of the second day?

Rav Yosef Chaim resolved this difficulty as follows: Light and darkness represent two opposing forces, they cannot function together. The division between these two opposite entities is thus a positive — and a necessary — act. For this reason it is entirely appropriate to refer to this division as "good." The division between the upper and lower waters, however, was a separation between two items of the same substance. When one separates light and dark, good and evil, that is good. But when there is a separation between forces that can work together, that is considered unfortunate, and thus undeserving of the appellation "good."

This distinction bears an important lesson for us in our dealings with others. As reprehensible as contention and controversy are, there are times when it is a necessary and good phenomenon. When struggling against the forces of evil we must implement a clear and total separation between ourselves and our opponents. It is in a situation in which two parties strive for positive goals, but disagree as to the manner of pursuing or presenting those goals, that divisiveness and strife must be avoided at all costs.

⊷§ The Lunar Cycle — Precise Calculation

וְהָיוּ לְאֹתֹת וּלְמוֹעֲדִים וּלְיָמִים וְשָׁנִים — *And they (the heavenly luminaries) shall serve as signs, and for festivals, and for days and years* (1:14).

One of the main functions of the sun and moon is to use their positions to measure time and calculate months and years. The Jewish calendar is unique in that it uses both the sun and the moon to determine dates and the transition of years.

The Sages, with their advanced astronomical knowledge, determined (see *Rosh Hashanah* 25a) that the average lunar month lasts 29 days and 793 "chalakim" (a "chelek" is 1/1080 of an hour, or 3.333 seconds).

Rav Yosef Chaim found an allusion to this figure in the phrase in *Tehillim* (104:19): עָשָׂה יָרֵחַ לְמוֹעֲדִים "He made the moon for determining times [of the year]," the numerical value of which is 793!

⊷§ Pride of the Moon

וַיַּעַשׂ אֱלֹקִים אֶת־שְׁנֵי הַמְּאֹרֹת הַגְּדֹלִים — *And God made the two great luminaries* (1:16).

Here both the sun and moon are described as "great luminaries," while immediately afterwards the Torah refers to them respectively as "the great luminary" and the "small luminary." Rashi cites the Midrash's explanation for this discrepancy: Originally the sun and the moon were the same size, both of them "great luminaries." The moon, however, came before God and complained, "It is impossible to have two kings reigning at the same time!" God responded, "Very well, go and diminish your size!" The moon protested, "Is it fair that just because I raised a valid point I should be punished by diminishing my size?!" (*Chullin* 60b).

The moon seems to have presented a good argument. Why was it fair to punish it with diminishment of its size? All it did was to point out a difficulty, which was in fact quite sound! Furthermore, the Sages intimate elsewhere that God Himself afterward admitted that decreasing the moon's size was indeed something of an unfair penalty (*Shevuos* 9a). How, then, should we understand the punishment in this story?

Rav Yosef Chaim explained that the message of this story is that humility demands not merely that we not consider ourselves greater than others, but that we actually view our fellow man as greater than ourselves. One who considers himself to be equal to his fellow deserves to be "cut down to size."

This sentiment is expressed in the words of the Ramban in his *Iggeres* (Epistle) as well: "Let your head hang low, and your eyes cast their glance downward while your heart is directed upward. Let every person seem greater than you in your eyes." Sometimes just considering oneself to be an equal is presumptuous!

⋙ Strife for Truth

וַיֹּאמֶר אֱלֹקִים נַעֲשֶׂה אָדָם — *And God said, "Let us make man"* (1:26).

*T*he Midrash relates that the angels were divided in their opinion as to whether man should indeed be created or not. Basing itself on the verse "Kindness and truth encountered each other; benevolence and peace collided" (*Tehillim* 85:11), it gives the following fascinating account of the debate:

Kindness said man *should* be created, for he bestows kindness on others; Truth, however, argued that man should not be created, for he is full of falsehood. Benevolence voted in favor of man's creation, for he is benevolent in nature; Peace was opposed to man's creation, for he is full of contention. [The vote was thus two against two.]

What did God do? He took Truth and cast it down to earth [leaving a majority in favor of the creation of man].

If God wanted to solve the deadlock by eliminating one of the votes against man's creation, why did He choose to cast Truth down to earth? He could just as well have eliminated Peace, the other opponent of the plan!

Rav Yosef Chaim proposed the following answer: By casting Truth down to earth, God was in effect removing its reason for opposition — that man was full of falsehood. Now that Truth was thrown to the earth, man would be endowed with the ability to act with truth and honesty. Man's other shortcoming — that he was full of contention and conflict — remained, however. Had God chosen to silence Peace by sending it down to earth, man's problem of contentiousness would have been ameliorated, but his flaw of tending toward falsehood would have remained.

By sending down Truth, explained Rav Yosef Chaim, God was teaching us that it is preferable to have a battle waged in an honest quest for truth, rather than have peace borne of falsehood!

⋖§ Man's Creativity

כִּי בוֹ שָׁבַת מִכָּל־מְלַאכְתּוֹ אֲשֶׁר־בָּרָא אֱלֹקִים לַעֲשׂוֹת — *Because on it He abstained from all His work which God created to make* (2:3).

What is meant by the seemingly superfluous words, "to make"? Rav Yosef Chaim explained that during the six days of creation God provided the world with an endless array of natural resources, but thereafter it became man's task to harness and develop these resources and *to make* something constructive out of the world in which he lives.

Rav Yosef Chaim provided a *gematria* allusion to this concept as well. In *Tehillim* 119:126 we read, "It is time to act" (*to act* and *to make* are represented by the same word in Hebrew, לעשות). The Hebrew word for *it is time* is עת, which has the numerical value of 470. Now, there are exactly 470 words in the Torah's story of the creation of the world, from *Bereishis* 1:1 to 2:4. The verse can thus be interpreted to mean, "The 470 [units that went into Creation] are for acting upon!"

Rav Yosef Chaim added a further insight into this idea. It is God's will that man strive toward his own personal development and perfect himself. This is why, unlike any other creature, he comes into this world utterly helpless, unable to move from place to place or even to eat without these necessities being directly provided to him by his parent. Growth to adulthood takes an incredible 13 years — all because God wants the development and upbringing of man, the crown of creation, to be gradual and to be accomplished only through a great deal of effort and thought.

An allusion to this concept is sometimes read homiletically into the verse, "The advantage of man over beast is nothing" (*Koheles* 3:19). Unlike animals, who are born with certain minimal capabilities required for survival — or attain them shortly thereafter — human beings are born totally incapable of doing anything for themselves. But this "flaw" is actually an indication of man's superiority over animals, as explained above. "The advantage of man over beast is [that he is born with] absolutely nothing!"

◄§ Unlimited Growth Potential

וַיִּפַּח בְּאַפָּיו נִשְׁמַת חַיִּים — *And He blew into his nostrils the soul of life* (2:7).

*M*an is unique in creation in that he carries within him a soul that emanates from on high, from God Himself.

One time, at the funeral of Rav Yitzchak Yerucham Diskin (the son of Rav Yehoshua Leib Diskin) on the Mount of Olives, someone took hold of Rav Yosef Chaim's arm to help him manage the steep descent from the hillside cemetery. He declined the assistance, asserting that he could manage fine on his own. When the man insisted, Rav Yosef Chaim waxed philosophical. "You are making a mistake," he told him. "You think it is more dangerous to walk down a hill than it is to ascend it! But the fact is that when a person descends there is a limit to how far he can go; eventually he gets to the bottom of the decline and regains his footing. When it comes to climbing up, however, there is no end to the heights to which a person can ascend. Man's soul emanates from the highest imaginable source, and his potential for growth and achievement is infinite!"

⋖§ Behind Every Great Man

אֶעֱשֶׂה־לּוֹ עֵזֶר כְּנֶגְדּוֹ — *I will make him a helper corresponding to him* (2:18).

There is an expression, "Who is a proper wife? One who does the will of her husband" (*Rema, Even Ha'ezer* 69:7, citing from *Tanna DeVei Eliyahu*). The simple understanding of this saying is that it is a commendable and primary attribute for a wife to be subservient and obedient to her husband. But Rav Yosef Chaim interpreted the maxim in an entirely different manner. As noted above (see previous piece), the Hebrew word for *to make* is the same as that used for *to act* (or *to do*) — לַעֲשׂוֹת. Instead of translating the word in this phrase as "who does," then, Rav Yosef Chaim rendered it as "who makes." A proper wife is one *who makes* and forms her husband's will. Shall his goals and aspirations be imbued with spirituality and righteousness, or will he be interested in nothing but the crass pursuit of wealth and comfort? Will he conduct himself in a noble and refined manner, or will he have an undignified, disorderly demeanor? The answer to these questions is dependent in large measure upon the tone and atmosphere that prevail in his household, which are set, for the most part, by the woman of the house. Thus, a proper wife is the one "who makes" and shapes the will of her husband into one which is virtuous and noble and brings credit to them both.

◀§ Sometimes Simple Is Best

עַל־כֵּן יַעֲזָב־אִישׁ אֶת־אָבִיו וְאֶת־אִמּוֹ וְדָבַק
בְּאִשְׁתּוֹ — *Therefore a man shall leave
his father and his mother and cling to
his wife* (2:24).

*R*av Yosef Chaim related that although he was extremely close with his rabbi and mentor, the *Ksav Sofer*, and always followed his guidance in all matters, there was one time when he could not agree with his rebbe's advice — when it came to choosing a wife. The *Ksav Sofer* was of the opinion that the best *bachur* out of the five hundred in the Pressburg yeshiva should not settle for anything less than the daughter of one of the most distinguished families in the community. In those days in Czechoslovakia and Hungary it was not uncommon to find men who excelled in Torah learning and at the same time enjoyed considerable monetary prosperity as well. It was a girl from such a background that the *Ksav Sofer* sought for his foremost student.

But Rav Yosef Chaim himself disagreed. He saw a wealthy upbringing as a drawback and not an advantage in a prospective mate. The trials and tribulations of life, he believed, were much easier to experience for a person who was not nurtured in the lap of luxury, but was used to a humble, simple way of life. Furthermore, Rav Yosef Chaim knew that it ran contrary to his nature to be dependent on the generosity of another person, even if that person would be the father of his wife; he preferred struggling on his own to benefiting from others. Moreover, from a purely practical standpoint, he felt it unwise to become used to a high standard of living — especially one which is based on the generosity of a single individual — for a man's good fortunes are never guaranteed, and if one's beneficiary suddenly falls upon hard times the resulting adjustment in lifestyle can be quite painful, and even lead to strife in family life. The Sages, after all, ruled that a man must provide his wife with a standard of living that matches or surpasses that to which she is accustomed (*Kesubos* 61a). A simple girl from a modest background, however, would be much more likely to deal with the cruel vicissitudes of life without undue emotional stress.

As it turned out, a confrontation with his rebbe was avoided, for it was when the *Ksav Sofer* was out of the country, recuperating from illness in a health spa, that Rav Yosef Chaim was introduced to Sarah, the daughter of Reb Shlomo Seltzer, a *shochet* from the village of Kubersdorf, and finalized his marriage arrangements with her.

◆§ Minding the Family Business

וַתֹּאמֶר הָאִשָּׁה הַנָּחָשׁ הִשִּׁיאַנִי — *The woman said, "The serpent enticed me"* (3:13).

*R*av Yosef Chaim, though constantly busy with the affairs of the community, always devoted a great deal of attention to the education and personal development of his children and grandchildren. When one of his sons would visit with a small grandchild who was just beginning to babble unintelligible sounds, he would take the baby on his knees and recite to him or her, "The Torah that Moses commanded us is the heritage of the Congregation of Jacob" (*Devarim* 33:4), and other similar verses (see *Sukkah* 42a).

One time Rav Yosef Chaim remarked to my father, "There were two events in history that were so momentous that they had an everlasting effect on all of mankind thereafter — Adam's eating from the Tree of Knowledge and Cain's slaying of Abel. These actions forever altered the course of history and the nature of man's life on earth. We must learn from these two fateful episodes that it is important for a man to be aware of the kind of associations his wife and children make, and the possible negative effects these relationships have on their spiritual well-being. Any shirking of this responsibility can lead ultimately to the most disastrous consequences! One must therefore always be aware of where his children are, whom they associate with and what their activities are."

✎§ The Struggle for Livelihood —
Curse or Blessing?

וַיֹּאמֶר ה' אֱלֹקִים אֶל־הַנָּחָשׁ כִּי עָשִׂיתָ זֹּאת אָרוּר
אַתָּה מִכָּל־הַבְּהֵמָה... וְעָפָר תֹּאכַל כָּל־יְמֵי חַיֶּיךָ
— *And Hashem God said to the ser-
pent, "Because you have done this, accursed are you beyond all the
animals... and dirt shall you eat all the
days of your life"* (3:14).

*T*he Sages make the following comment about the serpent's curse:

See how God's conduct is different from that of human
beings. When a human being angers his fellow, [the latter] ha-
rasses him viciously. But God is not like that. He cursed the
serpent, but as a result — [wherever he goes he finds his food (dirt)
ready for him:] when he goes up to a rooftop he finds food; when
he goes down again he finds food.

The question has been raised: In light of the Sages' comment,
how can God's judgment against the serpent be viewed as a punishment at all? What kind of punishment is it to be sentenced to
perpetual availability of sustenance?

The key to understanding this issue may be found in another
comment of the Sages (*Yevamos* 64a): "Why is it that our Matriarchs (Sarah, Rebecca and Rachel) were all barren at first? Because God yearns for the prayers of the righteous." It is not prayer
per se that God desires, notes the Maharal (*Chiddushei Aggados*
ad loc.), but specifically "the prayers of the righteous." This, he
explains, is because prayer is very often referred to in Scripture as
an analogue of sacrifice as a form of Divine service. Just as God
loathes sacrifices of the wicked (see *Mishlei* 21:27, *Isaiah* 1:11,
etc.), so does He reject their prayers. The more evil a person is,
the more God rebuffs his prayers.

Man realizes that the attainment of adequate sustenance for
himself and his dependents is a challenge and at times a difficult
task, and he turns to God to assist him in this quest — though

some people do so more directly and consciously than others. Even animals are "aware" of this reality of life, and they, too, in their own way, look toward God to supply them with the necessities of life (see *Tehillim* 104:27 and 145:15). As a result of the serpent's deplorable behavior, God sought to remove it from this order of things. By supplying the serpent with ever-available sustenance, He was in effect giving it the message, "Here is your food. Now I don't ever want to hear from you again!" Being deprived of one's connection and capability of communication with God is indeed a punishment — perhaps the most severe penalty of all. Conversely, sometimes the imposition of hardship and adversity can in fact serve as reminders of the connection that exists between man and God and of the wisdom of taking advantage of that relationship through prayer and repentance. As God is quoted as saying in the *Ha'azinu* song (*Devarim* 32:39), "I crushed, but I shall heal."

Rav Yosef Chaim applied this concept to explain yet another passage in the Talmud (*Pesachim* 118a):

When God told Adam, "Thorns and thistles will [the earth] sprout for you, and you will eat the herbs of the field" (*Bereishis* 3:18), Adam's eyes gushed forth with tears, and he exclaimed, "Master of the Universe! Shall I and my donkey eat from the same trough?!" When God added, "By the sweat of your brow you will eat bread" (3:19), he was appeased.

If a person is relieved of any participation in the process of finding sustenance, if he faces no challenge and bears no burden in providing for himself and his family, he is no different from his donkey, who also finds his food prepared for him without any toil on his part. They both are deprived of the critical sense of the relationship with the Divine. It was this fate that Adam so bitterly lamented, and it was only when he was told that he would produce his own food by his own toil, and thus be subject to the grace of God, that he was mollified.

◆§ The Serpent's Sin

וַיֹּאמֶר ה׳ אֱלֹקִים אֶל־הַנָּחָשׁ כִּי עָשִׂיתָ זֹּאת אָרוּר אַתָּה מִכָּל־הַבְּהֵמָה — *And Hashem God said to the serpent, "Because you have done this, accursed are you beyond all the animals"* (3:14).

*T*he Zohar teaches that the serpent was the personification of the *yetzer hara* (man's drive to do evil). The question thus arises: Why was the serpent punished for enticing Eve into eating the forbidden fruit? It is the job of the *yetzer hara* to tempt people to sin; this was the very purpose of its creation. The serpent should have been commended, not condemned!

Before answering this question, let us consider another problem related to this passage: What did God mean when He said, "Because you have *done* this"? The serpent did not "do" anything; he merely spoke words — and speech, according to the halachah (see *Makkos* 16a), is not considered to be an action!

If we contemplate these two questions, however, we will realize that one actually answers the other. The *yetzer hara's* function in the world is indeed to tempt man to transgress by introducing sinful thoughts into his mind, and thereby to increase his reward for resisting these temptations. However, the serpent went beyond his mandate, for, as the Sages tell us (see Rashi on 3:4), he actually pushed Eve into the tree to "prove" to her that it was perfectly harmless. This was an action, not mere words. It was this overstepping of the serpent's bounds that angered God, and earned him his curse. "Because you have *done* this, accursed are you!"

פרשת נח
PARASHAS NOACH

⋖§ Alcohol and the Flood

וַיָּחֶל נֹחַ אִישׁ הָאֲדָמָה וַיִּטַּע כָּרֶם. וַיֵּשְׁתְּ מִן־הַיַּיִן
וַיִּשְׁכָּר — *Noah, the man of the earth, debased himself and planted a vineyard. He drank of the wine and became drunk* (9:20-21).

*N*oah was 601 years old at the time of this incident. The question thus arises: Had Noah ever drunk wine before the Flood? It is hard to imagine that he had never tasted wine for 600 years! After all, in ancient times practically the only alternative to alcoholic beverage was water. On the other hand, if Noah had experienced this drink before, why did he suddenly overindulge to the point of such absolute, humiliating intoxication, as the Torah goes on to describe? Furthermore, Ham's reaction upon seeing his father in his drunken state seems to indicate that he was totally dumbfounded by his father's conduct; he had clearly never witnessed drunkenness before. How can this be explained?

I heard the following original and fascinating explanation for this from my grandfather Rav Yaakov Meir Sonnenfeld (*zatzal*). The Midrash teaches that many natural processes in the world underwent a radical change at the time of the Flood. The atmosphere before the Flood, for instance, did not contain the type of air that causes rot to occur in old fruits and vegetables. (This, explain the commentators, is why the sacrificial meat miraculously never became putrid during the days of the First Temple [*Avos* 5:5]; the air that prevailed inside the Temple was of the same pristine type that existed before the Flood.)

Now, if the process of putrefaction did not exist before the Flood, neither did fermentation, for this too is caused by bacterial decomposition of sugar into alcohol. This explains why Noah suddenly became intoxicated at this point in time. He was indeed used to drinking wine — but it had always been nonalcoholic, a mere grape-flavored drink. Now, however, when Noah sat down to drink the produce of his vine, he was in for a surprise, and he suddenly found himself shamefully drunk. Ham, of course, had never experienced drunkenness before either, so he was totally bewildered by his father's state, and went to tell his brothers about it.

↵§ Flee from Wickedness

מִן־הָאָרֶץ הַהוא יָצָא אַשּׁוּר — *From that land Ashur went forth* (10:11).

*R*av Yosef Chaim was known for his uncompromising insistence on the Orthodox community's total independence from and refusal to collaborate with any Jewish group that rejected the Torah as their supreme guide in life. In this he followed faithfully in the footsteps of his mentor, the *Ksav Sofer*, and those of the latter's father, the *Chasam Sofer*. He found in our verse a substantiation for this manner of conduct.

Why was it that Ashur left "that land" (Babylon) and moved elsewhere? Rashi explains that he saw that his children were being influenced by the evil teachings of Nimrod and his ilk, who were encouraging rebellion against God in building the Tower of Babel, and he immediately decided to move far away from this bastion of godlessness. According to *Piskei Tosafos* (*Megillah*, #23), it was for this reason that the Hebrew language and script are often referred to in the Talmud as *Ashuri*. It is called *Hebrew* because "Abraham the Hebrew" had spoken it, and *Ashuri* because Abraham had taught the language to Ashur, who repudiated the deniers of God and fled from them.

From this we learn the importance of rejecting any form of

association with those who deny God and rebel against Him. On the contrary, we are urged to shun them entirely, and flee from their nefarious actions.

⊷§ Man-Made Destruction

וַתְּהִי לָהֶם הַלְּבֵנָה לְאָבֶן וְהַחֵמָר הָיָה לָהֶם לַחֹמֶר
— *And the brick served them as stone, and the bitumen served them as mortar* (11:3).

*R*av Yosef Chaim always stressed the importance of recognizing God's hand in everything that occurs, and not falling prey to the arrogant notion that one's successes and accomplishments are the result of his own input alone, or, in the words of the Torah, that "my strength and the might of my hand have made me all this wealth" (*Devarim* 8:17). One must always remember that "it is God Who gives you the strength to make wealth" (ibid., v. 18).

This thought was expressed by Rav Yosef Chaim against an interesting historical background. In 1927, the president of Czechoslovakia, Dr. Tomas Masaryk, who was a great friend of the Jewish people, paid a visit to the Holy Land. He visited the old Orthodox communities of Jerusalem, where a reception was held for him at *Kolel Shomrei Hachomos*, whose ranks included a large number of Czech nationals. (Rav Yosef Chaim himself was a Czech citizen.) A festively decorated arch was erected at the entrance of the neighborhood, where Dr. Masaryk was met by Rav Yosef Chaim. From there the two of them strode side by side to the home in which the reception was held.

After the ceremony, Dr. Masaryk visited the *kolel* offices and inquired about its operation, its functions and its financial outlays, in particular to those of Czech and Austrian nationality. After this, he and Rav Yosef Chaim sat and began to discuss various other topics. One subject Rav Yosef Chaim brought up was the disturbing decline in the standards of modesty and decency in the world since the end of World War I, and the ascendancy of the attitude that man's own ingenuity and the steady strides of science could surpass the forces of nature in God's universe. Anything nature could do, it seemed to many at that time, technology could accomplish artificially, and could do it better. This estrangement from God and man's dependence on Him was bound to spell disaster for mankind, said Rav Yosef Chaim, illustrating his point from a verse in the Torah describing the building of the Tower of Babel: "And the brick served them as stone, and the bitumen served them as mortar." Why, he asked, did the Torah see fit to describe the particulars of the building materials used by these men in their rebellious project? Surely this trivial detail does not seem to contribute to the understanding of the narrative!

Upon closer reflection, however, Rav Yosef Chaim explained, the Torah is in fact making an important point for these details illustrate the extent of the builders' rebelliousness against God. The ordinary material used in building a large structure is stone. But these men declared, "We don't need nature's stones! We can make an even better material than that! *Let us make bricks and burn them in fire* (11:3)." Thus, *the brick served them as stone* (ibid.).

It was thus this attitude of exaggerated independence from God and the desire to circumvent all with which He provides us that laid the foundation of the builders' outright rebellion against God.

This concept can be applied to another difficulty in our passage as well, continued Rav Yosef Chaim. The people who were going to build the Tower of Babel "found a valley in the land of Shinar and settled there" (11:1). If they were planning to build a "tower that would reach into the heavens" (11:4), one would expect that they would begin their project with a head start, by building the tower on the highest mountain they could find. Yet the Torah tells us that, on the contrary, they chose a valley for the building site! How can we account for such seemingly illogical behavior? In light of the idea developed above, the answer to this question becomes apparent. It is true that the builders wanted to build an edifice towering up to the heavens, but they sought to do the job on their own, "without any help from God," as it were. If they had built it on a mountain peak, they would be availing themselves of a contribution of natural height supplied by God, and, as explained above, this was exactly what they sought to avoid at all costs.

This insight conveys an important message to us, for this spiritual malaise presents itself very often throughout history — from the days of the Generation of Dispersion down to Communism in our own day. In their zeal to prove that they have no need for God, such people elevate their godless ideologies to a supreme value, far more important than such issues as human compassion and individual rights. Human life has value only insofar as it functions to further the Great Cause. The Sages tell us that the builders of the tower would become greatly distraught when a tool or building material would break or become lost, for that particular item could not be replaced without added cost; but when a person was killed in a work accident, they would immediately refill his position without a second thought, for people to them were quite dispensable. In our own times, examples of such inhuman cruelty in the name of a greater cause are plentiful as well. Stalin's massacres, undertaken supposedly for the sake of the overall good of the U.S.S.R.; the Russian army's clearing of minefields by waves of footsoldiers, who would be killed or maimed in the process, in order to make way for tanks — the list is as long as history. But the lesson is clear: By forfeiting the recognition that God is the ultimate Power to Whom we are beholden, one inevitably ends up pursuing his goals without any moral compunctions whatsoever.

◆§ Sarah's Other Name

וְשֵׁם אֵשֶׁת־נָחוֹר מִלְכָּה בַּת־הָרָן אֲבִי־מִלְכָּה וַאֲבִי יִסְכָּה — *The name of Nahor's wife was Milcah, the daughter of Haran, who was the father of Milcah and Iscah* (11:29).

*T*he Iscah mentioned in this verse was none other than Sarah, the Sages tell us (see Rashi). And why was Sarah also known as Iscah (יִסְכָּה)? The Gemara (*Megillah* 14a) explains: "It was because she saw (סָכְתָה) hidden things through her Divine spirit. Another explanation: Because everyone gazed (סוֹכִין) at her beauty."

Two questions present themselves upon studying this comment of the Sages. First, why would something as external as physical beauty be considered a worthy reason to prompt a new name for Sarah? We can understand that a sublime characteristic like Divine inspiration should be grounds to supply a new name for her — but not physical beauty! Secondly, judging from the way the two explanations are presented, some relationship between them seems to be alluded to; yet they seem to be two independent, unrelated interpretations of the name *Iscah*.

Rav Yosef Chaim suggested that the key to understanding this passage lies in another story related by the Sages, in connection with another of the Matriarchs. Leah, we are told, had "tender (unattractive) eyes," unlike her sister Rachel, who was "beautiful in appearance" (*Bereishis* 29:17). The Midrash explains how Leah's eyes became adversely affected: "People used to say, 'Isaac has two sons, Esau and Jacob; and [his brother-in-law] Laban has two daughters, Leah and Rachel. The older daughter will be matched up with the older son, and the younger daughter with the younger son.' Leah was so distraught over her apparent destiny of marrying the wicked Esau that she wept constantly. That is how her eyes became 'tender.' "

It is quite possible, argues Rav Yosef Chaim, that a similar situation existed within Abraham's family. Terah had two surviving sons, Abraham and Nahor; Haran had two daughters, Milcah and Sarah. Surely the people in town expected Abraham to marry Milcah and Nahor to marry Sarah! Sarah, however, did not react to her situation with the same bitter resignation that plagued Leah. This is because Sarah, unlike Leah, possessed the powers of Divine inspiration, and was able to foresee that, despite popular gossip, she was actually going to marry Abraham. She was thus able to remain perfectly content, and did not develop the same disfiguring "tender eyes" that plagued Leah. As a result, she fully retained her original beauty.

Now we can understand the connection between the two explanations of the name Iscah given by the Gemara. Sarah "saw hidden things through her Divine spirit," and as a direct result of this fact, "everyone gazed at her unspoiled beauty."

פרשת לך לך
PARASHAS LECH LECHA

∽§ Subversive Support

וַיְהִי בִּימֵי אַמְרָפֶל — *And it happened in the days of Amraphel* (14:1).

*T*he Gemara (*Megillah*) tells us that whenever the words וַיְהִי בִּימֵי (*And it happened in the days of*) occur in *Tanach*, it is an ominous indication that something bad is about to happen. In our case, for instance, the Gemara points out that right after this phrase we read of the war of the four kings against the five kings, Lot's capture, etc. As another example, the Gemara cites the verse, "And it happened in the days of Ahaz" (*Isaiah* 7:1).

Ahaz was a notoriously wicked king of Judah. In fact the Midrash (on our verse) expounds upon his very name: "Why was he called Ahaz? Because he grasped (*achaz*) the *battei midrashim* (Torah study halls)."

What does the Midrash mean by this strange comment? If Ahaz closed down the *battei midrashim*, why do they refer to this action as "grasping" them? Apparently, then, Ahaz did not close them down, but gave them his support (*grasp*). What, then, was so reprehensible about Ahaz's behavior? Certainly the Sages did not mean to pay the evil king any compliments!

Rav Yosef Chaim explained that Ahaz indeed supported the *battei midrashim* — but his motivations in doing so were far from noble. His intention was to take control of these study houses and to use them as implements in promoting his own agenda — introducing some of his favorite topics, such as idolatry, Molech-worship, child sacrifice etc. (see *II Melachim* 16:3-4; *II Divrei Hayamim* 28:2-4). He realized that the key to controlling the hearts and minds of the Jewish people lay in these schools. By "grasping" the *battei midrashim*, and placing them under his patronage, he ensured that they would have to follow his program of study, or face closure for lack of support. This, in fact, the Midrash concludes, is why the phrase וַיְהִי בִּימֵי (*And it happened in the days of Ahaz*) is used here; such a program of "support" for Torah study is a major disaster, surely enough to warrant this ominous expression.

Upon examining the words of the Midrash, however, we will be struck with an apparent contradiction. The Midrash at first asks, "What was the tragedy in Ahaz's day (that warranted the use of the expression וַיְהִי בִּימֵי)? It was the fact that the Jewish nation was invaded by their enemies, 'the Arameans at the front, and the Philistines at the rear' (*Isaiah* 9:11)." How can we reconcile this with the fact that the Midrash subsequently gives another, unrelated explanation for the foreboding expression וַיְהִי בִּימֵי?

The answer to this question, suggested Rav Yosef Chaim, is that Ahaz could not simply take over the *battei midrashim* of Israel without any pretense; he had to provide a reason for his actions. The excuse he found was the perilous security situation. "The Arameans are at the front, and the Philistines at the rear!" he reminded his countrymen. "It is a time of grave danger. If you do not allow me to provide for you and administer the *battei midrashim*, all will be lost! This is no time for ideological stubbornness!"

There was thus only one reason for the use of the term וַיְהִי בִּימֵי — namely, Ahaz's takeover of the study halls of Torah. The fact that "the Arameans were at the front, and the Philistines at the rear" merely provided the catalyst and excuse for that action.

The lessons of this Midrash were taken in all seriousness by Rav Yosef Chaim, who applied them to his own times. There were many organizations and foundations that sought to provide financial assistance to the Jews of the old Orthodox community of Jerusalem. These offers of support, Rav Yosef Chaim taught, must be rejected if they might in any way compromise the spiritual and religious integrity and independence of the community.

⊸§ Don't Rush to Despair

וַתִּקַּח שָׂרַי... אֶת־הָגָר... מִקֵּץ עֶשֶׂר שָׁנִים לְשֶׁבֶת
אַבְרָם בְּאֶרֶץ כְּנָעַן וַתִּתֵּן אֹתָהּ לְאַבְרָם... לְאִשָּׁה
— *And Sarai... took Hagar... after ten years of Abram's dwelling in the land of Canaan, and gave her to Abram... as a wife* (16:3).

*T*he Gemara (*Yevamos* 64a) teaches that if a man does not have any children with his wife by the time ten years of marriage have elapsed, he must marry another woman, in order to fulfill the mitzvah to reproduce. Our verse is cited as an allusion to this law, for Abram, after ten years of living in *Eretz Yisrael* (their years of marriage outside of the Land did not count, explains the Gemara), took Hagar as an additional wife for the express purpose of bearing children through her.

One time a couple came to Rav Yosef Chaim and described their bitter personal predicament before him. The two, who were both from well-known families in the Orthodox Jerusalem community, had been married for ten years, and had not been blessed with children. In compliance with the halachah cited above, they had come to the conclusion that they would have to divorce in order to allow the husband to marry another woman. They came to Rav Yosef Chaim, who very often fulfilled the role of compassionate patriarch to all those of bitter hearts, to seek his guidance on the matter.

Rav Yosef Chaim looked the couple in the eye and asked, "What's the rush?"

The two were puzzled by this seemingly inappropriate question. "Are ten years of yearning and broken hopes called 'rushing'?" they asked incredulously.

"Well, I remember when you two were married," said the rabbi, who had officiated at their wedding. "The full ten-year period is not yet over. You still have a few months left. When the full ten years have elapsed, come back to me and then we will discuss what to do next. Meanwhile, trust in God, and may He grant His blessing to you!"

Somewhat encouraged, the couple went home, now equipped with the blessing of a great *tzaddik*.

As it happened, there was no need for them to return to Rav Yosef Chaim to discuss their problem again. The woman became pregnant, and the couple subsequently went on to have three children.

◈§ True Righteousness

> הִתְהַלֵּךְ לְפָנַי וֶהְיֵה תָמִים — *Walk before Me and be upright* (17:1).

After the birth of one of his sons, someone wished Rav Yosef Chaim, "May he grow up to be a *frumer Yid* (a pious Jew)." Rav Yosef responded, "First and foremost let him be an *ehrlicher mensch* (upright person)!"

Rav Yosef Chaim brought a proof for his approach from a verse in *Nehemiah* (9:7-8): "You chose Abram and took him out of Ur Kasdim, and changed his name to Abraham, and found his heart to be upright (נֶאֱמָן) before You, and You forged a covenant with him." At first Abraham was no different from any other Gentile in the world. It was only after God determined, through many trials and tests, that he had "an upright heart" that He forged His covenant with him, thereby initiating his unique relationship with Him. From this verse, Rav Yosef Chaim concluded, we may learn that the first step a person must take is to be "upright"; after this he can worry about becoming "pious."

A similar thought is found in the introduction to the Book of *Bereishis* in the Netziv's *Chumash* commentary, *Ha'amek Davar*. This book (*Bereishis*), he writes, is referred to (*Joshua* 10:13) as "The Book of the Upright," for in it are related the stories of Abraham, Isaac and Jacob, who were called "upright ones" (*Avodah Zarah* 25a). The uniqueness of the Patriarchs, he explains, was that not only were they righteous in their service of God, but they were honest and upright in their relationships with others. This is, alas, a rare virtue, the Netziv laments, for all too often people believe that acting "for the sake of Heaven" justifies disregarding the rights and privileges of others.

⇜§ Shrewd Innocence

> וַיֵּרָא ה׳ אֶל־אַבְרָם וַיֹּאמֶר אֵלָיו... הִתְהַלֵּךְ לְפָנַי וֶהְיֵה תָמִים — *Hashem appeared to Abram and said to him, "...Walk before Me and be upright* (or *innocent)"* (17:1).

*B*eing "upright (תָמִים — also *innocent, unassuming*) with God" is something that the Torah expects of all Jews (*Devarim* 18:13). Ironically, however, such simple ingenuousness is not an easy trait to come by. As the Kotzker once said, "How much cunning is necessary to achieve this innocence!"

This paradox constituted a marked facet of Rav Yosef Chaim's personality. On the one hand, his shrewd perceptiveness was well known to all, yet, at the same time, the overriding characteristic in his service of God was one of basic simplicity and innocence.

In discussing these personality traits, Rav Yosef Chaim used to say that shrewdness is comparable to medicine. When it is absolutely necessary it is a very helpful thing to have, but otherwise it should be totally avoided. When sharpness is called for — such as in curtailing sinful impulses or combating sinners — it is an indispensable tool, but as a general, pervasive character trait it is most reprehensible. The proof for this, he said, could be found in the Torah's depiction of Jacob. On the one hand, he is described as the ultimate אִישׁ תָּם, a "man of innocence." Yet when he had his first encounter with his notoriously dishonest uncle Laban, he warned him that he could prove to be "his brother in guile" (Rashi to 29:12) if the situation called for this, as indeed it subsequently did.

The word אִישׁ, translated here as "man," can also mean

"master" or "ruler," Rav Yosef Chaim noted. The depiction of Jacob as אִישׁ תָּם (rendered above as "a man of innocence"), then, can be interpreted to mean "one who rules over [the trait of] innocence." The Torah does not mean to tell us that Jacob was incapable of recognizing deceitful behavior, a naive pushover. Jacob was actually full of shrewdness, as the events of his lifetime proved time and time again. Rather, the Torah informs us that Jacob was "a master (אִישׁ) over innocence." He was basically an unassuming, artless person, but he possessed the unique ability to suppress this trait when it became necessary and could deal with deception effectively and forcefully.

⧉ Braving the Storm

וּבֶן־שְׁמֹנַת יָמִים יִמּוֹל לָכֶם כָּל־זָכָר לְדֹרֹתֵיכֶם —
At the age of eight days every male among you shall be circumcised, throughout your generations (17:12).

Despite his busy schedule and many responsibilities, Rav Yosef Chaim never turned down an offer to serve as *mohel* (circumciser) at a *bris*. His face would radiate sheer joy as he experienced the tremendous merit of "inducting another member into God's legion," as he put it.

He fulfilled this mitzvah with incredible dedication. Neither inclement weather nor perilous Arab disturbances nor any other conceivable difficulty could stand in the way of Rav Yosef Chaim Sonnenfeld when there was a *bris* to be performed!

In 1920 there was an extraordinarily heavy snowstorm in Jerusalem. The blizzard began on a Monday, and continued unabated for three days, blanketing the city with well over three feet of snow. Fences and walls were obscured, so that one could not tell when he was entering or leaving an enclosed area. There was a real danger of falling into one of the many pits and cisterns scattered throughout the city. Many a roof collapsed under the weight of the accumulated snow. In the Moslem quarter of the Old City several buildings caved in completely, killing and injuring many of the inhabitants of those houses.

Rav Yosef Chaim had been "booked," before the snowfall began, to perform a *bris* in the Meah Shearim neighborhood on that Wednesday morning. In the early morning, when there was barely a soul who ventured out onto the streets, the figure of an old man climbing his way over the mounds of snow was spotted by the residents of the Battei Ungarin buildings in Meah Shearim, making its way down St. Paul's Street (as *Rechov Shivtei Yisrael* was known then) from the Old City. It was not long before they realized that it was none other than Rav Yosef Chaim, at that time over 70 years old, who was on his way to perform the *bris*. Word quickly spread throughout the neighborhood, shouted from one window to the next, of the beloved rabbi's arrival.

One of the rabbi's grandsons immediately undertook the arduous task of plodding through the snow to meet his grandfather at the *bris*. When he arrived, he saw Rav Yosef Chaim, weary, but beaming with joy that he had overcome such tremendous odds and had succeeded in reaching his destination to perform his sacred task. The grandson asked him, "Zeidy, why did you undertake such a treacherous walk all the way from the Old City? What would have been so bad if one of the local *mohalim* would have been called upon to perform the *bris*? Surely you didn't think that the *bris* would be postponed to another day if you didn't come!"

"Of course not," replied the elderly rabbi. "I knew that in any event the *bris* would be performed today, on the baby's eighth day, as required by Torah law. However, I was concerned that the child's father might delay the *time* of the *bris* to later in the day, when he could ascertain whether I, the scheduled *mohel*, would be coming or not. Another willing *mohel* might be difficult to find under the present difficult circumstances, and furthermore he would certainly hesitate to do the *bris*, out of respect for me, until the last moment. Therefore, I decided to rise before dawn and make my way over here, in order to ensure that the *bris* would take place without undue delay!"

פרשת וירא
PARASHAS VAYEIRA

✥ Priorities in Education

כִּי יְדַעְתִּיו לְמַעַן אֲשֶׁר יְצַוֶּה אֶת־בָּנָיו וְאֶת־בֵּיתוֹ
אַחֲרָיו וְשָׁמְרוּ דֶּרֶךְ ה' — *For I have loved him, because he commands his children and his household after him that they keep the way of Hashem (18:19).*

*G*od's foremost commendation of Abraham was that he was faithful in transmitting the all-important values of charity and fear of God to his family and descendants. This is the sacred charge entrusted to each and every Jew, from our first ancestor down to our own day.

Rav Yosef Chaim's struggle for the purity of Torah-true education for children was one of his greatest legacies. He spoke out harshly against those who sent their children to secular schools so that they could get "a better education." The Gemara teaches that if a person recites the *Shema*, which speaks of the requirement to don tefillin, and is not wearing tefillin himself, this amounts to a declaration of self-hypocrisy — "he is bearing false testimony against himself," as the Gemara expresses it. The same logic holds true — and even more so — Rav Yosef Chaim argued, if one declares in the *Shema*, "You shall teach them [the words of Torah] to your sons," while his children are enrolled in a school in which they are inculcated with anti-Torah and heretical ideas!

"Imagine," he continued, "what would happen if a world-famous doctor would declare that he had discovered a wonder drug that guaranteed long, healthy life to all who took it. A parent with a sick child would give all of his or her money to obtain the medicine, even selling his last possessions to finance the purchase! Now, the Healer of all flesh, the Master of all nature, promises us that the Torah is 'your life; and with this thing you will have long life upon the land' (*Devarim* 32:47). We echo these sentiments ourselves daily, declaring in the prayers, 'they [the words of To-rah] are our lives and the length of our days.' Thus, parents who refrain from sending their children to Torah schools out of vague considerations of 'learning a livelihood' are actually compromising their children's health both physically and spiritually. They are able to guarantee the child's spiritual well-being — and thereby his material satisfaction as well — and they are furthermore commanded to do so in any event, yet they relinquish this sacred duty and rely on miracles that their child will somehow emerge a good Jew. On the other hand, when it comes to providing the child with the supposed opportunity to earn a livelihood — a matter which is in fact not in man's hand at all, but is determined by God — these same parents spend sleepless nights worrying about the proper education that will make him 'educated' and 'enlightened.' But how can a person be considered 'enlightened' if he lacks basic knowledge of the Torah, without which a man is no better than a beast?

"Even if we adopt the opinion recorded at the end of *Kiddushin* (82a) that a father should see to it that his son is trained in a profession, before a boy is well grounded in his knowledge of the Talmud, how is it possible to even consider diverting him from Torah study and endangering his entire spiritual existence? We have seen with our own eyes what happened to so many of these people who were so concerned about their sons' futures, when they and their descendants fell into spiritual oblivion for the sake of the pursuit of some dubious academic pursuit, and over the course of only a few generations their connection to the Jewish people has vanished altogether.

"And let no one argue," he concluded, "that due to the difficulties of our exile, we Jews must work ever harder to achieve success in the harsh world that surrounds us. On the contrary, it is in times of adversity that we must redouble our dedication to our holy Torah, which protects us from harm (*Sotah* 21a). To cite the parable of Rabbi Akiva (*Berachos* 61b): Though the fish fear for their lives from predators and fishermen when they are in the water, they would certainly be worse off if they left the water! If we find ourselves subject to persecution and danger while immersed in the Torah, how much more so if we abandon it!"

✑§ Don't Venture Too Far Afield

*T*he following story also illustrates Rav Yosef Chaim's outlook on the question of livelihood vs. spiritual welfare.

A certain Sephardic Jew in the Beis Yisrael neighborhood near Meah Shearim was blessed with a very large family. When it came to financial well-being, however, he was considerably less blessed. In his great desperation he accepted an offer from an acquaintance to have his daughter work as a salesgirl in a store in the Machaneh Yehudah marketplace. A rabbi of the neighborhood admonished him for this, reminding him that such a workplace was no place for a "nice Jewish girl," and that her carefully nurtured innocence and piety would be jeopardized there. The man said that he was aware of the danger, but felt that he had no choice in light of his difficult financial situation. The discussion went on and on, until the two agreed to put the question before the great sage and kabbalist Rav Shlomo Eliezer Alfandri.

Later that day they made their way to the Old City, to Rav Alfandri's home. After hearing the two sides of the issue, the venerable rabbi (who was 100 years old at the time!) told them that since he had been somewhat removed from firsthand experience with current events and the actual situation in the marketplace for quite some time, he felt that he was not qualified to adjudicate the argument. He suggested they seek the advice of Rav Yosef Chaim, for he possessed both the Torah insight and worldly knowledge necessary to render a decision in this matter.

Since it was only several days before Shavuos, the two men

decided that they would stop in to visit Rav Yosef Chaim after holiday prayers at the Western Wall, and would present the question to him at that time.

After hearing the two sides of the argument, Rav Yosef Chaim responded as follows. "I believe that the answer to your question can be found in a comment of Rashi's on the Book of *Ruth*, which we just read today. When Ruth left home to pick up gleanings in Boaz's field, the Midrash tells us that she carefully took note of various landmarks along the way to ensure that she would be able to find her way back home. At certain intervals along the route she would practice the return trip home, following the landmarks she had designated. If she was successful in retracing her steps, she would go on to the next leg of the trip, and so on.

"This could be seen as a metaphor for any person who embarks on a new path in life," continued Rav Yosef Chaim. "He or she must proceed slowly, with small steps, all the while ensuring that the return to one's place of origin is safely secured. Whenever the situation arises that this 'return journey' might no longer be possible, however, the excursion must be stopped immediately.

"In your case," he concluded, "you seek to send your daughter off on a 'journey' into new, uncharted 'territory,' where she will be faced with many challenges and possible pitfalls. Unless you have some guarantee that she will always be able to 'trace her way home' and retain her present spiritual purity, you must not endanger her in this manner. I would suggest that you decline this offer. God will surely reward those who make their decisions based on considerations of faith and religious purity, especially when the decision is a difficult one!"

In the end, these words of blessing uttered by Rav Yosef Chaim came true. The man went into business himself, and was quite successful, enabling him to support his family amply and honorably.

ᴥৡ Never Too Late for Repentance

וַיִּגַּשׁ אַבְרָהָם וַיֹּאמַר... אוּלַי יֵשׁ חֲמִשִּׁים צַדִּיקִם
בְּתוֹךְ הָעִיר... אִם־אֶמְצָא בִסְדֹם חֲמִשִּׁים צַדִּיקִם
בְּתוֹךְ הָעִיר וְנָשָׂאתִי לְכָל־הַמָּקוֹם בַּעֲבוּרָם —
*Abraham came forward and said,
"...Perhaps there are fifty righteous people in the midst of the city..." And Hashem said, "If I find in Sodom fifty
righteous people in the midst of the city,
then I will spare the entire place on their
account"* (18:23-26).

Why did God say, "If I find in Sodom"? God did not have
to search Sodom and "find" what was there; He surely
knew the results of this investigation already! We
would have expected Him to say, "If there *are* fifty righteous people
in Sodom..." Furthermore, since God obviously knew that there
were *not* even five righteous people in Sodom, why didn't he simply
tell Abraham, "Save your breath; there are no righteous people in
Sodom"? Why did He allow him to continue arguing and suggest
the possibility of fifty, then forty-five, etc. righteous people?

The answer to these questions, my father once said, lies in the
basic article of faith that God gives man freedom of choice:
Although He *knows* what a person's decision will be, He does not
influence that decision. Thus, even if there were no righteous
people in Sodom at the time of Abraham's discussion with God,
this did not mean that the situation could not change at any
moment. The gates of repentance are always open to all men,
even to Sodomites; it was still possible that some of that city's
residents would change their ways and thereby alter its doomed
fate. In fact, the Midrash tells us (*Bereishis Rabbah* 49:6), God
tried, through a series of natural disasters, to persuade the Sodomites to repent for twenty-five years, but it was to no avail. Thus,
the relevant question was not, "*Are* there fifty righteous people in
Sodom?" but, "*Will* there be (or, *Will I find*) fifty righteous people
in Sodom when the time comes to pass judgment on them?"

◆§ The Progenitor of the Messiah

לְכָה נַשְׁקֶה אֶת־אָבִינוּ יַיִן... וּנְחַיֶּה מֵאָבִינוּ זָרַע — *Let us ply our father with wine... that we may give life to offspring through our father* (19:32).

*L*ot's daughters, who were afraid that there was no one left on earth to marry them, wanted to become pregnant through their father and thereby give birth to children. But the daughter quoted in this verse does not speak of giving birth to "a child," but to "offspring." The Midrash comments on the use of this expression: "It does not say *a child*, but *offspring*. This refers to the distant descendant that would emerge from this union, the king Messiah — זֶה מֶלֶךְ הַמָּשִׁיחַ." Moab, one of the children born of Lot's incestuous relations with his daughters, was the ancestor of Ruth the Moabite, who was the progenitor of King David, who is in turn the forebear of the Messiah. It was this descendant, far in the future, that Lot's daughter unwittingly referred to when she spoke of "giving life to offspring."

Rav Yosef Chaim found a *gematria* allusion to the Midrash's interpretation of the Torah's words. The phrase וּנְחַיֶּה מֵאָבִינוּ זָרַע (*that we may give life to offspring through our father*) is exactly equal in numerical value to the Midrash's assertion of זֶה מֶלֶךְ הַמָּשִׁיחַ (*This refers to the king Messiah*) — 465!

◆§ Mitzvah Enhancement —
Better than Mitzvah Reward

וַיָּמָל אַבְרָהָם אֶת־יִצְחָק בְּנוֹ — *Abraham circumcised his son Isaac* (21:4).

*I*t is from this verse that the Talmud (*Kiddushin* 29a) learns that it is a father's duty to circumcise his son. If he is not capable of discharging his duty personally, he may appoint another person to act in his stead, but it is primarily the father's own mitzvah.

When Rav Yosef Chaim's wife was expecting their first child (while they were still in Europe), Rav Yosef Chaim prepared himself for the possibility of the baby's being a boy by studying the art of circumcision from a *mohel*, so that he would be able to perform the mitzvah himself. Nevertheless, when the baby boy was born, he decided to honor his rabbi, Rav Avraham Shag, to perform the circumcision. Rav Shag, however, declined the offer, giving Rav Yosef Chaim the following explanation.

"We read in *Tehillim* 112:1, 'Praiseworthy is the man who fears Hashem, who greatly desires His commandments.' The Sages (*Avodah Zarah* 19a) note that it says, 'who desires His commandments,' and not 'who desires the *reward* of keeping the commandments.' One should love God's mitzvos for their own sake, not for the sake of their reward.

"Now, if I circumcise your son, I will be rewarded for having performed this great mitzvah, while if you perform the circumcision, I will, of course, get no reward whatsoever for that act. However, there is a rule that 'It is a greater mitzvah to fulfill a commandment personally than to delegate its performance to another person' (*Kiddushin* 41a). Thus, the performance of the mitzvah will be enhanced if you yourself do the circumcision. I prefer that the mitzvah be carried out in the best possible manner rather than personally receiving reward for participating in the mitzvah when it is carried out in a less optimum fashion. In keeping with the Sages' maxim, I desire mitzvos for their own sake, not the reward for mitzvos!"

◆§ The Belated Question

בַּיּוֹם הַשְּׁלִישִׁי... וַיֹּאמֶר יִצְחָק אֶל־אַבְרָהָם אָבִיו... הִנֵּה הָאֵשׁ וְהָעֵצִים וְאַיֵּה הַשֶּׂה לְעֹלָה — *On the third day... Isaac said to Abraham his father... "Here are the fire and the wood, but where is the lamb for the offering?"* (22:4-7).

The question has been asked: Why did Isaac wait until the third day to ask why they had not taken along a lamb? He surely noticed the absence of an animal as soon as they left home!

A possible answer is that Isaac suspected that he might possibly be the "lamb" to be sacrificed. so he held his silence about the issue. On the third day, however, he heard his father tell the attendants, "Stay here while I and the boy go over there; we will worship and we will return to you" (22:5). When he heard the words, "*we* will return to you," he began to doubt his hypothesis. "If 'we' — both of us — will be returning from Mount Moriah to rejoin the attendants," he thought, "then I am apparently not going to be sacrificed." It was therefore at that point that he asked, "Where is the lamb for the offering?"

◆§ Spare the Child

וַיֹּאמֶר אַל־תִּשְׁלַח יָדְךָ אֶל־הַנַּעַר וְאַל־תַּעַשׂ לוֹ מְאוּמָה כִּי עַתָּה יָדַעְתִּי כִּי־יְרֵא אֱלֹקִים אַתָּה וְלֹא חָשַׂכְתָּ אֶת־בִּנְךָ אֶת־יְחִידְךָ מִמֶּנִּי — *And he said, "Do not stretch out your hand against the boy nor do anything to him, for now I know that you are a God-fearing man, since you have not spared your son, your only one, from Me"* (22:12).

The word "spared" (חָשַׂכְתָּ, usually used for saving oneself an expense) seems to be out of place. A more appropriate word might have been "refuse" (מֵאַנְתָּ).

The solution to this problem can be best understood through a parable: There was once a wealthy businessman who was approached by his rabbi, who asked him to donate a large amount for an urgent community matter. The businessman promised to produce the requested sum and bring it to the rabbi the next day. When he came to deliver the money, however, he was told that the urgent matter had been unexpectedly resolved; his donation would now be unnecessary. The rich man felt doubly fortunate; not only did he show full cooperation — at great personal expense — in this tremendous mitzvah, but he would go home without having spent a penny!

When Abraham was told that he would not have to sacrifice his son after all — "Do not stretch out your hand against the boy" — we would have expected him to be overjoyed. However, the Midrash tells us that the angel had to add, "Do not do *anything* to him," because Abraham had argued, "If I am not to sacrifice him, at least let me draw a bit of blood!" Instead of being relieved, Abraham was disappointed! He did not regard himself as having been "spared" the trauma of the sacrifice. It was this attitude of superhuman devotion that prompted God to tell him, "Now I know that you are a God-fearing man, for you have not *spared* your son from Me." Thus, the very next verse goes on to tell us that "Abraham went and offered it up [a lamb] in place of his son." Explaining the expression "in place of his son," Rashi writes: "At every step of the sacrifice process Abraham declared, 'May this be considered before You as if I had done this to my son.'"

פרשת חיי שרה
PARASHAS CHAYEI SARAH

ᵔᶴ Women and Shabbos's End

וַיְבִאֶהָ יִצְחָק הָאֹהֱלָה שָׂרָה אִמּוֹ — *And Isaac brought her into the tent of Sarah his mother* (24:67).

ashi (citing the Midrash) explains the meaning of this phrase: "He brought her into the tent, and found that she was just like Sarah his mother. As long as Sarah was alive there was a candle lit from Friday to Friday. When she died, it ceased. Then, when Rebecca came it returned."

In a letter to Rav Yissachar Shlomo Teichtal, Rav Yosef Chaim discussed a question raised by Rav David Lakenbach, the *dayan* of Pressburg. It is customary that women do not partake of the wine over which *Havdalah* was recited. Now, when a festival falls out on a Sunday, the *Kiddush* for that festival on Saturday night is combined with *Havdalah* for Shabbos, and both are recited over the same cup of wine. The question is: Should women refrain from drinking from that wine, on the grounds that it was used for *Havdalah* as well? Or should the *Havdalah* aspect of the cup of wine for some reason be ignored?

Rav Yosef Chaim noted that when Pesach begins on a Saturday night, this combination *Kiddush*-and-*Havdalah* is actually one of the four cups of wine of the Seder. It is, of course, impossible to suggest that women should refrain from drinking this cup in this instance, as women are obligated to partake of the four cups of wine just as men are. From this case we may derive that in general whenever *Kiddush* and *Havdalah* are recited over the same cup of wine, women may drink from this cup.

Expanding upon the topic of this custom (that women refrain from drinking of the *Havdalah* wine), Rav Yosef Chaim suggested the following reason behind the practice. The *Talmud Yerushalmi* (*Ta'anis* 1:6; cited in *Tur*) mentions that there is a custom that some women observe, not to engage in any work for a certain amount of time on Saturday night after Shabbos is over. Thus, we may suggest that when women avoid drinking from the wine of *Havdalah* this is intended to be a sign indicating that although Shabbos is officially ended, they intend to "ignore" the *Havdalah* and continue observing Shabbos, by refraining from doing work, for a while longer. An allusion to this custom of women's extending Shabbos observance beyond its actual time frame may be found in our verse, wrote Rav Yosef Chaim. Sarah's Shabbos candles, lit on one Friday, remained until the next Friday — "from Friday to Friday" — an indication that the sanctity of Shabbos in Sarah's tent was retained throughout the week.

If this is indeed the reason that lies behind the custom of women not drinking the *Havdalah* wine — that it is a sign that they intend to continue observing the Sabbath's cessation from work — then it is, of course, not applicable at all when a festival falls out on Saturday night, when it is in any event forbidden to do any work because of the festival. This explains why, as Rav Yosef Chaim proved above, there is no problem for women to drink from the cup of wine over which both *Kiddush* and *Havdalah* were recited.

◆§ Hidden Allusions

וְלִבְנֵי הַפִּילַגְשִׁים אֲשֶׁר לְאַבְרָהָם נָתַן אַבְרָהָם מַתָּנֹת וַיְשַׁלְּחֵם מֵעַל יִצְחָק בְּנוֹ בְּעוֹדֶנּוּ חַי קֵדְמָה אֶל־אֶרֶץ קֶדֶם — *But to Abraham's concubine children Abraham gave gifts; then he sent them away from Isaac his son, while he was still alive, eastward to the land of the east* (25:6).

*R*av Yosef Chaim was fond of finding hints and allusions to all facts and historical events in the Torah. As is known to those familiar with the history of those times, Rav Yosef Chaim, as a staunch opponent to the secular

Zionist movement, held contacts with certain Arab leaders, in order to seek friendly relations with their constituents. At a meeting with the sharif Hussein ibn Ali, he was asked by the Jordanian foreign minister, through his interpreter Rav Avraham Chaim Naeh, the following question: "You believe that everything that happens has an allusion in the Torah. Can you tell me where the Moslem holy city Medina is mentioned?"

In only a fraction of a second Rav Yosef Chaim came up with the answer to the query. "The Torah tells us that Abraham sent all his children, except for Isaac, to a place called the 'land of the east.' The Aramaic translation of this place, in *Targum Onkelos*, is 'the land of Medinha.' "

Impressed with this response, the minister tried his luck again. "And where is the Balfour declaration (to wit: 'His Majesty's Government view with favour the establishment in Palestine of a national home for the Jewish people it being clearly understood that nothing shall be done which may prejudice the civil and religious rights of existing non-Jewish communities in Palestine') to be found in the Torah?" he asked.

Once again, Rav Yosef Chaim answered without missing a beat. "It is found in the curses of *Devarim* 28: 'You will be swept away from the ground to which you are coming to possess.' The word used for 'swept away,' וְנִסַּחְתֶּם, can also mean 'you will be the victims of a *formula* or *statement* (נוּסַח).' The Torah foretells that there will be a time when a declaration will be made, but it will be formulated in such a way that both sides will be able to interpret it to their own advantage, and this will be a major cause for strife for the Jewish people in their relations with the other nations!"

✑§ Banishment to the East

וַיְשַׁלְּחֵם מֵעַל יִצְחָק בְּנוֹ בְּעוֹדֶנּוּ חַי קֵדְמָה אֶל־ אֶרֶץ קֶדֶם — *He sent them away from Isaac his son, while he was still alive, eastward to the land of the east* (25:6).

*W*hy are the words, "while he was still alive," necessary? It goes without saying that whatever Abraham did he did while he was alive! Another question on this passage is: The Torah tells us that Abraham sent his sons off toward the east; what information is added by the vague description of their destination as "the land of the east"?

Rav Yosef Chaim addressed these problems as follows. Abraham sought to fulfill the command that God had given him previously, to accede to Sarah's demand: to "drive away this slavewoman with her son [Ishmael]," because "it is through Isaac that offspring will be considered yours" (21:10,12). That is: "In order to ensure that your spiritual legacy will be carried on by Isaac, you must rid your household of all those who would exert a negative influence upon him." Abraham could have given instructions to have this unpleasant task done by others, after his death, but he chose to undertake it himself, "while he was still alive." Furthermore, in order to ensure that the desired effect was accomplished effectively and thoroughly, he sent his other children off "to the land of the east," that is, to the easternmost and farthest land from *Eretz Yisrael*.

The Torah alludes to this idea here when it tells us, "Abraham gave all that he had to Isaac; but to Abraham's concubine children Abraham gave gifts." Abraham gave all of his substantial material wealth that he had received as tributes from others (see Rashi) to his other children; however, he gave "all that he had" — that is, what he regarded as his only important possession, his spiritual legacy — to Isaac.

פרשת תולדות
PARASHAS TOLDOS

❧ Persuasive Prayer

וַיֶּעְתַּר יִצְחָק לה׳ לְנֹכַח כִּי עֲקָרָה הִוא אִשְׁתּוֹ
אִשְׁתּוֹ כִּי עֲקָרָה הִוא וַיֵּעָתֶר לוֹ ה׳ — *Isaac entreated Hashem opposite his wife, because she was barren, and Hashem allowed Himself to be entreated by him* (25:21).

$\mathcal{C}$oncerning the unusual expression וַיֵּעָתֶר (translated here as *He allowed Himself to be entreated*), Rashi explains: "He allowed Himself to be importuned, to be appeased, to be persuaded." The Torah very often speaks of God simply "hearing the prayers" of someone. Why in this instance was there a need for being "appeased, persuaded, etc."?

Later on in this passage, when the Torah relates that Jacob cooked a stew of lentils (v. 29), the Midrash (cited in Rashi) explains that this was a customary food for mourners, and Jacob was preparing it on account of his grandfather Abraham's death. Although he died at the age of 175, the Midrash continues, Abraham was supposed to have lived another five years (just as Isaac lived 180 years). God brought about his early demise, however, in order that he not be distressed at witnessing his own grandson, Esau, rejecting his traditions and embracing instead a life of violence, crime and sin at the age of 15. Since it was this very day that Esau had undergone this transformation, God caused Abraham's immediate, "untimely" death.

It emerges from this Midrash, noted Rav Yosef Chaim, that according to the original "schedule," Abraham should have died five years later than he did, and Esau, who became corrupted at age 15, should have been born five years later than he was, in order not to distress Abraham. There was, therefore, a good reason why the birth of Esau and Jacob should be delayed. Hence, it was only due to Isaac's intense prayers that God "allowed himself to be persuaded" to move up the time of Rebecca's giving birth by five years, although this would ultimately lead to an earlier death for Abraham.

Rav Yosef Chaim bolstered this insight by noting that the *gematria* value of the words וַיֵּעָתֶר לוֹ ה׳ (*and Hashem allowed Himself to be entreated by him*) is equal to that of the words חָמֵשׁ שָׁנִים (*five years*) — 748.

◄§ Prayers of the Righteous

וַיֵּעָתֶר לוֹ ה׳ — *and Hashem allowed Himself to be entreated by him* (25:21).

Although both Rebecca and Isaac prayed to God (as the Torah states, "Isaac entreated Hashem opposite his wife"), it was specifically to Isaac's prayers that God responded — "Hashem allowed Himself to be entreated by *him*." The reason for this, explains Rashi, is that "the prayer of a righteous person (in this case, Isaac) who is the child of a righteous person (Abraham) is not comparable to that of a righteous person (Rebecca) who is the child of a wicked person (Bethuel)." This explanation is taken from the Talmud (*Yevamos* 64a).

The question has been asked by many: If two equally righteous people pray, why should the prayer of the one whose father was righteous as well be more effective than the other, whose father was a bad person? If anything, the opposite should be the case: It is not so hard to be righteous when one is brought up in a home saturated with sanctity and piety, being raised by a Sarah and an Abraham! For Rebecca to have become the saint that she was, she faced infinitely greater challenges and obstacles. It was a much greater accomplishment for her to emerge a righteous person than it was for Isaac, and she should be given more credit than he, not vice versa!

Rav Yosef Chaim proposed a novel, completely different understanding of the Talmud's comment, which removes this question. The halachah is that when one prays for a person he should mention that person's full name — that is, his or her name and that of the person's father or mother, as in "Reuven son of Shimon," or "Yehudah son of Devorah." However, if the object of one's prayer is present before him at the time, it is unnecessary to be so specific about the name. This is derived (in *Berachos* 34a) from the incident in which Miriam was stricken with leprosy, and Moses, who was there at the time, prayed simply, "Please, Hashem, heal *her* now" (*Bamidbar* 12:13). Now, since Isaac was praying in the presence of Rebecca ("opposite his wife"), he did not have to specify that he was praying for "Rebecca daughter of Bethuel," but could suffice with simply "Rebecca." This prayer, in which the name of the wicked person is omitted, is more acceptable to God than one in which the name of the offending party is mentioned. This, Rav Yosef Chaim, is what the Talmud means when it says that "the prayer of a righteous person who is the child of a righteous person is not comparable to that of a righteous person who is the child of a wicked person" — a prayer on behalf of "Rebecca" cannot be compared to one on behalf of "Rebecca daughter of Bethuel." The Talmud's comment, according to this novel interpretation, is thus addressing the words "opposite his wife," and not the words "Hashem allowed Himself to be entreated by him," as the conventional interpretation understands it.

As to why Isaac chose to pray for Rebecca specifically in her presence, it is interesting to note a comment made by the Radak in his commentary on *I Melachim* 17:19. The prophet Elisha, when he prayed to God to restore the life of a young boy, spread himself out over the boy's body, placing his mouth over his, his eyes over his, his hands over his, etc. (*II Melachim* 4:34). The reason for this, explains Radak, was "in order that his prayer should be with the utmost focus and concentration, while he was lying and stretched out right over him. In a similar manner, 'Isaac prayed opposite his wife' in order that he should better focus his prayers on her behalf."

◆§ Character Control — Even for Innocence

וְיַעֲקֹב אִישׁ תָּם — *But Jacob was a man of innocence* (25:27).

*A*bove, on 17:1, the word תָּם (translated here as *innocent*) was discussed, and the following observation of Rav Yosef Chaim was made:

The word אִישׁ, translated here as "man," can also mean "master" or "ruler." The depiction of Jacob as אִישׁ תָּם (rendered above as "a man of innocence"), then, can be interpreted to mean "one who rules over [the trait of] innocence." The Torah does not mean to tell us that Jacob was incapable of recognizing deceitful behavior, a naive pushover. Jacob was actually full of shrewdness, as the events of his lifetime proved time and time again. Rather, the Torah informs us that Jacob was "a master (אִישׁ) over innocence." He was basically an unassuming, artless person, but he possessed the unique ability to suppress this trait when it became necessary, and deal with deception effectively and forcefully.

Even a positive character trait must be subjected to moderation. Innocence is undoubtedly a beneficial characteristic to have, but too much innocence leads to outright naivete. The same goes for compassion. Although it is one of the most important of all traits, and is considered to be one of the basic positive qualities of the Jewish people (*Yevamos* 79a), there are times when pity is inappropriate. As the Sages (in *Midrash Koheles*) tell us, "He who shows pity where cruelty is called for will ultimately end up showing cruelty when mercy is called for." The proof for this assertion, the Midrash teaches, is King Saul, who was too meek and kind to destroy the Amalekites, and ended up slaughtering all the Kohanim of Nob for no reason. If one cannot control his natural inclinations in one direction, he will not be able to restrain them in the other direction either.

✑§ Why Isaac Favored Esau

מִי־אֵפוֹא הוּא הַצָּד־צַיִד וַיָּבֵא לִי וָאֹכַל... וָאֲבָרְכֵהוּ
גַּם־בָּרוּךְ יִהְיֶה — *Who, then, is the one who hunted game and brought it to me... Indeed, he shall remain blessed!* (27:33).

*I*saac's reaction in this situation is somewhat puzzling. Having just discovered that Jacob had stolen the blessings from Esau by taking advantage of his blindness and deceiving him, Isaac, instead of condemning him for his act of deception and retracting the blessings, actually confirms them. This is especially surprising given Isaac's initial reaction when he realized what had happened — "he trembled with a very great trembling" (27:33). What caused Isaac to suddenly decide now that Jacob should have the blessings after all, especially in light of Esau's bitter protestations?

In order to answer these questions, let us first examine the nature of Isaac's preference for Esau in the first place. How could Isaac have chosen the wicked Esau to be the beneficiary of his blessing? Surely this great patriarch was not a fool; he obviously knew that Jacob was a "man of innocence" while Esau was a "man of the field." Even if we take into consideration the flattery with which Esau plied his father, it is inconceivable that he should have been blinded to his base nature; and even if he himself could not find fault with Esau, why did Rebecca not inform him of his misjudgment? Furthermore, the Torah testifies that Esau's wives were "a source of spiritual bitterness" to both Isaac and Rebecca.

The explanation for Isaac's behavior, suggested Rav Yosef Chaim, was that he thought the blessings to be suited for Esau precisely because of his base nature. Isaac knew that Esau was prone to indulging his numerous physical desires. But he reasoned that if Esau would not be blessed with "the fat of the land" and with "dominion over his brother," he would resort to even more violent means to gratify his wanton passions. The blessings, therefore, were seen as a means of containing the damage inherent in Esau's hedonistic tendencies. Furthermore, Isaac figured that Esau would in any event share his good fortune with his twin brother.

Jacob, on the other hand, had no such need. On the contrary, abundant wealth and earthly possessions would surely distract him from his "abiding in the tents of Torah" and his devotion to the service of God. In any event, an innocent Torah scholar would probably not know how to manage such wealth; it would only go to waste.

These were the considerations of the saintly, purebred Isaac. Rebecca, however, had firsthand experience in dealing with greedy and wicked people, for in her upbringing in the house of Bethuel and Laban she had been exposed to many such individuals. She knew that Isaac's expectations that material wealth would serve to restrain Esau's evil impulses, and that he would be glad to share his wealth with his brother, were not practical. This was the basis of her disagreement with Isaac, and explains why she knew what he did not — that the blessings had to go to Jacob.

Isaac fully expected to follow through with his intentions to bless Esau, and he was shocked when his plans were thwarted. However, as soon as he comprehended how Jacob managed to outsmart him, he came to the realization that Jacob was not as "innocent" and simplistic as he had appeared to be. If he was able to implement a plan involving goatskins, wearing Esau's clothing, etc., then it was no longer unfeasible to give him the blessings. He would indeed be able to manage the wealth that would come about through these blessings, and to take full advantage of it. He therefore declared, "Indeed, he shall remain blessed!"

⇜ Jacob's Cunning

בָּא אָחִיךָ בְּמִרְמָה וַיִּקַּח בִּרְכָתֶךָ — *Your brother came with guile and took your blessing (27:35).*

Onkelos renders the word בְּמִרְמָה (*guile*) into Aramaic as בְּחָכְמְתָא (*wisdom*). Why does Onkelos veer from the plain meaning of the word? What was the great wisdom involved in Jacob's actions?

Rav Yosef Chaim noted that according to the Sages this episode took place on Pesach eve (see Rashi on v. 9). The two goats that

Jacob brought to Isaac served as the *Chagigah* and the *Pesach*, the two sacrifices that are brought on that day. One of the laws governing the Pesach offering is that its meat is eaten at the very end of the meal (called *afikoman*), and no other food may be eaten after that. Now, when Esau entered Isaac's tent with his game, he told him, "Let my father rise and eat of his son's game, so that your soul will bless me" (v. 31). He expected that this food would supply the vehicle through which Isaac would attain the requisite level of Divine inspiration to deliver his blessing, as Isaac himself had told him (v. 4). In fact, even if Jacob had already usurped the blessing intended for Esau, this did not exclude the possibility of Esau receiving a blessing as well, for surely Isaac had more than one blessing to give (v. 38)! The problem, however, was that when Jacob fed his father the Pesach sacrifice, he was thereby ensuring that Isaac would no longer be able to eat Esau's food! Jacob therefore effectively ensured not only that he would be blessed by his father, but that Esau would not be. This was indeed a very clever plan. This is why *Targum Onkelos* refers to it as חָכְמְתָא, *wisdom*.

Where did Onkelos see any allusion to such a plot in the Hebrew words? Rav Yosef Chaim noted that the *gematria* value of בְּמִרְמָה (*with guile*) is the same as אֲפִיקוֹמָן (*afikoman*) — 287.

⋙§ Reflected Feelings

> וַיְשַׁבְתָּ עִמּוֹ יָמִים אֲחָדִים עַד אֲשֶׁר־תָּשׁוּב חֲמַת אָחִיךָ, עַד־שׁוּב אַף־אָחִיךָ מִמְּךָ — *And remain with him a short while until your brother's wrath subsides, until your brother's anger against you subsides (27:44-45).*

The repetitiousness of this sentence is striking. Why did Rebecca speak of Esau's wrath subsiding twice in succession, with almost the identical words?

Another question that is sometimes asked here is: How was Jacob to know when it was time to come home? How could he, in a faraway land, ever be sure of the fact that Esau's wrath had subsided?

It has been suggested that in fact these questions complement each other; one supplies the answer to the other. There is a maxim in *Mishlei* (27:19) that states, "As water reflects a face back to a face, so one's heart is reflected back to him by another." A person's feelings toward his fellow do not exist in a vacuum; emotions shown toward another — whether contempt, love, hatred, etc. — are usually met with reciprocal sentiments in return.

Rebecca told Jacob to flee and remain in hiding until "your brother's wrath subsides," i.e., until Esau's hatred toward him would cease. And how would Jacob know when that point in time has arrived? Rebecca supplied the answer to that obvious question by adding, "until the anger of your brother subsides *from you* (מִמְּךָ, translated above as *against you*)." When your own anger and hatred toward Esau (*the anger of your brother*) subsides from your own heart, you will know that Esau's enmity toward you has also come to an end.

The question now arises, however: We understand why Esau hated Jacob, but why should Jacob reciprocate this feeling? Esau had not wronged him; he had no reason to hate him at all!

The answer to this question may be found in a comment found in *Tosafos* on *Pesachim* 113b, which discusses the verse, "If you see the donkey of someone you hate crouching under its burden you shall surely help him" (*Shemos* 23:5). This "someone you hate," explains the Gemara (ibid.), refers to someone whom you know to be a sinner, in which case it is permitted — and even commendable — to hate him (for it is generally forbidden to hate one's fellow [*Vayikra* 19:17], and the Torah would not speak of a case in which a person hated someone wrongfully — *Rashbam*). *Tosafos's* question is: The Gemara elsewhere (*Bava Metzia* 33b) writes of the same verse that the Torah teaches us the importance of overcoming our hostility toward others; therefore it commands us to go against the dictates of our feelings and extend a helping hand to those we hate. How can the Gemara (in *Bava Metzia*) speak of subduing and overcoming our feelings of hatred toward our fellow man, when in *Pesachim* the Gemara teaches that the "fellow man" in question is a sinner whom we are actually *required* to hate?

The answer, *Tosafos* writes, is that while the hatred of A (the helper who sees the crouching donkey) toward B (the hated person, who, according to the Sages, is a known sinner) originates out of noble motivations and is perfectly justified, B inevitably will reciprocate with equally hostile feelings toward A, and this will in turn cause A's hostility toward B to become personal rather than an act of piety. It is this secondary hatred that the Torah wants us to curb. The lesson of the Torah is that while it is sometimes permitted to hate someone for religious reasons, one must not allow this hatred to degenerate into personal vindictiveness.

What we can derive from this *Tosafos*, for purposes of our own discussion, is that the verse about "one's heart being reflected back to him by another" applies even when the hatred in one direction is well deserved and understandable. The fact that B is hated by A for a perfectly valid reason does not in the least impede the reflex reaction of B developing mutual hatred toward A. Here, too, although Esau had reason to resent Jacob, but not vice versa, it was only natural for Jacob to develop reciprocal enmity toward the source of this hatred. When he would feel that hatred subside, he would know that it was time to go home.

פרשת ויצא
PARASHAS VAYEITZEI

◆§ Thanks for Everything

> וַתַּהַר עוֹד וַתֵּלֶד בֵּן וַתֹּאמֶר הַפַּעַם אוֹדֶה אֶת־ה׳
> עַל־כֵּן קָרְאָה שְׁמוֹ יְהוּדָה — *She conceived
> again and bore a son, and declared,
> "This time I shall give thanks to Ha-
> shem"; therefore she called his name
> Judah (29:35).*

*T*he Talmud (*Berachos* 7b) comments on this verse, "From the day God created His world, there was never any person who gave thanks to God, until Leah came along and gave thanks to Him." This assertion seems quite puzzling. Did Abraham or Isaac never thank God for all the bounty and good fortune that He bestowed on them? Is it conceivable that Abraham did not thank God when he emerged unscathed from Nimrod's furnace? Didn't Noah express his thanks to God, in the form of sacrifices, after emerging from the Ark (ibid. 8:20)?

The explanation for the Talmud's comment, said Rav Yosef Chaim, citing his rabbi the *Kesav Sofer*, is that indeed we may assume that thanks had been expressed by others before Leah. However, these expressions of gratitude came in the wake of some miraculous event or salvation. What the Talmud means to say is that Leah was the first person to ever thank God for a mundane, natural occurrence. There is nothing so out of the ordinary about giving birth to a child — especially after three other healthy children have already been born. Women give birth all the time, and they always have done so. Nevertheless, Leah saw fit to praise God for being the Prime Cause behind the forces of nature that we tend to take for granted, and this was the practice that she originated.

◆§ Gratitude to God — the Essence of Judaism

וַתֹּאמֶר הַפַּעַם אוֹדֶה אֶת־ה' עַל־כֵּן קָרְאָה שְׁמוֹ יְהוּדָה — *And she declared, "This time I shall give thanks to Hashem"; therefore she called his name Judah* (29:35).

The Gemara (*Megillah* 13a) tells us, "Mordechai was from the tribe of Benjamin. Why, then, was he called 'Mordechai the Jew (Judahite)' (*Esther* 5:13)? Because whoever rejects idolatry is called 'a Judahite,' as it says, 'There are Judahite men who do not bow down to your god' (*Daniel* 3:12)."

Anyone who belongs to the Jewish religion — who thus rejects idolatry — is called a *Yehudi* in Hebrew, even if he is not descended from Judah. Similarly in almost every other language, the name for our people is derived from the name "Judah" in that language. Why was Judah, of all the twelve tribes, chosen for this distinction? Why are we not referred to as "Reubys" or "Simonis" rather than "Jews"?

Rav Yosef Chaim, in a letter to Rav Yissachar Shlomo Teichtal, explained that the answer to this question can be found in the reason the Torah gives for Leah's choice of this name for her child. "This time I shall give thanks to Hashem." One who acknowledges the existence of God, and rejects all forms of idolatry, realizes that his entire existence revolves around the obligation to praise and give thanks to God. The appellation "Jew" (an abbreviated form of "Judahite"), then, is not so much an indication of lineage as a mark of one's belief and conviction that his life is centered around the service of God and the need to constantly be aware of our need to praise Him for all that He has done for us.

פרשת וישלח
PARASHAS VAYISHLACH

✥ Brotherly Love

בָּאנוּ אֶל אָחִיךָ אֶל־עֵשָׂו וְגַם הֹלֵךְ לִקְרָאתְךָ
וְאַרְבַּע־מֵאוֹת אִישׁ עִמּוֹ — *We came to your brother, to Esau; moreover, he is heading toward you, and four hundred men are with him (32:7).*

The four hundred men accompanying Esau were not exactly a welcoming committee for Jacob; Esau had mustered them together to fight his brother and to overcome him. As Rashi comments on the words, "We came to your brother, to Esau," the messengers were intimating to Jacob, "You refer to him as 'your brother,' but in reality he is still 'Esau' (bent on destroying you)." Yet, despite Esau's preparations for warfare, when he saw Jacob he embraced and kissed him (33:4). The Midrash (cited in Rashi) takes note of the abrupt shift in Esau's mood, commenting, "It is a given, known fact that Esau hates Jacob. Nevertheless, at this time his compassion was stirred, and he kissed him in all sincerity." What brought about Esau's sudden change of heart, turning his emotional disposition from vicious vengeance to reconciliation? Rashi explains, "When he saw Jacob bowing to him so many times his compassion was stirred." Rav Yosef Chaim, in the wake of a personal experience, explained more specifically what lay behind Esau's abrupt transformation.

The old Orthodox Jewish community of Jerusalem, with Rav Yosef Chaim at its helm, was fiercely independent of the Zionist movement that saw itself as the sole representatives of the Jewish community in *Eretz Yisrael* as a whole. The Zionists were not pleased — to use an understatement — with the independent course taken by this group, which they saw as a threat to their authority and hence their effectiveness. One time a group of thugs barged into Rav Yosef Chaim's house as he was learning with his grandson. This is how the youth later described the incident:

"They were big, brawny young men, with an audacious and terrifying appearance. They shouted all sorts of threats and curses at my grandfather, denouncing the 'traitors' and 'collaborators' of the Orthodox community, who dared to undermine the 'official leadership' of the Jews of Palestine. As a youngster, I was terrified of these hoodlums, and ran for cover. My grandfather remained in his chair, however, with a calm, peaceful demeanor, and gazed at them with an expression that revealed pity and sorrow for those who had abandoned their exalted heritage of Torah and traditional Jewish values and descended to the level of worthless thugs and murderers.

"My grandfather's cool composure in the face of their threats unnerved them, and they began to physically threaten him with their fists. He then rose from his chair and began to unbutton his shirt, until he bared his heart. He looked them straight in the eye and told them defiantly, 'I am ready to give my life in sanctification of God's Name. Shoot me, right here and now. I promise you I will not resist. Then go and tell those who sent you that the Orthodox community will not allow itself to be intimidated by worthless, vile people. We do not have any influence over your course of actions, but we expect that you in turn will not interfere in our matters and allow us to operate independently. No threats will deter us from our determination!'

"Grandfather's courageous defiance infuriated them even further, and it seemed to me that they were about to attack him. But then suddenly they turned and left."

Rav Yosef Chaim, some time later, analyzed what exactly had taken place in that encounter. "I thought of the meeting of Jacob with his estranged brother Esau," he said. "It is axiomatic that 'Esau hates Jacob,' as the Sages tell us, but we must remember that 'Jacob hates Esau' as well, for it is written, 'Those who hate You,

Hashem, I hate' (*Tehillim* 139:21). But when Jacob saw Esau and his four hundred men coming toward him, what did he do? 'He bowed to the ground seven times, until he reached his brother' (*Bereishis* 33:3). We can understand this verse figuratively, as indicating that Jacob repressed and overcame his feelings of animosity toward Esau, focusing his mind on whatever positive traits Esau had and repressing the evil ones, 'until he reached his brother,' that is, until he was actually able to feel true closeness and brotherly affection for him. It was this attitude of genuine care and love that radiated from Jacob which changed Esau's disposition toward him in return.

"This is the attitude that we must exhibit toward our own brethren who have gone astray as well," concluded Rav Yosef Chaim. "We must train ourselves to judge them favorably and discover the good that lies in the hearts of each of these people. Although we are involved in a bitter struggle against them, this struggle must be pursued with love rather than personal animosity. It is only in this manner that there is a possibility that their eyes may become open and they may realize the error of their ways.

"This is how I related to those young men who came to attack me. I looked at them as brothers, full of compassion and sympathy. This, in turn, forced them to change their attitude toward me as well, and they left without causing any harm."

As can be seen clearly from these words of Rav Yosef Chaim, he was extremely hesitant to speak harshly against any Jew, even those with whom he was engaged in bitter controversy. This fact is borne out further by the end of the story begun above: When the police (of the British mandatory force) heard about the incident with Rav Yosef Chaim, they came and questioned him about it. "Were these thugs who came to you Jews?" they asked.

"I'm not sure," answered the rabbi.

"Well, did they speak to you in Hebrew?" they questioned further.

"I understand that there are many Arabs who speak Hebrew quite well," he answered, completely evading the police's line of questioning.

"Would you like us to have a bodyguard stationed at your home to prevent further incidents?" they asked him.

"No, thank you," he replied. "I have no need for a guard."

פרשת וישב
PARASHAS VAYEISHEV

⋑ Tamar's Moral Commitment

> הִיא מוּצֵאת וְהִיא שָׁלְחָה אֶל־חָמִיהָ לֵאמֹר וכו׳
> — As she was taken out, she sent word
> to her father-in-law, saying (38:25).

amar did not want to explicitly implicate Judah in her pregnancy, in order to avoid embarrassing him, although this discretion was very likely going to cost her her life. The Sages learned from Tamar's behavior that "It is better for a person to have himself thrown into a fiery furnace rather than cause his fellow embarrassment in public" (*Berachos* 43b).

Many people, when they face difficult decisions in life, equiv-ocate and seek ways to evade what they know to be the Torah guidelines to their situation. In weighing pros and cons, they bring up various considerations and mitigating circumstances, and convince them-selves that these are compelling reasons — all for Heaven's sake, of course — to override what the halachah dictates. In such situations, we should take our inspiration from Tamar. Here were the lives of three human beings — Tamar and her unborn twins, one of whom was the progenitor of the Davidic line and the Messiah. All this was at risk of annihilation, just in order to save a person some embar-rassment. How tempting it would be for someone in Tamar's posi-tion to rationalize that this was too great a price to pay for preser-ving a person's honor. Surely the disadvantages outweighed the advantages! Yet Tamar withstood that temptation, imparting to us the eternal lesson that no matter how great the sacrifice seems to be, and no matter how noble one's excuses may be, one must always follow the course of action that is dictated by the Torah.

⋙ Morality Is not Relative

וַתִּתְפְּשֵׂהוּ בְּבִגְדוֹ לֵאמֹר שִׁכְבָה עִמִּי — *She caught hold of him by his garment, saying, "Lie with me!"* (39:12).

ashi cites the Gemara's description of what went through Joseph's mind at this point. "An image of his father appeared to him in the window and said to him, 'Joseph! In the future your brothers are going to have their names inscribed on the stones of the *Kohen Gadol's* breastplate, and you are supposed to be there with them. Do you wish that your name should be removed from among them?!'"

Rav Yosef Chaim derived an important lesson from this story: A person must never judge himself in comparison with others. If Joseph had compared his own position with that of his brothers, he would surely have judged himself to be more righteous than they. He had been kidnapped as a boy and shipped off to Egypt, living all alone in a land known for its rampant immorality and promiscuity. His master's wife was seducing him — practically ordering him — to commit this sin; how could he defy her? He was a young slave boy, with no friends or family to encourage him and reinforce him in the imperatives of decency and moral conduct. Surely, if he would yield to temptation he could not be held fully responsible for his actions! Surely he would be forgiven for his lapse under such conditions of duress! His brothers, on the other hand, were far worse than he was. They took their own flesh and blood, whom, as their younger brother, they should have protected and guarded from harm, and sold him into slavery to Ishmaelites, for absolutely no reason, bringing untold anguish upon their beleaguered father. Whose name, then, should be erased from the breastplate?! Surely he deserved to be on those stones more than they did!

This is what Joseph might have thought, and we would have to fully understand him if he did. But this is not, in fact, how things work. Jacob's message was that when a person's actions are judged by God, what other people do is not a relevant consideration. Comparison is not a mitigating factor. Joseph realized that to yield to Potiphar's wife would be a sin, and that if he did not desist from it, he would jeopardize his standing as one of the twelve founders of the tribes of Israel.

✢§ Consistency in Righteousness

וְלֹא־זָכַר שַׂר־הַמַּשְׁקִים אֶת־יוֹסֵף וַיִּשְׁכָּחֵהוּ. וַיְהִי מִקֵּץ שְׁנָתַיִם יָמִים — *The chamberlain of the cupbearers did not remember Joseph, but he forgot him. It happened at the end of two years* (40:23-41:1).

*R*ashi comments (from the Midrash): "Because Joseph put his faith in the cupbearer instead of in God, he had to languish two more years in prison before being called to Pharaoh." This harsh treatment of Joseph seems quite puzzling. Throughout the ages, whenever a Jewish individual or community has found itself in trouble or danger, it was always understood that they would avail themselves of any means possible — bribery, ingratiation, intercession, etc. — to alleviate their difficulties with the authorities. The Sages teach that in fact it is forbidden to sit back and rely on God's miraculous salvation. Why, then, was Joseph held to task for seeking the help of the cupbearer to bring up his case with Pharaoh?

In a correspondence with Rav Avraham Stern, the rabbi of Novozamky in Czechoslovakia, Rav Yosef Chaim discussed the sin and punishment of Nadav and Avihu, and came to a conclusion which is relevant to the case of Joseph as well. Why did these two sons of Aaron pay with their lives simply because they brought an extra offering in the Mishkan, "which God did not command"? They were only trying to serve God! The answer, suggested Rav Yosef Chaim, is that this incident of the "extra offering" was in fact not the direct cause of the punishment meted out to Nadav and Avihu. Rather, it was the sin of the Golden Calf that was responsible for their harsh treatment. For why did they, the oldest sons of Aaron, not protest when the Jewish people turned to idolatrous worship at Mount Sinai? The immediate excuse that protected them at the time was that they could not be expected to take action in the presence of their father; this would be considered a show of disrespect and insubordination. Now, however, they showed that they were quite capable of defying authority and acting independently. When they wanted to initiate an unwarranted offering, they suddenly knew how to assert themselves! The excuse that had protected them from prosecution for their silence during the Golden Calf incident had now become suddenly invalid; it was for this reason that they were punished so severely.

Now, let us return to the case of Joseph. The Ramban poses the following question: Why did Joseph, during all his years in Egypt, not send a letter to his father to inform him that he was alive and well — especially after he became a senior government official, when such correspondence could easily have been arranged? Why did he allow his father to mourn his disappearance for so many years, agonizing over not knowing the fate of his most beloved son? The Ramban answers that because Joseph considered his meteoric rise to power in Egypt to clearly be the result of the supernatural guidance of God, he was sure that the dreams he had dreamt while still a youngster would yet materialize and his father and brothers would one day come down to Egypt and meet him face to face.

Joseph thus curbed his natural yearning to communicate with his father and ease his pain because of his great trust in God that his prophetic dreams would yet come true. When he met the cupbearer, however, and he realized that he might provide him with a chance to extricate himself from prison, he decided to seek this avenue of escape. The objection was then raised toward him: When it comes to alleviating the suffering of your old father who mourns for you every day, you excuse yourself on the grounds that you have complete faith in God that he will eventually come to see you in Egypt. Yet when it comes to your own personal welfare, you suddenly decide that there is nothing wrong with exerting a bit of human effort, and not relying completely on God to handle matters! It was because of this inconsistency that Joseph was punished so severely.

It is interesting to note that the very same Midrash that admonishes Joseph for his lack of faith in seeking the assistance of the cupbearer quotes the verse, "Fortunate is the man who makes Hashem his trust" (*Tehillim* 40:5), and takes it as a reference to Joseph. How can the Midrash portray Joseph as the epitome of "one who makes Hashem his trust" and criticize his reliance on the cupbearer in the same breath? According to what we have established above, the words of the Midrash make perfect sense. It was precisely *because* Joseph's level of trust in God was so extraordinary that he was held accountable for turning for help to the cupbearer.

פרשת מקץ
PARASHAS MIKEITZ

◆§ Famine in the Midst of Plenty

וַתֹּאכַלְנָה הַפָּרוֹת רָעוֹת הַמַּרְאֶה וְדַקֹת הַבָּשָׂר
אֶת שֶׁבַע הַפָּרוֹת יְפֹת הַמַּרְאֶה וְהַבְּרִיאֹת — *The
cows of ugly appearance and gaunt
flesh ate the seven cows that were of
beautiful appearance and robust* (41:4).

his detail of the dream was interpreted by Joseph to
mean that the seven years of famine would be so drastic
and severe that they would cause the seven years of
plenty that preceded them to be forgotten. But the image of the
gaunt cows swallowing the other cows does not seem to correspond exactly to the idea it was meant to represent. The seven
years of famine might be calamitous and oppressive in their own
time, but they did not in any way diminish the comfortable level
of living that was enjoyed during the years of famine. The seven
lean cows might have been shown as being more formidable or
frightening than the first cows, but they should not have eaten
them!

Rav Yosef Chaim explained that in fact the Torah teaches us
here a great lesson in human nature. Even if a person is blessed

with abundant prosperity and wealth, he is unable to enjoy his good fortune if he is constantly overcome with a sense of impending doom. It is difficult to imagine that a prisoner who is fed his favorite meal just before his execution derives any pleasure from this food. The Egyptians, too, were aware throughout the seven years of plenty that this bounty was only temporary and that disaster was soon to strike, and this knowledge gnawed away at their nerves each time they took a bite of food. The dream was thus quite accurate in its depiction of the years of plenty and famine. The seven years of famine would actually erode the enjoyment of the seven years of plenty, and "the abundance will be unknown in the land, in the face of — *in anticipation of* — the subsequent famine" (v. 31).

◆§ Don't Fault Others

> וַיֹּאמְרוּ אִישׁ אֶל־אָחִיו אֲבָל אֲשֵׁמִים אֲנַחְנוּ —
> *They said to one another, "Indeed we
> are guilty!"* (42:21).

After the bloody Arab riots of 1929, in which many Jews were killed, a group of *kolel* students that had gathered together in Rav Yosef Chaim's house for Torah study began to discuss the grim situation. "It is because of the ball games that are held on Shabbos that all this is happening to us!" declared one of the young men, confident that he had discovered the cause for God's wrath at His people. The others nodded in approval.

At that point Rav Yosef Chaim got up from his chair and declared emotionally, "I disagree with your assessment, that it is because of these misguided youth that these misfortunes have befallen us! Who are these unobservant Jews who are behind these Shabbos desecrations? Most of these people were drafted into the various European armies during the World War I. There is no doubt that during the war they were forced many times to eat nonkosher food, to violate Shabbos, etc., and thus, through the course of time, their observance of Judaism weakened drastically.

After their release from the army they returned to their towns and families in Russia, Ukraine, etc., and found themselves facing the pogroms of Petlyura (the infamous nationalist Ukrainian leader just after the Communist Revolution) and his cronies, in which many Jewish women and children were massacred. And perhaps among the victims was someone's father who was killed in front of his eyes, while wrapped in his tallis and tefillin.

"So now I ask you — what do you want from such people, who have been through so much trauma and disruption in their lives? Is their sin so great to warrant that all of the Jewish people should suffer such calamity on their account?"

"If so," the students asked him, "with whom does the blame lie?"

"Indeed *we* are guilty!" Rav Yosef Chaim responded, paraphrasing our verse. "We were never forced by extenuating circumstances to eat nonkosher food, to desecrate the Shabbos, to violate any mitzvos! Our parents were not murdered by anti-Semitic mobs in front of our eyes. We have merited to live a life of peace and tranquility, here in the holy city, Jerusalem, sheltered in a totally Torah-oriented environment, surrounded by Torah scholars and rabbis. Therefore, much more is expected of us by God. And if we are not completely righteous in all our ways — who knows if it is not this imperfection that has brought about this terrible suffering for the Jewish people!"

This was typical of Rav Yosef Chaim's approach. He always protested whenever anyone would voice incriminations about the spiritual shortcomings of the Jewish people. He would silence those who searched for imperfections in the deeds of others and dwelled on these misdeeds. He compared this to a son who disgraced and cursed his father: Anyone who relates to others what the son did only adds to the father's disgrace. By focusing and dwelling on the sins of others we contribute nothing toward the glory of God.

⁓§ Joseph's Clever Plan

וַיִּקַּח מֵאִתָּם אֶת־שִׁמְעוֹן — *And he took Simeon away from them* (42:24).

*R*av Yosef Chaim suggested an interesting motive behind Joseph's holding Simeon as hostage while the others returned home. The brothers were commanded to bring their younger brother Benjamin from Canaan, over the strenuous objection of their elderly father. What would prevent them from simply taking any young boy off the street and presenting him as Benjamin? It would be impossible for the viceroy of Egypt to ever be able to detect such a ruse. They would be able to bring him a "Benjamin" and still avoid breaking their father's heart! In order to forestall such a tactic, Joseph held Simeon captive. When the brothers would return with Benjamin, Joseph could bring him in to Simeon and ask him if he could identify him. If he could not, he would know that the brothers had deceived him. Thus, the detention of Simeon was a clever plan to ensure that the brothers did indeed bring Benjamin back with them the next time they came.

פרשת ויגש
PARASHAS VAYIGASH

∾§ Joseph's Admonition

> וַיֹּאמֶר יוֹסֵף אֶל־אֶחָיו אֲנִי יוֹסֵף, הַעוֹד אָבִי חָי?
> — וְלֹא־יָכְלוּ אֶחָיו לַעֲנוֹת אֹתוֹ כִּי נִבְהֲלוּ מִפָּנָיו
> *And Joseph said to his brothers, "I am*
> *Joseph! Is my father still alive?" But his*
> *brothers could not answer him because*
> *they were confounded before him (45:3)*

*M*any commentators ask: After Judah's lengthy address, which focused almost exclusively on his father and how he would suffer if Benjamin would not be allowed to return home, how could Joseph now ask, "Is my father still alive?" It was already made quite clear to him that Jacob was alive!

Another question is asked in connection with a passage in the Talmud (*Chagigah* 4b) that relates to this verse: "Rabbi Elazar would cry when reading this verse, saying, 'If such confoundedness is the reaction to the admonishment of a human being, how much more so when we face the admonishment of God!" What "admonishment" did Rabbi Elazar see in these words of Joseph? All he said was, "I am Joseph!"

Rav Yosef Chaim answered these two questions as follows.

Among the many personal details the brothers mentioned to Joseph was the fact that they had once had a twelfth brother who was now dead (42:13, 42:32, 44:20). Joseph knew, of course, that this was not true. He assumed that most probably this detail was added in order to arouse sympathy to their case in the face of the harsh accusations that were cast at them. Perhaps, then, there was no elderly father eagerly anticipating Benjamin's return either; perhaps this too was a ploy to arouse Joseph's compassion. Hence, Joseph told them, "*I am Joseph!* Your claim that I was dead is false. Now tell me the truth about Father. *Is my father still alive?* Or is that also a fabrication?"

Joseph's question to his brothers can be understood in another manner as well. He told them, "You present yourselves as being so intensely concerned over the welfare of your father and the hazard to his health that my withholding Benjamin might cause. Well, *I am Joseph!* Why did you not show the same concern for your father's feelings when you sold me into slavery? In light of your description of our father's attachment to Benjamin and his certain death if he would not return home, I can only wonder in amazement, *Is my father still alive* now, despite the loss of his favorite son twenty-two years ago?"

פרשת ויחי
PARASHAS VAYECHI

❧ Joseph's Oath to Jacob

וַיֹּאמַר אָנֹכִי אֶעֱשֶׂה כִדְבָרֶיךָ. וַיֹּאמֶר הִשָּׁבְעָה לִי
וַיִּשָּׁבַע לוֹ — *He said, "I will do as you
have said." He replied, "Swear to me,"
and he swore to him* (47:30-31).

W hy did Jacob wait until Joseph acceded to his request
before asking him to swear to him? It would seem
that after having received Joseph's word on the matter, it was somewhat inappropriate to ask for an oath, which bears
the implication that Jacob did not fully trust his son. If he wanted
Joseph to swear over the matter, he should have said from the
outset, "Swear to me that you will bury me in Canaan."

Before answering this question, let us discuss another point in
this narrative. Jacob asked Joseph to perform "kindness and
truth" (v. 29) for him in following his burial requests. Rashi explains that kindness done for the dead is called "kindness of truth"
because it is wholly altruistic; one cannot expect to ever have his
favor repaid in any manner. The Sages (in *Kesubos* 72a) tell us,
however, that when a person shows respect for the dead by eulo-
gizing or lamenting them at their funerals, his reward will be that
the same honor will be accorded to him when his time comes to
depart from this world. If so, kindness done for the dead is in fact

subject to recompense, no less than kindness done for any living person!

Rav Shmuel Nadash (Rav Yosef Chaim's grandfather) suggested the following approach in answering both these questions. When Jacob at first requested from Joseph that he transport his body for burial in *Eretz Yisrael,* he did not even consider the possibility that Joseph himself might seek the same burial arrangement for himself. He therefore asked him to perform "kindness of truth" in bringing his remains to Canaan, for there was no possibility of repayment for such an act. If Joseph would agree to undertake such a tremendous favor for his father, such acceptance would be considered an undertaking to perform a mitzvah, which may not be retracted. Joseph's acceptance of Jacob's request would be sufficient to guarantee that the deed would be done. This is why Jacob did not originally seek an oath to reinforce Joseph's personal assurance.

However, to Jacob's surprise, Joseph told him, "I will do as you have said." According to *Da'as Zekeinim* (quoting a midrash), what Joseph meant to say was, "I, too, plan to have the same thing done to my remains when I die, requesting burial in *Eretz Yisrael. I will do* (for myself) just *as you have said* (for yourself)." At that point, Jacob knew that Joseph might have ulterior motives when transporting his body to *Eretz Yisrael,* thinking, "One day this honor that I am showing for my father will be repaid to me!" Joseph's acceptance of Jacob's request was now no longer a purely altruistic matter; there were personal considerations involved as well. It was no longer a simple case of "accepting upon oneself to do a mitzvah," which may never be retracted. Therefore, after hearing Joseph's response, Jacob told him, *"Swear to me that you will fulfill my request,"* for only through an oath would Joseph's compliance with his wishes be guaranteed.

ספר שמות
SHEMOS / EXODUS

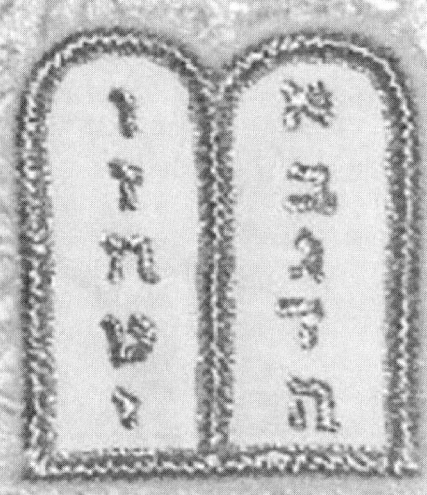

פרשת שמות
PARASHAS SHEMOS

⋙ The Balance Between Good and Evil

וַיְצַו פַּרְעֹה לְכָל־עַמּוֹ לֵאמֹר כָּל־הַבֵּן הַיִּלּוֹד
הַיְאֹרָה תַּשְׁלִיכֻהוּ — *Pharaoh commanded his entire people, saying, "Every son that will be born — into the river shall you throw him"* (1:22).

ashi comments that when Pharaoh said "every son," he meant that *all* newborn boys in Egypt — not only the Jewish ones — were to be killed.

The Talmud (*Chagigah* 15a) interprets the verse, "God has made one opposite the other" (*Koheles* 7:14), as follows: "Everything that God created in His world, He created an opposite to it. He created the righteous; He created the wicked. He created *Gan Eden*; He created *Gehinnom*."

Every spiritual phenomenon in the world has an equal and opposite one corresponding to it. It stands to reason, then, that when Moses was born, embodying one of the purest and most righteous souls ever to exist, a corresponding force of evil entered the world at the same time. Pharaoh was told by his astrologers that a savior would be born to the Jews, and that he was destined to meet his end through water; this is why he decreed that all

Jewish boys should be killed by throwing them into the river (v. 16; see Rashi to v. 10). Since it was Pharaoh's plan to eliminate the tremendous positive spiritual force that was personified by Moses, it was inevitable that the opposite force of evil had to cease to exist as well. This, explained Rav Yosef Chaim, is why it was fated that Pharaoh decree that on the day Moses was born *all* children had to be killed.

Rav Yosef Chaim applied the same concept to explain another situation described in the Torah. Toward the end of the Book of *Bamidbar* (31:2), God tells Moses, "Take vengeance for the Children of Israel against the Midianites; afterwards you will be gathered unto your people." As Rashi (ibid., v. 3) mentions, this verse implies that God made Moses' death contingent upon the war against the Midianites. But why was this so? What connection was there between these two events?

Moses was the greatest prophet who ever lived (*Devarim* 34:10). As such, he represented an unsurpassed spiritual force in the world. Balaam, the Sages tell us, was Moses' counterpart in the non-Jewish world; his powers of sorcery and impurity matched those of Moses for sanctity and prophetic ability. These two opposing powers had to coexist. If Moses was about to depart from this world, Balaam had to go as well. This is why the battle against Midian had to be waged before Moses' death, for it was in that battle that Balaam was killed (*Bamidbar* 31:8).

פרשת וארא

פרשת וארא
PARASHAS VA'EIRA

◆§ True Fear of God

הַיָּרֵא אֶת־דְּבַר ה׳ מֵעַבְדֵי פַּרְעֹה הֵנִיס אֶת־עֲבָדָיו
וְאֶת־מִקְנֵהוּ אֶל־הַבָּתִּים. וַאֲשֶׁר לֹא־שָׂם לִבּוֹ אֶל־
דְּבַר ה׳ וַיַּעֲזֹב אֶת־עֲבָדָיו וְאֶת־מִקְנֵהוּ בַּשָּׂדֶה —
*Those among the servants of Pharaoh
who feared the word of Hashem hurried
his servants and his livestock into
houses. And those who did not take the
word of God to heart left his servants
and livestock in the field (9:20-21).*

The Torah describes here the actions of two opposite types
of people in these verses — those who "feared the word
of Hashem" and those who "did not take the word of God
to heart." Since these two classes of people are supposed to be
antithetical to each other, we would have expected the Torah to
contrast "those who feared the word of God" with "those who did
not fear the word of God." Why does it instead refer to the second
group as "those who did not take the word of God to heart"?

The Torah, explained Rav Yosef Chaim, is teaching us an important lesson here in what "fear of God" means. A person who lacks

this quality is not necessarily someone who commits sacrilege or other sinful acts. The mere fact that someone "does not take the word of God to heart," and relates to God's commands with apathy and indifference already qualifies him as a person who has no fear of God. There are many people who are totally observant of all the mitzvos, but only out of habituation and conditioning. They conduct their religious lives in an unemotional, apathetic manner. The "word of God" does not mean anything to them; it does not truly penetrate their heart. Such people, according to our verse, cannot really call themselves "those who fear God."

פרשת בא
PARASHAS BO

◄§ The Dismissal of Moses and Aaron

וַיְגָרֶשׁ אֹתָם מֵאֵת פְּנֵי פַּרְעֹה — *And he drove them away from the presence of Pharaoh* (10:11).

*T*he word פְּנֵי (*the presence of*) seems to be superfluous; What would have been lacking had the Torah said simply וַיְגָרֶשׁ אֹתָם מֵאֵת פְּנֵי פַּרְעֹה — *he drove them away from Pharaoh*?

The word פְּנֵי, wrote Rav Yosef Chaim, bears the connotation that the unceremonious dismissal of Moses and Aaron took place only *in the presence* of Pharaoh. Once they exited Pharaoh's chamber, however, they met with a different attitude entirely. There, out of Pharaoh's sight, they were accorded the greatest respect, for, as the Torah tells us later, "the man Moses was very great in the land of Egypt, in the eyes of the servants of Pharaoh and in the eyes of the people" (11:3).

◄§ Of Dogs and Donkeys

וּלְכֹל בְּנֵי יִשְׂרָאֵל לֹא יֶחֱרַץ־כֶּלֶב לְשֹׁנוֹ — *Against all the Children of Israel, no dog shall whet its tongue* (11:7).

*A*s a reward for holding their tongues, the *Mechilta* (cited by Rashi below, 22:30) teaches, dogs were the recommended beneficiaries when an animal is found to be *treifah* (nonkosher by virtue of a wound): "You shall not eat the flesh of an animal that was torn (*treifah*) in the field; to the dog shall you throw it" (ibid.).

A similar thought is found regarding another verse, at the end of our *parashah*: "Every firstborn donkey you shall redeem with a lamb" (13:13). Rashi comments: "This law applies to firstborn donkeys only, not to the firstborn of other unkosher animals. This is because donkeys played a role in the Exodus, for every Israelite took many donkeyloads of spoils from the Egyptians." The donkeys, too, were rewarded for their "good behavior" during the Exodus.

The question arises, however: Why is it that the donkeys' reward consists of an exalted status of sanctity being appended to their firstborn, while dogs are rewarded by being fed unkosher, defiled meat? Why are the dogs treated with less respect than the donkeys?

Rav Chaim gave the following explanation for the difference in treatment between the two animals. The donkeys' good deed consisted in actually exerting themselves in providing assistance to the Israelites. For helping another person bear his burden, one earns the merit of being blessed with added sanctity. All the dogs did, by contrast, was refrain from barking. This was an admirable manner of behavior indeed, but totally passive; no effort or exertion was required. Therefore, their reward consists of nothing more than being fed scraps of rejected meat.

Rav Yosef Chaim provided another insight into the midrash about the donkey and its reward as well. As is well known, Rav Yosef Chaim was opposed to Chief Rabbi Kook's tolerant and kind indulgence of the secular, often anti-religious Zionists. One time Rav Kook advanced the following argument: We find that the Torah rewards the donkey — an "unclean," unkosher animal — because of a single righteous act that it performed at one moment in history. The Zionists, too, do many good deeds in their efforts in setting up the foundations of the growing Jewish community in Israel — providing hospitals, organizational institutions, urban infrastructures, making the desert bloom, etc. For all these services that they do for the Jewish people, they should be regarded in a positive light, certainly no less than the donkey!

When Rav Kook's line of reasoning was told to Rav Yosef Chaim, he countered as follows: It is true that the donkey, an unclean animal, was invested with a certain degree of sanctity because of its role in the Exodus. However, let us examine what the com-

mandment of the firstborn donkey actually entails. The owner of
the donkey is supposed to transfer the firstling donkey's sanctity
onto a sheep, which is then given to a Kohen (13:13). The lesson
of this mitzvah, then, is that sanctity and nonsanctity cannot coexist in the same object; they must be separated into distinct entities. If this separation does not take place, in fact, the Torah
commands that the donkey be killed (ibid.).

The lesson to be applied vis-a-vis the Zionists, then, concluded
Rav Yosef Chaim, is that we must pray that these pioneers and
builders of the Jewish homeland speedily repent and turn to the
Torah-true way of life, so that their merits and good deeds may
dwell in the bodies of holy people!

⋲§ Pharaoh and His Servants

> וְיָרְדוּ כָל־עֲבָדֶיךָ אֵלֶּה אֵלַי וְהִשְׁתַּחֲווּ־לִי לֵאמֹר
> צֵא — *Then all these servants of yours*
> *will come down to me and bow to me,*
> *saying, "Leave!"* (11:8).

As Rashi notes, it was not Pharaoh's servants, but
Pharaoh himself, who went to Moses when the Plague
of the Firstborn struck and begged him to leave.
Moses couched his defiant warning in terms of Pharaoh's servants, however, because it is inappropriate to show disrespect to
a king — even one as wicked as Pharaoh.

Does this mean that Moses' statement was untrue? Did he actually lie out of respect for the king? Rav Yosef Chaim explained that
actually what Moses said was true in the literal sense as well.
Moses did not speak of "servants" in general, but of "*these* servants *of yours*," referring to the personal attendants of Pharaoh,
who were standing in his presence at that time. Now, it is well
known that a king does not simply go about from place to place
without a large retinue of attendants. Even in an emergency,
Pharaoh would certainly take along a servant or two if he went
anywhere. Thus, when Moses told Pharaoh that "these servants of
yours" would be paying him a visit, he was actually intimating to
him that he (Pharaoh) himself would be coming to him (Moses),
accompanied by his personal servants.

✥ The Difference Between Rosh Chodesh and the Festivals

הַחֹדֶשׁ הַזֶּה לָכֶם רֹאשׁ חֳדָשִׁים — *This month shall be for you the beginning of the months* (12:2).

*I*n the festival liturgy, the *Musaf* prayer begins with the words, "You chose us out of all peoples; You loved us and showed favor to us, for You gave us this _____ holiday." In the *Rosh Chodesh* prayers, however, this formula is not used. What is the reason for this change?

Rav Yosef Chaim explained that when the laws of *Rosh Chodesh* were given to us, it was before the giving of the Torah on Mount Sinai — for the concept of *Rosh Chodesh* was introduced in Egypt, as our verse indicates — and thus, it preceded God's choosing of the Jews as His nation. The idea that "You chose us out of all peoples" is thus an irrelevant theme on *Rosh Chodesh*, and it is therefore omitted from the prayers.

The same reason may be applied to explain why Israel's chosenness is not mentioned in the Shabbos *Musaf* either, for the commandment of observing Shabbos was also given to the Jews before Sinai, while they were still at Marah (*Shemos* 15:25; see Rashi ibid.). In fact, an allusion to Marah can be seen in the words of the Shabbos *Musaf* prayer, Rav Yosef Chaim noted. We say אָז מִסִּינַי נִצְטַוּוּ עָלֶיהָ — "then, at (lit., *from*) Sinai, they were commanded about it." The word אָז (*then*) has the numerical value of 8. The phrase can thus be translated as, "eight [steps] from Sinai they were commanded about it." Marah was the Jews' eighth encampment before they arrived at Mount Sinai (*Bamidbar* 33:8-15)!

✥ Custom and Compassion

הַחֹדֶשׁ הַזֶּה לָכֶם רֹאשׁ חֳדָשִׁים — *This month shall be for you the beginning of the months* (12:2).

*T*here is a custom observed by many women to refrain from doing certain chores on *Rosh Chodesh* (see *Shulchan Aruch*, O.C. §417).

In Rav Yosef Chaim's day, washing machines were still quite uncommon in Israel, and certainly in the impoverished neighborhoods of the old Orthodox community. A washerwoman would be hired on laundry day, and she would slave over a tub and washboard, scrubbing each item individually, from dawn to dusk — all for a very modest wage. Understandably, it was generally women from very poor families who engaged in this occupation.

One *Rosh Chodesh* day, before Rav Yosef Chaim set out for prayers, a loud commotion was heard from down the block. The Rav asked his daughter-in-law, who had moved in, along with her family, after the Rebbetzin's death, if she might go out and see what the fuss was all about.

It seems that one of the women who lived in Battei Machaseh (Rav Yosef Chaim's neighborhood in the Old City of Jerusalem) had hired a Yemenite washerwoman to come to do her laundry that day. When the woman arrived in the predawn darkness to begin her work, however, her would-be employer told her that she had forgotten that that day was *Rosh Chodesh*. The custom was not to do laundry on *Rosh Chodesh*, and the woman was adamant about scrupulously observing this practice. She therefore told the laundress to go home. The dismayed washerwoman explained that if she did not work on that day, she would literally not have any money to feed her children, since her husband was incapacitated and she was the sole supporter of the family. An argument ensued, and this was the early-morning commotion that Rav Yosef Chaim — and the rest of the neighborhood — had heard.

When Rav Yosef Chaim heard what had happened, he quickly asked his daughter-in-law, "Do we have any dirty laundry in the house, for which to employ this woman?"

The daughter-in-law replied that she thought she could round up a bit of work for the laundress to do.

"Quickly, then," Rav Yosef Chaim urged her. "Go bring the woman to our house for a few hours. To cause sorrow and pain to a poor Jewish woman like this is a much more serious sin than breaking a religious custom!"

The daughter-in-law ran to call the woman to her house before she had a chance to leave the neighborhood. She set up the tub and washboard, and brought in the laundry for the washerwoman. Just then, there was a knock on the door. It was the woman who had originally hired the laundress.

"If the Rav can have his laundry done on *Rosh Chodesh*, then so can I!" she declared, and she rehired the Yemenite woman for the day.

⋘ Safeguarding Matzos and Mitzvos

וּשְׁמַרְתֶּם אֶת־הַמַּצּוֹת — *You shall safeguard the matzos* (12:17).

By altering the vowel marks of מַצּוֹת (*matzos*) the word can be read as מִצְוֹת (*mitzvos*). The Sages (cited in Rashi) thus comment, "Do not read, 'safeguard the *matzos*,' but 'safeguard the *mitzvos*.' When a mitzvah becomes available to you, attend to it immediately, not allowing it to 'ferment.'"

Rav Yosef Chaim took painstaking care when baking his matzos that everything should proceed according to the strictest standards. It once happened that one of those assisting him in matzah baking pointed out to him that one of the workers who was kneading the dough was not doing such a good job. He suggested to Rav Yosef Chaim that the worker be admonished and told to work faster and more efficiently.

Rav Yosef Chaim declined, however, saying, "I refuse to distress a poor worker by admonishing him to work harder than he already does, just because I want my matzos to be a notch more *mehudar* (strictly kosher)! I, for my part, am willing to undergo the greatest effort and expense to improve the quality of my matzah. Furthermore, I pray that God grant me the merit of having matzah that meets the strictest standard, and I trust that God will accept my prayer, for He knows how intense my desire is to fulfill this mitzvah in the best possible manner. However, to obtain *mehudar* matzos at the expense of rebuking a poor laborer — the gain in terms of mitzvah-quality would be canceled out by the loss!

"Perhaps this is what the Sages had in mind," he concluded, "when they said, 'Do not read *safeguard the matzos*, but *safeguard the mitzvos*.' When baking matzos, one must remember that there are other mitzvos besides matzah in the Torah, and that care should be taken to observe them scrupulously as well!"

A similar story is told about the *Chasam Sofer*: Matzos for the needy in town were distributed out of the *Chasam Sofer's* house.

One time the maid made a mistake and accidentally gave away the *Chasam Sofer's* own extra-*mehudar* matzah to a poor man instead of the ordinary ones that were generally given out. As soon as she realized her mistake, the maid was beside herself with apprehension over what the Rav's reaction to her mistake would be. When she told the Rebbetzin what she had done, she too was distraught, and tried to think of a way to break the news to her husband without making him too upset.

When the *Chasam Sofer* arrived home just before the holiday began, he immediately noticed the worried look on everyone's faces and asked what had gone wrong. When he was told about the matzos, he turned to the Rebbetzin and said, "Don't worry. Nothing so terrible happened. It is better that we should eat ordinary matzos this year like all other Jews than allow ourselves to yield to the evil and reprehensible emotion of anger!" (Or, according to another version, he said, "It is better to put ourselves in a position of eating food that might possibly involve a small trace of *chametz* than to express even a small trace of anger!")

◆§ Soldiers of God

וַיְהִי בְּעֶצֶם הַיּוֹם הַזֶּה יָצְאוּ כָּל־צִבְאוֹת ה' מֵאֶרֶץ מִצְרָיִם
— *It was on this very day that all the legions of Hashem left the land of Egypt* (12:41).

*W*hy are the people of Israel referred to as "the legions of Hashem," as if they were some sort of army?

Rav Yosef Chaim explained that here the Torah teaches us that at all times, in all situations, a Jew must serve as a soldier for God. Just as a soldier, in times of battle, must subsist on meager rations of dried bread, so the Jews are commanded to spend seven days each year eating matzah, to recall the Exodus from Egypt, when they first became known as "the legion of Hashem." And just as a soldier must often sleep alone in the field, sheltered only by a tent or makeshift hut, so too are we commanded to spend seven days living in the sukkah, which is, by definition, a temporary dwelling, to instill in our hearts the transience of our lives here in this world.

פרשת בשלח
PARASHAS BESHALACH

✦ Where Did all Those Chariots Come From?

וַיִּקַּח שֵׁשׁ־מֵאוֹת רֶכֶב בָּחוּר וְכֹל רֶכֶב מִצְרָיִם —
He took six hundred elite chariots and all the chariots of Egypt (14:7).

The *Mechilta* (cited in Rashi) asks where the Egyptians acquired all the horses to pull these chariots! The Ten Plagues had already decimated all the livestock of Egypt (above, 9:6)! Rashi answers that these horses came from "those who feared the word of Hashem," who moved their livestock indoors whenever Moses announced an impending plague (9:20). It was thus those Egyptians who feared God that supplied the horses that gave chase to the Jews, in an attempt to kill and plunder them (below, 15:9). The *Mechilta* concludes, "Even the most worthy of the Egyptians you must kill; even with the nicest snake, you must smash its head."

A question arises concerning the *Mechilta's* observation. It is logical to assume that Pharaoh took horses for his army without asking their owners for permission. Even nowadays, in enlightened, democratic countries, citizens' cars and other personal property are pressed into military service with or without their owners' consent — and all the more so in an ancient, despotic system of government!

How, then, does the *Mechilta* see any proof here to its assertion that even the most worthy Egyptians were wicked and menacing? Perhaps they did not have any say in the matter!

Rav Yosef Chaim explained that while it is true that Pharaoh could have pressed his citizens' horses into service without their consent, this would have taken considerable organizational effort and coordination, which would have required at least several days' delay. But Pharaoh gave chase to the Jews almost immediately after they left. The only way he could have found enough horses to drive all those chariots on such short notice was if the Egyptians voluntarily dedicated all their efforts to donate their possessions to Pharaoh's "great military venture." The fact that the livestock owners did so as well indeed teaches us the lesson that in warfare, "Even the most worthy of the Egyptians you must kill."

❧ Mighty Forbearance

מִי־כָמֹכָה בָּאֵלִם ה׳ — *Who is like You among the heavenly powers, Hashem?* (15:11).

he Talmud provides a homiletical interpretation of this phrase involving the alteration of the word אֵלִים (*heavenly powers*) into אִלְּמִים (*mute, silent*). Sometimes God shows His might through His remarkable forbearance. Even in the face of the most vile sacrilege and blasphemy — such as the destruction and desecration of the Temple by the Romans — God remains silent (*Gittin* 56b). The question arises, however: While this observation may be true, what is its relevance to the Song of the Sea? The drowning of the Egyptians in the Red Sea was an example of God's action in decimating His enemies, not one of His forbearance and patience in the face of provocation!

The answer to this question, explained Rav Yosef Chaim, is that it was precisely at this time, when the Israelites saw God's harsh judgment unleashed with such unrestrained wrath, when all the nations of Canaan "heard and were agitated, were gripped with terror, confounded and trembling with fear" (vv. 14-15), that they realized the extent to which God was willing to devastate those who angered Him. It was at that point that, in retrospect, they realized how reserved and restrained God had acted during their 210 years of repression and enslavement by the Egyptians. They could only now appreciate that the lengthy period of time during which the Egyptians were shown grace and forbearance indeed proved God's tremendous "might" in His tolerance of sin and provocation.

✑§ Amalek and Tomorrow

וַיֹּאמֶר מֹשֶׁה אֶל־יְהוֹשֻׁעַ בְּחַר־לָנוּ אֲנָשִׁים וְצֵא הִלָּחֵם בַּעֲמָלֵק מָחָר אָנֹכִי נִצָּב עַל־רֹאשׁ הַגִּבְעָה — *Moses said to Joshua, "Choose people for us and go do battle with Amalek; tomorrow I will stand on top of the hill"* (17:9).

The Gemara (*Yoma* 52b) lists the word מָחָר in this verse as one of the words in the Torah that can be interpreted as either belonging to the preceding phrase ("Go do battle with Amalek tomorrow; I will stand on top of the hill") or the following phrase ("Go do battle with Amalek; tomorrow I will stand on top of the hill").

What, we may ask, is the importance of the word "tomorrow" altogether in this narrative? What element of insight does the Torah impart to us by telling us when the battle against Amalek was to be undertaken?

Rav Yosef Chaim saw an allusion in this word to a deeper concept. Amalek represents the forces of evil in man's heart — the *yetzer hara* (see following piece). It is the function of the *yetzer hara* to tempt man to sin. Sometimes, however, outright incitement does not work. The *yetzer hara* cannot convince a sane, composed person to go and commit murder, for instance. It is difficult, in fact, for the *yetzer hara* to drive a religious person to directly break any of the commandments. Therefore it acts in more discreet, sinister ways. One of its most potent tools is that of "tomorrow." The *yetzer hara* assures its victim that, "Yes, of course you are going to do that mitzvah. Of course you will give your due to *tzedakah*, you will increase your time allotted for

Torah study. But not today. You will start tomorrow." In this manner, with one "tomorrow" leading to the next, and with each passing day diminishing the person's resolve to do the good deed that he had intended to do, the *yetzer hara* outwits and overpowers its victim. It is this facet of "Amalekism" that the Torah tells us to eradicate — we must take immediate action to implement mitzvos that present themselves to us, and not allow lethargy to lead to endless procrastination. This idea, said Rav Yosef Chaim, is alluded to further in v. 11: "It happened that when Moses raised his hand Israel was victorious, and when he lowered his hand Amalek was victorious." When a person "raises his hand," i.e., he lifts up his hands in action and deed, he defeats Amalek — the personification of the *yetzer hara*. But when he "lowers his hands," when he becomes inactive and lazy, postponing action for a later time, Amalek has achieved victory.

∽§ What Amalek Stands For

וַיֹּאמֶר ה׳ אֶל־מֹשֶׁה כְּתֹב זֹאת זִכָּרוֹן בַּסֵּפֶר... כִּי־ מָחֹה אֶמְחֶה אֶת־זֵכֶר עֲמָלֵק — *Hashem said to Moses, "Write this as a remembrance in the Book... that I shall surely erase the memory of Amalek"* (17:14).

It is one of the mitzvos of the Torah that we not forget what Amalek did to us, and that we obliterate the Amalekites "from under the heavens" (*Devarim* 25:19). All this is due to the fact that Amalek engaged Israel in a war, which he lost in any event. Why does the Torah deal with Amalek so severely? There were so many nations that did much more harm to the Jewish people over the years, and we do not find that any of them were slated for destruction — except for Amalek.

Furthermore, as this mitzvah is one of the 613 that are applicable for all time, we must ask: What exactly does the Torah expect of us in terms of compliance with this commandment? There is no longer a specific country or nationality called "Amalek," so it is impossible for us to destroy it. Perhaps some people in the world today are descended from the original Amalekites, but it seems totally illogical to imagine that the Torah desires us to figure out who these individuals are and to unceremoniously put them to death. And if one should suggest that the Torah wants us only to "blot out the memory" (ibid.) — but not the physical entity — of Amalek, this too is impossible. For the Torah is eternal, and it itself reminds us of Amalek and even exhorts us not to forget them (ibid.). (See *Ha'amek Davar*, which deals with these issues.)

Rav Yosef Chaim interpreted the Torah's mitzvah of "blotting out Amalek" to be a conceptual one. We are commanded to eradicate from our minds the negative spiritual influences which Amalek embodied. And what exactly did Amalek's detrimental spiritual force consist of? In *Devarim* 25:18 the Torah relates that "Amalek encountered you (קָרְךָ) on the way [as you were going out of Egypt]." The Sages interpret the word קָרְךָ in a different manner as well — "he cooled you off." After the Israelites left Egypt, having just experienced the miracles of the Exodus and the Red Sea, an intense faith in the certainty of God and His Providence were deeply ingrained in the people's consciousness. When Amalek came along and attacked, killing some of the weak and defenseless people, he suddenly "cooled off" this profound faith, injecting an element of doubt and skepticism into the hearts of the people, who actually wondered, "Is Hashem in our midst or not?" (*Shemos* 17:7). (Rav Yosef Chaim noted further that the numerical value of עֲמָלֵק [*Amalek*] and סָפֵק [*doubt*] are each 240.) It is this attitude of skepticism and uncertainty in faith — personified by Amalek — that the Torah commands us to eradicate from our midst.

פרשת יתרו
PARASHAS YISRO

✒ The "Path and Deeds" of Rav Yosef Chaim

וְהִזְהַרְתָּה אֶתְהֶם אֶת־הַחֻקִּים וְאֶת־הַתּוֹרֹת וְהוֹדַעְתָּ
לָהֶם אֶת־הַדֶּרֶךְ יֵלְכוּ בָהּ וְאֶת־הַמַּעֲשֶׂה אֲשֶׁר יַעֲשׂוּן
— *You shall caution them regarding the decrees and the teachings, and you shall make known to them the path in which they should go and the deeds that they should do* (18:20).

After informing the people of God's "decrees and teachings," what else was left for Moses to tell them that might be incorporated under the categories of "the path in which they should go and the deeds that they should do"? The Sages of the Talmud (*Bava Metzia* 30b) explain that "the path" mentioned here refers to acts of kindness, and "the deeds" refer to conducting oneself in a manner that goes beyond what is strictly required by law.

Rav Yosef Chaim personified these traits in his selfless dedication in showing concern and providing assistance to others, which he pursued to a remarkable degree, as some of the following anecdotes reveal.

As the foremost figure in the Orthodox community of Jerusalem, Rav Yosef Chaim often received donations from abroad to be distributed among the poor. One time he received a sum of money that was earmarked for a particular needy Torah scholar. He went to deliver it personally to the specified address. Told that the man was not at home, Rav Yosef Chaim turned around and returned to his house. When the man in question returned home, his family told him that Rav Yosef Chaim had been looking for him, and he immediately and hastily set out for his house, wondering what urgent matter could have brought the Rav to his home. When he was told that the cause of the visit was a sum of money that the Rav had sought to deliver to him, he was astounded.

"The Rav did not have to trouble himself to go all the way to my house just for that," the man told him apologetically. "He could have sent it with someone else!"

"But the donor wrote in his letter, 'Please deliver this money to So-and-so,' " explained Rav Yosef Chaim. "If I was entrusted with this task, it would have been negligent on my part if I had delegated it to anyone else!"

Rav Yosef Chaim was always the first one to arrive in the synagogue in the morning, and the last to leave. There was no other commitment or distraction that could prevent him from promptly heading out to prayers when the time came. Thus, the congregants in the synagogue were quite surprised one Shabbos when they saw Rav Yosef Chaim disappear early on in the prayers. After a short while, some concerned members of the congregation went downstairs, where Rav Yosef Chaim's apartment was located, to look for him. When he was not found there, their apprehension became even greater.

One of the congregants soon discovered what had happened. Rav Yosef Chaim had noticed that a certain elderly man, who was childless and lived alone, had not come to the synagogue for prayers. Concerned over his absence, the Rav went to his apartment to see if he was perhaps not feeling well, or might need assistance. When his knocks at the door went unanswered, he took an axe and broke the door down, for, though it was Shabbos, he thought the old man might be in mortal danger. As it turned out, the man had unfortunately died in his bed during the night.

Such was Rav Yosef Chaim's tremendous concern for others, that it was only he who noticed that this lonely old man had not arrived at the synagogue on time, and that he personally took responsibility for searching for him and determining the cause of his absence.

A Jerusalem resident recounted that one time, on a rainy day, he was shopping in the Machaneh Yehudah market. When the rain began to pour particularly heavily, he took shelter under one of the many awnings in the area, and stood there next to several other shelter-seekers, among them a woman from Battei Machaseh — Rav Yosef Chaim's neighborhood — who was clutching a baby close to her, protecting it from the harsh weather. Suddenly he noticed that a horse-drawn carriage pulled up to the spot where he was standing. Rav Yosef Chaim quickly got out of the covered part of the carriage and spryly — though he was nearly 80 years old! — jumped into the empty seat next to the driver, which was completely exposed to the elements. He told the woman to get into the carriage with her baby, for he was on his way to Battei Machaseh. The woman declined the offer, saying that she would in no way travel in a carriage while the Rav sat outdoors in the rain. Rav Yosef Chaim, already quite drenched, was insistent. He told her that in any event he would not go back inside the carriage, for he had already "donated" the seat for the purpose of performing a mitzvah, and could not retract the gesture. Since he would be riding next to the driver anyway, he explained to the woman, she might as well sit in the empty carriage! The woman finally consented, and got home safe and sound — and dry.

◄§ Despising Money

וְאַתָּה תֶחֱזֶה מִכָּל־הָעָם אַנְשֵׁי־חַיִל יִרְאֵי אֱלֹהִים אַנְשֵׁי אֱמֶת שֹׂנְאֵי בָצַע — *And you shall discern from among the entire people, men of accomplishment, God-fearing people, men of truth, people who despise money* (18:21).

The *Mechilta* elaborates on the quality of "despising money": "This refers to people who despise their own money when it [interferes with] justice, and all the more so the money of others." This trait, too, was exemplified by Rav Yosef Chaim.

There was a rule in the charter of *Kolel Shomrei Hachomos* that every member was entitled to a grant of ten napoleons (gold coins) when marrying off a son or daughter, to assist in the expenses of the wedding. For some reason, when Rav Yosef Chaim was about to marry off his son Rav Yaakov Meir, the treasurer of the *kolel* completely forgot to provide him with the grant money — despite the fact that Rav Yosef Chaim himself was at the helm of the administration of the *kolel*. The weeks and months went by, the wedding day was approaching, but the money was not delivered. It was not Rav Yosef Chaim's nature to demand money from others, even when it was his own money that others rightly owed him — and certainly not to demand funds from others. He thus did not raise the issue with the treasurer of the *kolel*. He disdained borrowing money as well, but he soon realized that he had no other option, and was forced to undertake a loan to pay for the wedding expenses.

On the morning of the wedding day, the treasurer of the *kolel* suddenly realized his oversight. He ran to Rav Yosef Chaim's house, bearing the ten napoleons of the "wedding stipend" and profuse apologies for his forgetfulness.

To his surprise, however, Rav Yosef Chaim declined the money. "I am not entitled to this grant," he declared, as he adamantly refused to accept the coins. "The rule states that ten napoleons should be given for the purpose of assisting in 'covering wedding expenses.' I have already borrowed all the funds I need for the wedding. What I have now is debts. The ten napoleons are specifically designated for a 'wedding stipend,' and I cannot accept them to use as a 'debt-repayment' stipend!"

ᴇ§ The Light of Shabbos

זָכוֹר אֶת־יוֹם הַשַּׁבָּת לְקַדְּשׁוֹ — *Remember the Sabbath day to sanctify it* (20:8).

*T*he honor of Shabbos was one of Rav Yosef Chaim's foremost concerns, and he wrote many letters of support and encouragement to the *Mishmeres Shabbos* committees that made the rounds in Jerusalem urging stores, businesses, etc. to close on Friday afternoon in time for Shabbos.

When he was older, Rav Yosef Chaim walked with the aid of a cane, but on Shabbos he refrained from using the walking stick. Since he was so used to walking with the cane, and he did not want to experience discomfort on Shabbos, he would spend the whole day Friday walking without it, so that when Shabbos arrived he would be somewhat accustomed to walking unaided.

One time, on a Friday night, Rav Yosef Chaim's rebbetzin became ill, and it was necessary to summon a doctor. The Rav immediately set out to call Dr. Schwartz, a Viennese physician who was patronized by the Orthodox Jewish community, especially those of Austro-Hungarian descent. Responding to the knocking, Dr. Schwartz came to answer the door with a lantern in his hand. Rav Yosef Chaim was very disappointed and saddened to see the Shabbos desecrated in such a casual and unnecessary manner, but he restrained himself from saying anything to the doctor; this was not the time to engage in religious discussions and remonstrations!

The Rav led the doctor to his house, where he examined the Rebbetzin and administered some medication, which soon brought a marked improvement in her condition. Rav Yosef Chaim thanked the doctor for his services, and began to accompany him back to his house, as the first light of dawn began to rise in the eastern sky.

On the way, Rav Yosef Chaim turned to the physician and asked him, "Tell me, Doctor, what is the relative size of the head, compared with the body as a whole? As a medical man, you certainly are able to tell me that!"

Dr. Schwartz was somewhat puzzled by the seemingly irrelevant question, but he provided the Rav with the information he sought. "The human head takes up approximately one seventh of the entire body."

"Only a seventh part!" exclaimed Rav Yosef Chaim, as he prepared to make his point, through an allegory. "Imagine this," he began. "All the limbs and organs of the body united against the head, declaring, 'It's not fair! We do all the work — the hands fashion, the feet walk, and every other part of the body has an important function to fulfill. But when it comes time to eat, it's the head that opens up its mouth and devours all the food! Furthermore, when it comes time to express an opinion, again it is the mouth that arrogates for itself the position of spokesman! We protest!'

"But the head easily countered their arguments. 'You are right that the eating and the talking emanate from me. But this is only right, for it is I who directs and orchestrates all the actions of the body, and it is I who enables their functioning. If not for me, you would all be worthless hunks of flesh!'"

"That was a good, cogent argument!" the doctor said approvingly, entertained by the Rav's story, though still puzzled by what the point was supposed to be.

Once the Rav saw that he had loosened up the normally somber mood of the doctor, he continued, "The ratio of the head's size to the rest of the body is exactly the same ratio with which God has divided up man's days — six days of physical, material pursuits, and one day of rest, during which man can refresh his spiritual essence. From this day of rest man draws his inspiration and blessing for the other six days of the week. As the author of the *Lechah Dodi* poem puts it, Shabbos 'is the source of blessing' — כִּי הִיא מְקוֹר הַבְּרָכָה. Just as the head exerts its control and guidance over the rest of the body, so Shabbos is the one day that endows the rest of the days with meaning and perspective. If not for the opportunity that Shabbos provides to restore the spiritual and social balance that is upset during the six weekdays of incessant materialistic pursuits, man would become an indentured servant to his passions and monetary aspirations. His spiritual and intellectual side would be totally subdued, if not eliminated; man and his donkey would stride side by side as they sweat and toil pulling the plow. Now that God has given us this great gift of Shabbos, however, it preserves man's spiritual integrity, and imbues all the days of the week with purpose and meaning. We should therefore take the utmost care in preserving the Shabbos, just as it preserves *us*, in body and spirit!"

Rav Yosef Chaim's words, which were uttered in fluent, elegant German idiom, impressed the doctor greatly, and he pledged, "From now on I will let the Shabbos — not a lantern — light up my path!"

✌§ The Mitzvah with a Reward

כַּבֵּד אֶת־אָבִיךָ וְאֶת־אִמֶּךָ לְמַעַן יַאֲרִכוּן יָמֶיךָ עַל הָאֲדָמָה — *Honor your father and your mother, so that your days will be lengthened upon the land* (20:12).

his is one of the very few mitzvos concerning which the Torah explicitly promises a reward in return for its observance. Why indeed does the Torah see fit to provide this guarantee in this particular case?

Rav Yosef Chaim explained the reason for this as follows. The halachah states that when honoring one's parents one need not incur a personal monetary loss; the expenses for the mitzvah may be taken from the parents' own funds (*Kiddushin* 32a). But, as the familiar saying goes, "Time is money." What of the valuable time that a person invests in giving honor to his parents? How is one reimbursed for this "expense"? This is why the Torah informs us here that the reward for honoring parents is "lengthened days," or long life. One need not be concerned over "losing time" when honoring his parents, for all such "losses" will be returned — with interest — in the form of added longevity.

פרשת משפטים
PARASHAS MISHPATIM

✑§ The Best of Doctors

וְרַפֹּא יְרַפֵּא — *He shall provide for healing* (21:19).

he Talmud (*Bava Kama* 88a) learns from this verse that it is permissible for the ill to seek — and for the physician to provide — medical care for illness and disease (and doing so is not considered to be an act of defiance against God, Who inflicted the condition in the first place — Rashi). Nevertheless, the Sages declare, "The best of doctors (lit., *the good of the doctors*) ends up in *Gehinnom*!" Why do the Sages provide doctors with such a dismal prognosis for their condition in the Next World?

Rav Yosef Chaim interpreted the Sages' dictum in the following manner: "If one is to be a good doctor, he must sometimes be prepared to risk his share in *Gan Eden* (and thus end up in *Gehinnom*)." This is because the halachah declares that when a person is near death, it is forbidden to move him or alter his situation in any way, lest it inadvertently hasten his death in the process, which would be tantamount to murder. A doctor, however, is often able to save a patient's life in such situations, and bring him back from the brink of death, and he is, in fact, *obligated* to try to do so. It emerges, therefore, that a doctor must often gamble with his reward in the Next World when he treats patients who are gravely ill. On the one hand, he is obligated to provide treatment, for there is no task more sacred than saving a person's life; yet, if he ends up hastening the patient's death instead of prolonging his life, he will emerge from the ordeal a "murderer." Any "good doctor" is expected, of course, to risk the consequences of *Gehinnom* and provide the necessary treatment, in the hope that it will achieve the desired result.

Rav Yosef Chaim had a very friendly relationship with Dr. Moshe Wallach, the founder and director of Shaarei Tzedek Hospital. One time, while the two men were engaged in friendly conversation, Rav Yosef Chaim offered the following humorous explanation of the Sages' saying about doctors. "You are such a dedicated doctor," he told Dr. Wallach. "You often work days and nights without stopping to rest, especially in times of emergency. Doctors like you don't have any place in *Gan Eden*, for everyone there will be in perfect condition. In *Gehinnom*, however, according to kabbalistic teaching, those who sinned with their hands will have their hands missing, those who had sinful eyes will find themselves without eyes, and so on for all the limbs of the body. They will be in very poor shape indeed! That's where 'the best of doctors' are really needed!"

In those days, there was a certain well-known doctor by the name of Bufeles. He was an observant and pious Jew, but he always charged a very high price for his services. People used to ask him why he did not show a bit more charitableness in determining his fees.

"Do you know why good doctors are destined for *Gehinnom*?" he asked in response to this question. "It is because illness is an instrument by which God brings punishment upon man for his sins. Now, let us say that God has determined that a certain person must suffer an illness that will cost him such and such an amount of money. If a doctor is 'good' (טוב, which can also mean *kindly*, or *disposed toward generosity*), and charges, say, $50 per visit instead of $100, he is in fact doubling that person's suffering, for it will take him twice as long to reach the amount of money that had been decreed that he lose to this illness! Therefore, the 'nice doctors,' who have pity on their patients and charge less, are in fact bringing extra distress upon the patient, and will end up in *Gehinnom*!"

✑§ Care for the Downtrodden

כָּל־אַלְמָנָה וְיָתוֹם לֹא תְעַנּוּן — *You shall not cause pain to any widow or orphan* (22:21).

*R*av Yosef Chaim's concern for the downtrodden, and his extent to which all his considerations and decisions in life were so delicately balanced, are illustrated in the following story:

Rav Nachum Bergman served for many years as the *chazan* on the High Holy Days in the shul in Battei Machaseh. One year, he passed away at the end of Elul, just over a week before Rosh Hashanah. The question of who would take Rav Nachum's place as *chazan* on such short notice immediately arose. Although Rav Nachum's sons were quite capable of following in their father's footsteps and filling his position as *chazan* — and it was fully assumed that one day they would indeed do so — it is customary that during the year of mourning for a parent, one does not lead the services on Shabbos or *Yom Tov*. One of the congregants offered his services as a temporary replacement, but Rav Yosef Chaim declined to accept his offer. He told the *gabbaim* who were in charge of organizing the services that they should not worry about who would serve as *chazan* on Rosh Hashanah. The *gabbaim* understood that Rav Yosef Chaim himself wanted to lead the prayers this year, and they removed the issue from their holiday agenda.

When it came time for *Musaf* on the first day of Rosh Hashanah, however, the *gabbaim* were quite surprised to see Rav Yosef Chaim approaching Rav Shimon Bergman, Rav Nachum's son, and asking him to approach the podium and serve as *chazan*. The *gabbaim* — along with everyone else in shul — were puzzled at the Rav's unconventional actions.

After the prayers were finished, Rav Yosef Chaim shared his reasons for his decision with the curious congregants. "The reason that a mourner is not generally allowed to lead the services on Shabbos and *Yom Tov*," he explained, "is because it is considered to be a display of a lack of sensitivity and respect toward the congregants. Now, let us make a calculation. The unfortunate widow, who has just lost her beloved husband so suddenly, is sitting in the women's section. When the soulful tones of the introductory prayer of *Musaf, Hineni he'ani,* begin to resonate in the shul, she will be overcome with emotional distress and grief when she suddenly hears the voice of a stranger filling the position of her husband. Hearing her son taking the place of their father, however, will be a great source of solace and comfort for her. Now, causing pain to a widow constitutes a Torah prohibition (as our verse states). I submit that it is perfectly in line with the requirement of showing respect to the congregation if Rav Nachum's son is allowed to lead the prayers, despite the fact that he is a mourner, if this somewhat eases the plight of this unfortunate woman!"

Another story comes to mind when speaking of Rav Yosef Chaim and his concern for the feelings and welfare of orphans.

Rav Yosef Chaim served as the head of the Diskin Orphanage in Jerusalem. One time the administration found it necessary to dismiss a certain teacher who, it was felt, was not doing such a good job. A group of well-meaning individuals, who had pity on the poor fellow who suddenly found himself out of a job, approached Rav Yosef Chaim and argued that although the teacher might have certain shortcomings, perhaps he should be shown leniency, taking into consideration the fact that he had no source of income with which to feed his wife and many children.

Rav Yosef Chaim refused to accept their plea, however. He turned to them and said, "It's really very unfortunate that he doesn't have what to eat. But just because of that we should allow him to eat (devour) orphans?!"

◆§ A Curse and a Blessing

אֱלֹהִים לֹא תְקַלֵּל — *You shall not curse a judge* (22:27).

av Yosef Chaim served for a short time as head of the *beis din* of Rav Yehoshua Leib Diskin. During his tenure as *av beis din,* he was confronted with a bitterly disputed divorce case. After he ruled in favor of the husband's side, the members of the wife's family, who felt that the ruling was unjust, barged into Rav Yosef Chaim's house and began shouting and cursing at him. The men were so vicious and violent that the Rebbetzin, who was sitting in an adjacent room and witnessed the entire event, began sobbing uncontrollably. It was a week before Rosh Hashanah, and, being so close to the days of judgment, their cruel words grated most harshly on her sensitive heart.

Throughout the outburst, Rav Yosef Chaim remained seated peacefully and didn't even lift his head up from his Gemara. When the shouting and commotion began to get out of hand, however, Rav Yosef Chaim arose, looked them straight in the eye, and declared sternly, "Listen now to what I have to say!" A sudden silence fell upon the room.

"If you are correct in your claims and accusations against me, and I and my *beis din* erred, you have already registered your complaint with the One Above. May He have mercy on us, for a judge is only human and can rule only in accordance with what his eyes see before him.

"But if we are correct and you are wrong, if our ruling is indeed justified, then — " Rav Yosef paused for a moment, as the protesters braced themselves for some scathing words of rebuke. "Then, I want you to know that I forgive you with a full heart for your disgraceful outburst, and for all the pain you have caused me and the members of my family, and I wish you to be inscribed for a good year!"

The men were shocked — and overcome with embarrassment — by the Rav's humility, and left in disgrace, as the neighbors were beginning to congregate to see what the commotion was all about.

Some days later, on erev Yom Kippur, as Rav Yosef Chaim was returning from prayers at the Western Wall, the ringleader of the unruly men who had insulted him approached him and asked his forgiveness for his impudent behavior. Rav Yosef Chaim reaffirmed that he indeed forgave him with all his heart, and the man was greatly relieved. Rav Yosef Chaim then asked him the curious question, "Tell me, have you bought an *esrog* yet?"

"What a question!" the man replied with a slight overtone of pride. "I found myself a real 'beautiful fruit,' as it says in the Torah (*Vayikra* 23:40), if there ever was one! It cost me half a napoleon (a gold coin), but it was well worth it!"

Rav Yosef Chaim then continued, "Let's make a calculation now. You know, in order to fulfill a positive commandment, such as holding an *esrog* on Sukkos, one is obligated to spend no more than one fifth of his money. Yet in order to avoid transgressing a negative commandment one is required to forfeit everything he has. Now, there is a negative commandment of 'You shall not curse a judge.' What is the Torah referring to with these words? Is it addressing the party in whose favor the judge has ruled? It hardly seems likely, for that party would be more inclined to bless the judge than curse him! No, it is certainly referring to the one who lost the case. Now, if he realizes that the judge has ruled fairly and that he is indeed guilty as charged, he also has no reason to curse the judge. We must conclude, therefore, that the Torah's prohibition is addressed to someone who believes with all his heart that the judge has made a mistake and miscarried justice in ruling against him.

"Now, I ask you, in comparing this negative commandment with the Torah's positive commandments, which must be taken more seriously? Where is the sense of proportion?!"

◆§ A Bribe for the Righteous

וְשֹׁחַד לֹא תִקָּח כִּי הַשֹּׁחַד יְעַוֵּר פִּקְחִים וִיסַלֵּף דִּבְרֵי צַדִּיקִים — *Do not accept a bribe, for the bribe will blind those who see and corrupt the words of the righteous* (23:8).

Commenting on the words, "corrupt the words of the righteous," the Gemara (*Kesubos* 105a) writes, "Even a completely righteous person who takes a bribe will eventually have his opinions distorted." The depiction of a thoroughly righteous person taking a bribe is somewhat puzzling — if someone accepts a bribe he is, by definition, not completely righteous!

With the help of the following story about Rav Yosef Chaim and his phenomenal integrity we will be able to better understand the Sages' statement.

It was toward the end of World War I, when the World Zionist Organization was beginning to assert its control over the Jewish community in *Eretz Yisrael* — a development which the old

Orthodox community strongly opposed. Rav Yosef Chaim came home from prayers one morning and, without stopping to eat breakfast, put on his hat and coat and left home. His son, Rav Yaakov Meir, knew that Rav Yosef Chaim never left home for the day without having a bite to eat first, and quickly realized that something unusual was going on. He decided to accompany his father to wherever he might be headed so urgently.

Rav Yosef Chaim, accompanied by his son, left the Old City through Jaffa Gate and headed for the bank. He approached the clerk who was in charge of overseas money transfers and told him that he wanted a $100 transfer that had been sent to him returned to the sender. Rav Yaakov Meir could not contain his amazement.

"Surely you know, Father," he protested, "that your children and grandchildren suffer from poverty and hunger at this time — including me and my children! If you did not want to keep the donation for yourself, you could have at least forwarded it to us, to provide sustenance for our families until the situation improves and life gets back to normal!" (A hundred dollars went a long way in those days!)

"You are right, my son," replied Rav Yosef Chaim apologetically. "I have never accepted a free gift from anyone in my life. Even if I would want to compromise on this principle in this case, to ease the plight of my family, I cannot do so in this instance. You see, the donation was sent to me anonymously, and I am afraid that it was sent from the Zionists in an attempt to buy my support for their cause. One day they may come forward and argue before me, 'Don't you remember the $100 you received a while back? Well, what about some reciprocal good will?' I cannot allow this possibility. Therefore I decided to return the gift hastily and immediately, before I had a chance to be tempted to change my mind about it! As for my hungry children and grandchildren — God has ways to provide them with sustenance without resorting to methods involving compromise on matters of principle!"

This anecdote illustrates clearly how it is possible for a "bribe" to find its way into the hands of a fully righteous person and ultimately influence his ability to act with impartiality.

פרשת תרומה
PARASHAS TERUMAH

◆§ For God's Sake

> דַּבֵּר אֶל־בְּנֵי יִשְׂרָאֵל וְיִקְחוּ־לִי תְּרוּמָה —
> *Speak to the Children of Israel that they take to Me a portion* (25:2).

ashi explains that the word לִי (*to Me* or *for Me*) indicates here *for My sake* — that is, "with the intention of giving it to Me."

The Gemara (*Sotah* 13b) relates that upon Moses' death God Himself eulogized him, declaring, "Who will rise up for Me against evildoers? Who will stand up for Me against those who commit iniquity?" (*Tehillim* 94:16). Now that Moses was gone, who would take his place in fulfilling these important roles?

The question presents itself, however: Joshua and the seventy elders had been duly appointed as Moses' successors; why could they not "stand up against evildoers and those who commit iniquity"? Were they inadequate for these roles in some way?

The answer to this question is supplied by Rashi's commentary on the Gemara (ibid.). Commenting on "stand up for Me against evildoers," Rashi writes, "to admonish them *for My sake*." Once again, Rashi explains that the word לִי is to be understood as "for My sake." Moses had a relationship with God that was unparalleled in human history (see *Yevamos* 49b; Rambam, *Hil. Yesodei HaTorah* 7:6); he was the only one about whom it could be said, "God knew him face to face" (*Devarim* 34:10). For this reason, when he rebuked a person wholly "for the sake of God," he was able to do so on a level that could not possibly be achieved by any other person. This is why God lamented over him, "Who will now rise up *for My sake* against evildoers? Who will stand up *for My sake* against those who commit iniquity?"

פרשת כי תשא
PARASHAS KI SISA

◄§ The Half and the Whole

זֶה יִתְּנוּ כָּל־הָעֹבֵר עַל־הַפְּקֻדִים מַחֲצִית הַשָּׁקֶל
— *This shall they give — everyone who passes through the census — a half shekel* (30:13).

When the Temple was standing, every adult male Jew had to give a half-shekel donation each year, to contribute to the maintenance of the public sacrificial service. Some commentators suggest that the reason this particular denomination — a half shekel, as opposed to a whole unit — was chosen for this purpose was to intimate the lesson that each Jew is incomplete as an individual, and only when he joins together with the community does he become whole and fully functional.

Rav Yosef Chaim applied this explanation to shed light on the words of the Mishnah (*Shekalim* 1:1): "On the first of Adar announcements are made concerning the donation of the *shekalim* and concerning *kilayim* (crops that are commingled in a forbidden manner)." What is the connection between these two seemingly disparate matters — *shekalim* and *kilayim* — that the Mishnah *juxtaposes them? Rav Yosef Chaim explained the relationship as follows. It is important for a person to cultivate social relationships with other people ("Acquire for yourself a friend" — Avos 1:6), for if he carries out a totally individualistic, self-centered life, he is considered to be an incomplete person, as* explained above. Nevertheless, when choosing his friends he must be sure to associate with the appropriate group of people, for just as certain mixtures of crops are forbidden, so is it unwise to affiliate oneself with people of questionable or incompatible character.

Rav Yosef Chaim offered a further support for this idea, noting that in *Pirkei Avos* (2:9), when Rabbi Yehoshua was asked what the most important focus of a man's life should be, he said, "[Having] a good friend." When asked what a man should most avoid in life, he responded, "A bad friend." As important as friendship is to a person's character fulfillment, it is just as important to ensure that the pursuit of this vital objective should not turn into a source of disruption in one's life rather than one of contentment.

◆§ Purim and the *Ketores*

וְאַתָּה קַח־לְךָ בְּשָׂמִים רֹאשׁ מָר־דְּרוֹר וכו' —
Now you take for yourself choice spices
— pure myrrh, etc. (30:23).

The Gemara (*Chullin* 139b) sees an allusion to Mordechai (of the story of the Megillah) in these words, for מָר דְּרוֹר (*pure myrrh*) is rendered by Onkelos as מֵירָא דַכְיָא, the letters of which are virtually identical to מָרְדְּכַי (*Mordechai*). Rashi explains what the allusion is supposed to indicate: The righteous are compared to fragrant spices (see *Megillah* 13a, *Shir Hashirim Rabbah* on 1:13, etc.). Pure myrrh is referred to as "the choicest spice," indicating that Mordechai was the foremost of the righteous of his day, the Men of the Great Assembly.

Rav Yosef Chaim added that just as Mordechai's name is alluded to among the fragrant spices of the "oil of anointment," so can an allusion to Haman's name be found among the spices of the *ketores* (incense). One of the ingredients of the *ketores* is *chelbenah* (galbanum), a bitter, pungent-smelling herb. Now, it happens that חֶלְבְּנָה (*chelbenah*) has the same numerical value as הָמָן (*Haman*) — 95!

פרשת ויקהל
PARSHAS VAYAKHEL

✍ Shabbos — Eternal Covenant

שֵׁשֶׁת יָמִים תֵּעָשֶׂה מְלָאכָה וּבַיּוֹם הַשְּׁבִיעִי יִהְיֶה
לָכֶם קֹדֶשׁ שַׁבַּת שַׁבָּתוֹן — *On six days work
may be done, but the seventh day shall
be holy for you, a day of complete rest*
(35:2).

*T*he commentators deal with the placement of this command of Sabbath observance in this particular place in
the Torah, where it does not seem to be relevant to its
context. A similar problem exists with the Sabbath command
found above, in 31:12-17: "You shall observe My Sabbaths, for it is
a sign between Me and you for your generations, etc." Rav Yosef
Chaim suggested a novel explanation to account for both of these
passages.

The Talmud (*Shabbos* 87a) tells us what went through Moses'
head just before he decided to break the Tablets of the Law that
God Himself had given him. "Concerning the Pesach sacrifice,
which is only one of the mitzvos of the Torah," he reasoned, "the
Torah says, 'No alienated person (apostate) may eat of it.' Here I
have the *entire* Torah, and all Israel has become estranged from
their faith. Can I possibly give it to them?" Moses thus felt that

the Jewish people had forfeited their privilege of receiving God's Torah.

Elsewhere as well, the Sages teach that through the episode of the Golden Calf and the consequent breaking of the Tablets, the Jewish people's unique relationship with God was severed in a sense.

Now, the Talmud (*Sanhedrin* 58b) teaches that it is forbidden for a non-Jew to observe Shabbos. The Israelites, after realizing the extent to which they had angered God, were despondent (see above, 33:4). They were afraid that now that they had become estranged from Him, they were no longer entitled to the rights and privileges of God's favored people, and that, as virtual non-Jews, they would have the gift of the Shabbos taken away from them. Therefore, the Torah records the command to observe the Sabbath immediately prior to the story of the Golden Calf (above, 32:12ff), and immediately thereafter (our verse), as if to reassure the Jewish people, "Just as you were considered full-fledged Jews before you lapsed, to whom the Shabbos applies, so you remain true, complete Jews after God forgave you for your sin!"

פרשת פקודי
PARASHAS PEKUDEI

❧ The Temple as Collateral

אֵלֶּה פְקוּדֵי הַמִּשְׁכָּן מִשְׁכַּן הָעֵדֻת — *These are the reckonings of the Tabernacle, the Tabernacle of Testimony* (38:21).

Why is the word "Tabernacle" stated twice? Rashi, employing a play on the word מִשְׁכָּן (*Tabernacle*), which can also mean "collateral," writes: "This is an allusion to the Temple, which was taken as collateral twice, when the two Temples were destroyed, because of the sins of Israel."

A young student once asked Rav Yosef Chaim, "If the destruction of the Temple is compared to the taking of collateral for the sins of Israel, why doesn't God return the pledge to us, especially since we long and yearn for it so much?"

Rav Yosef Chaim told him that there is a law in the Torah that requires the lender to return a security taken for a loan when the borrower is poor and is in need of the pledged object. For instance, if the collateral is a blanket, and the borrower has no other blanket to use, it must be loaned back to him every night (above, 22:25-26; *Devarim* 24:12-13). If the poor man has another blanket, however, it is not necessary to return it to him until he pays his debt.

"Now, do you want to know why God does not return our 'collateral' that He has taken from us?" Rav Yosef Chaim answered the boy. "It is because most Jews are perfectly content with the way their lives are in exile. They have wealth, comfort and prestige. They are quite satisfied with their present situation, and do not feel the urgent need for an end to our exile and the return of God's *Shechinah* to the Temple. There is thus no requirement for Him to return this 'collateral' as yet!"

Expressing similar sentiments, the *Shelah* wrote long ago, "My heart aches within me when I see that the Jews build beautiful houses for themselves, like palaces of princes, making permanent, long-lasting dwelling arrangements for themselves. This gives the impression that they have a lack of appreciation and expectation for our Messianic redemption."

ספר ויקרא
VAYIKRA/LEVITICUS

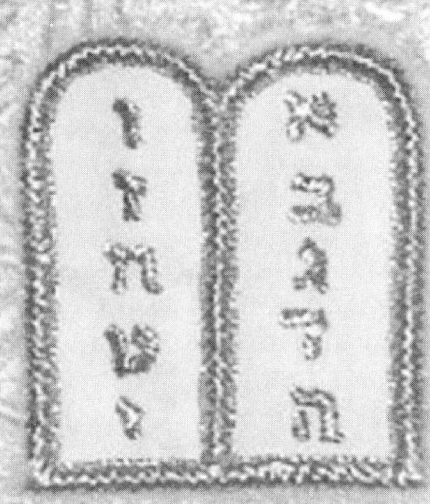

פרשת ויקרא
PARASHAS VAYIKRA

◄§ The Torah Forbids It

כִּי כָל־שְׂאֹר וְכָל־דְּבַשׁ לֹא־תַקְטִירוּ מִמֶּנּוּ אִשֶּׁה לַה׳
— For you shall not burn any leaven or
honey as a fire offering to Hashem (2:11).

*I*n the *Talmud Yerushalmi* (*Yoma* 4:5, excerpted in the
morning prayers), we are taught concerning the daily incense offering: "Bar Kappara taught: If they would have
included in [the incense's] composition a *kortov* (a minuscule
amount) of honey, it would have been impossible for anyone to stand
[in its presence], because of its [overwhelmingly fragrant] scent. So
why didn't they include honey in it? Because the Torah said, 'You
shall not burn any leaven or honey as a fire offering to Hashem.' "

If the addition of honey to the incense offering would have
rendered it overwhelming and unbearable to man, this should be
enough of a reason to explain why it was omitted from the incense
formula. Why, then, is the biblical verse adduced as proof?

The lesson of Bar Kappara's teaching is profound and universal
in its application, said Rav Yosef Chaim. Even when there is a
compelling reason to initiate or reject a certain proposal, if there
is a source in the Torah that relates to that issue, it is the Torah's
injunction that should be the guide in arriving at the final decision,
and not the practical or logical deliberations.

פרשת צו
PARASHAS TZAV

◄§ Thanksgiving and Kohanim

אִם עַל־תּוֹדָה יַקְרִיבֶנּוּ וְהִקְרִיב עַל־זֶבַח הַתּוֹדָה
— *If he offers it for thanksgiving, he shall offer with the thanksgiving sacrifice* (7:12).

*I*n the previous *parashah, Vaykira*, all the basic information about the various sacrifices was told to Moses, for him to relay "to the Children of Israel" (1:2, 4:2), so that they would know which sacrifices to bring upon which occasions. In our *parashah, Tzav*, the Torah supplies further details about these various sacrifices, addressed to the Kohanim ("Aaron and his sons" — 6:2, 6:18), who had to know how to administer and execute these sacrifices. The question thus arises: Why was the thanksgiving offering, of all the sacrifices, totally omitted from *Vayikra*? Why is it mentioned for the first time only in *Tzav*, which is addressed to the Kohanim?

In order to answer this question, let us first clarify the exact nature of the thanksgiving offering. Rashi writes that this sacrifice was brought by an individual "in recognition of a miraculous deliverance from harm, such as those who travel at sea, traverse the desert, are released from incarceration, or recover from illness

— the four types of salvation mentioned in *Tehillim* 107, of which it is written, 'They proclaim thanksgiving to Hashem for His kindness.' "

These are the occasions in one's life when a person comes to recognize God's hand in the events of the world, as manifested in His provision of guidance and protection from harm — which one perceives as "miraculous," although the ordinary laws of nature might not necessarily have been abrogated in these incidents. The Kohanim, however, were witnesses to an even higher level of exposure to God's immanent presence in this world, for, as we are taught in *Pirkei Avos* (5:5), there were ten overt miracles that were witnessed in the Temple on a regular basis. The idea of expressing one's recognition of God's intervention in our everyday lives by bringing a thanksgiving offering, then, is ever more applicable to the Kohanim, who experienced this intervention through manifest miracles on a daily basis. It is for this reason, explained Rav Yosef Chaim, that the entire discussion of the thanksgiving offering is deferred to *Tzav*, which speaks directly to the Kohanim, rather than to the common people.

Another explanation might be offered in light of an insight that was mentioned above, on the verse, "She (Leah) conceived again and bore a son, and declared, 'This time I shall give thanks to Hashem' (*Bereishis* 29:35)." The Talmud (*Berachos* 7b) comments, "From the day God created His world, there was never any person who gave thanks to God, until Leah came along and gave thanks to Him." It was noted above (in a comment on this verse, *Bereishis* 29:35) that the Talmud's assertion appears to be somewhat puzzling. The Gemara relates elsewhere that Adam was the author of Psalm 139, which includes praises of God. Furthermore, Noah expressed his thanks to God, in the form of sacrifices, after being spared from the Flood (*Bereishis* 8:20).

As we wrote above (ibid.), Rav Yosef Chaim cited the explanation of his rebbe, the *Kesav Sofer*, that indeed people did express their gratitude to God before Leah. However, these expressions of thanksgiving were offered as a result of a miraculous salvation. Leah, on the other hand, was the first person to ever thank God for a purely natural event, such as childbirth.

Bearing this explanation in mind, let us return to the question raised above: Why is the entire discussion of the thanksgiving offering addressed specifically to the Kohanim, rather than to the public at large? The answer may be that the Kohanim, owing to their constant devotion to the service of God and Torah study and their relative abstention from the more materialistic pursuits of life, were more spiritually sensitive and attuned to perceiving, as Leah did, the Divine guidance and providence that lies in the everyday events of life. It is thus they who would be the most likely to express feelings of thanksgiving to God.

פרשת שמיני
PARASHAS SHEMINI

๛ The Pig as Symbol

אַךְ אֶת־זֶה לֹא תֹאכְלוּ... אֶת־הַחֲזִיר וכו' —
*However, these you may not eat... the
pig, etc.* (11:4-7).

*T*he Gemara (*Bava Kamma* 82b) relates the following
story:
When the members of the Hasmonean family (Aristo-
bulos and Hyrcanos) were warring against each other (and the
Temple was besieged), each day the men in the Temple would
lower down money in a box to men waiting below, who would then
send up animals for sacrifices in return.

One day a certain elder who was familiar with "Greek wisdom"
told them, "As long as they continue the sacrificial service, you
will never be able to conquer them."

The next day, when the box of money was lowered, they sent up
a pig instead of a sheep. When the pig was halfway up the Temple
wall, it dug its claws into the stones, and the entire *Eretz Yisrael*
trembled At that time they declared, "Cursed be the man who
teaches his children 'Greek wisdom.' "

The story, in addition to its historical aspect, seems to be
fraught with allegorical meaning as well. Why did they send up a

pig specifically, rather than any other unkosher animal — such as a dog or cat, which surely would have been more easily accessible? Why did the pig "dig its claws" into the Temple wall? What is the significance of the tremor that reverberated throughout *Eretz Yisrael*?

Rav Yosef Chaim answered these questions as follows. At that time in history, besides the internecine strife between the various Hasmonean factions, there was a cultural war going on as well. It was between those Jews who were in favor of adopting Greek culture, which was the dominant intellectual force in the world then, and those who wished to preserve Judaism in its pristine, Torah-true form, unadulterated by imported "improvements" and "modernizations." This struggle was, in a sense, a precursor to the conflict between Reformists and Orthodox Judaism in our own day.

The pig is the only animal that has split hooves (one of the two requirements for classification as a kosher animal) but does not chew its cud (the other requirement). (Besides being a zoological reality, this fact is noted in *Chullin* 59a.) Because it possesses the outward sign of being a kosher animal but lacks the inner one, it is often used as a metaphor of sanctimonious hypocrisy, deceptively displaying its exterior signs of kosherness when it knows it is absolutely unkosher.

The Hellenists of old worked hard to show off to others how "kosher" their brand of Judaism was. The teachings of the Torah came to life and were enriched, they claimed, by the admixture of the "advanced" Greek culture. The adulteration of the Torah by means of the addition of external ingredients, however, is inherently "unkosher." The "beast" the Hellenists sought to create, like the pig, touted its kosher qualifications, when in fact it was devoid of halachic acceptability. This is why it was specifically the pig that was chosen by the man of "Greek wisdom" in the story cited above. It also explains the symbolism of the pig's insertion of its claws into the wall of the Temple; it represented the Hellenists' desire to exhibit how authentic and kosher they were, and to infiltrate their way into the very heart of Torah Judaism, the Temple Mount. It was upon this disgraceful show of hypocrisy and deception that the Land of Israel, representing the Jewish people as a whole, shuddered to its very core.

The danger to the Jewish heritage presented by Jews who seek to initiate "improvements" from within, concluded Rav Yosef Chaim, is far greater than that posed by its enemies from the outside.

⊷§ Defilement Leads to Defilement

אַל־תְּשַׁקְּצוּ אֶת־נַפְשֹׁתֵיכֶם בְּכָל־הַשֶּׁרֶץ הַשֹּׁרֵץ וְלֹא תִטַּמְאוּ בָּהֶם וְנִטְמֵתֶם בָּם — *Do not make yourselves abominable through [eating] any crawling thing; do not defile yourselves through them, lest you become defiled through them* (11:43).

*T*he end of this verse is difficult. We are told not to "defile ourselves through them," lest we "become defiled through them." How is the result (*defilement*) of the sin different from the sin (*defilement*) itself? The Gemara (*Yoma* 39a), addressing this difficulty, interprets the verse as follows: "If a person defiles himself a bit (by eating these forbidden foods), he will find himself defiled (by eating) even more; if he defiles himself (on earth) below, he will find himself defiled from (Heaven) above; if he defiles himself in this world, he will find himself defiled in the Next World."

Concerning the danger of one defilement by unkosher food leading to another, Rav Yosef Chaim used to relate the following story pertaining to the *Chasam Sofer*, the father of his rebbe, the *Kesav Sofer*.

In Pressburg (now Bratislava, Slovakia), there lived two wealthy Jewish merchants, who had studied under the *Chasam Sofer*. The two were business partners, and earned their livelihood from extensive international trade. At one point they procured a ship of their own to facilitate the importing and exporting of goods. They would always accompany the merchandise personally, and thus spent most of their time traveling.

One day, as the ship was sailing near the coast of Spain, it was stopped by the Spanish navy, who suspected that it was carrying goods that had been stolen from another ship by the pirates who frequented the area at the time. The ship was taken to Barcelona, where it was to be inspected for contraband by the authorities.

In those days Spain had friendly relations with the Austro-Hungarian Empire, of which Pressburg was a part, and the two merchants were thus treated most cordially pending the completion of the investigation. They were taken to the homes of senior Spanish customs officials to be hosted for their two- or three-day stay.

It is important to recall that in those days (the early 19th century) the "Spanish Inquisition" was still technically operative in the country. (It was abolished in 1834.) It was officially illegal in Spain for anyone to practice Judaism; if such a person was caught he was punished severely, and could even be put to death. Understandably, the two merchants did not divulge their Jewishness; they presented themselves as ordinary Austrian citizens.

As one of the merchants arrived at his host's home, he saw that the table was being set for a fine feast, in honor of the illustrious guest from Austria. The merchant was filled with anxiety by what he saw. He, of course, could not eat any food cooked by the kitchen staff; he would not even be able to drink the wine served. What could he do to avoid the detection of the reason for his refusal to eat? He had no choice. He would have to partake of the food; it was *pikuach nefesh*, a matter of life and death. The host noticed that his guest was becoming tense and nervous, and perceived that it was the food preparations that were making him so upset.

"Come with me," said the Spaniard to the merchant. "I'd like to show you something!" He then led the Austrian down to the dark, damp cellar of the house — which only served to heighten the merchant's apprehension.

Once the two were alone, the host turned to the merchant and said, "I can tell from your reaction to the food preparations that you are not able to eat our food. You must be a Jew!" The merchant was terrified. He had been discovered! What would become of him now?

"Well, don't you worry about a thing!" the host continued. "I am also a Jew, a descendant of the *Anusim* (Marranos). My family has carefully observed the laws of *kashrus* down through the generations. Whenever we have meat, I slaughter all the animals myself — with this." He then pulled out a box from the back of a closet, opened it up, and unwrapped from a cloth a perfectly sharpened *shechitah*-knife!

The merchant's surprise at his host's revelation was matched only by his relief. Finally he was freed from his fear of detection as a Jew! Even more important, he would be spared the need to partake of nonkosher food. (And he would at last have some food to eat as well!)

After the investigation of the merchandise was completed, and the ship was cleared, the two merchants were reunited as they prepared to set sail after their ordeal. Each man began to relate to the other what had transpired over the last few days. It turns out that the second merchant had also been hosted by a senior official, and was also treated with the utmost courtesy and hospitality. But when it came to the food situation, he was not so lucky. After much hesitation, and to his great revulsion, he was forced to partake of the unkosher food that had been served him. Since he was a very pious man, he was most upset by this incident. Why was this sin brought upon him? What had he ever done to deserve being put in a position in which he would have to eat prohibited foods?

When the merchants returned to Pressburg, they related their adventures to the *Chasam Sofer*. The second merchant broke out into tears. "Rebbe, why do you suppose I was put into such a terrible position, while my friend merited to be miraculously spared from defiling himself?"

The *Chasam Sofer* cast a soothing look at the merchant as he tried to comfort him. "Tell me," he asked. "Did you ever in your life partake of unkosher food before this? Or did you perhaps once eat food of questionable *kashrus*?"

"Heaven forbid!" declared the merchant, plainly insulted by the insinuation. "I would never allow a morsel of forbidden or questionable food to enter my mouth!"

"Search your memory," the *Chasam Sofer* persisted. "Perhaps there was some incident one time in your life that you have forgotten."

The man thought a bit harder. This time he remembered something. "Oh, I just recalled a certain incident. It was right after my marriage. My wife brought home a chicken from the butcher, and when she opened it up she found a *sheilah* (a *kashrus* problem requiring a halachic decision). Having just received my *semichah* (rabbinical authorization) I looked at the chicken myself, and decided that it was kosher. My wife was not so convinced, and she insisted on taking it to the local rabbi and getting a ruling from him. The rabbi was quite hesitant about the matter, and he advised her not to cook the chicken. I, however, was quite sure of myself, and besides that, was upset with my wife for not trusting my opinion. I therefore demanded that she cook the chicken and serve it to me."

"That's it!" declared the *Chasam Sofer*. "I have the tradition from my rebbe, Rav Noson Adler, that if someone is strict with himself never to eat any food about which there exists the slightest question of *kashrus*, he is guaranteed to be guarded from Heaven, to be spared from ever having to eat unkosher food under life-threatening situations. Your friend was apparently more careful than you in the past; he therefore merited this Heavenly protection, while you did not!"

פרשת תזריע
PARASHAS TAZRIA

✥ Why Circumcision Is Done on the Eighth Day

וּבַיּוֹם הַשְּׁמִינִי יִמּוֹל בְּשַׂר עָרְלָתוֹ — *On the eighth day the flesh of his foreskin shall be circumcised* (12:3).

The Gemara (*Niddah* 31b) suggests a reason why circumcision is deferred to the eighth day of the child's life: It is so that there should not be a situation in which "everyone else is happy, and the parents of the child are sad." As Rashi explains (ad loc.), a woman is ritually unclean — and is prohibited to have physical contact with her husband — for seven days following the birth of a boy. If the circumcision would be held before the eighth day, it would be a joyous occasion for all the guests, but the joy would be somewhat diminished for the boy's parents.

Rav Yosef Chaim offered a different interpretation of the Gemara's statement that the parents would be "unhappy" if the circumcision would be performed prior to the eighth day.

The *Shulchan Aruch*, in its discussion of the laws of Yom Kippur (*O.C.* 617:4), rules that during the first three days after childbirth, a woman is considered to be a critically ill person and is permitted to eat on Yom Kippur, even if she herself does not feel the need to do so. Between the third and seventh day, the law depends on the woman's feelings: If she feels that she is weak and needs to eat, she may do so; if she feels that eating is unnecessary, she must fast. From the eighth day and on, she is like any other person — meaning that she must fast unless this would clearly endanger her health.

A woman after childbirth is thus considered to be ill until the eighth day, at which point her status returns to that of a person of ordinary health. Rav Yosef Chaim therefore suggested that the Torah — whose "ways are ways of pleasantness" (*Mishlei* 3:17) — did not wish to impose upon the father to have two sick people, namely his wife and his newly circumcised son, on his hands at the same time. This would clearly impose a hardship upon both parents. Therefore the Torah postponed the circumcision to the eighth day, when the mother would have regained her health.

Rav Yosef Chaim saw an allusion to this idea in a verse in the Torah. In *Bereishis* 21:8, we are told that Abraham made a great feast on the occasion of his son's "weaning" (הִגָּמֵל). *Tosafos* (*Shabbos* 130a), citing a midrash (*Pirkei d'Rabbi Eliezer*), interprets this word to refer not to the time of Isaac's weaning, but to the day of his circumcision, for הִגָּמֵל can also be read as ה"ג מָל — "he circumcised on the eighth," as ה"ג has the numerical value of 8. Now, apart from the fact that הִגָּמֵל can be split up into two words in this manner, with the first of the two a *gematria* allusion — what is the plain translation of the word הִגָּמֵל according to the midrash's interpretation, that the word refers to the day of circumcision? Rav Yosef Chaim answered that the word refers to the day on which the mother has officially passed the stage of the danger of childbirth — the eighth day. Now she can pronounce the thanksgiving blessing הַגּוֹמֵל, praising God for "having bestowed (גָּמַל) favors to the undeserving."

פרשת מצורע
PARASHAS METZORA

∾§ The Power of the Mikveh

וְרָחַץ אֶת־בְּשָׂרוֹ בַּמַּיִם וְטָהֵר — *He shall immerse his flesh in water, and he will become pure* (14:9).

av Yosef Chaim went to the *mikveh* often. In his younger years he would frequent the *mikveh* next to the Shiloah Stream at the foot of Jerusalem's Old City, known as "Rabbi Yishmael Kohen Gadol's *mikveh*." One time he related to his grandson, "I used to have a large wart next to my eye, and on one of my trips to Rabbi Yishmael's *mikveh*, it suddenly disappeared completely!"

When Rav Isser Zalman Meltzer, the *Rosh Yeshivah* of Slutzk, arrived in Jerusalem, where he assumed the post of *Rosh Yeshivah* of Etz Chaim, Rav Yosef Chaim went to welcome him, accompanied by a group of *talmidei chachamim*. While there, they discussed various Torah topics with Rav Isser Zalman. Afterwards Rav Isser Zalman remarked to someone how impressed he was with the sharpness and clarity of thinking that these Jerusalemite scholars possessed.

Some time later, Rav Isser Zalman went to pay a return visit to Rav Yosef Chaim. When he arrived at the Rav's house, the members of the household told him that he had gone to the *mikveh* and would be back shortly. Upon the Rav's return, the two of them once again engaged in learned Torah discourse. At one point during the conversation, Rav Isser Zalman let his curiosity get the better of him. He asked Rav Yosef Chaim why it was that he immersed himself in the *mikveh* so often, a practice not ordinary followed by rabbis such as he. Rav Yosef Chaim explained the reason for his custom. "The Gemara tells us," he began, "that if a prospective convert undergoes circumcision, but does not immerse himself in a mikveh, he is not considered a valid convert, but remains a total non-Jew (*Berachos* 47b). It is only when he goes to the *mikveh* that he becomes a Jew according to the halachah. Now, if immersion in a *mikveh* has the power to transform a non-Jew into a Jew, how much more so does it have the power to make someone who is already a Jew into a holier Jew!"

פרשת אחרי מות
PARASHAS ACHAREI MOS

⊸§ The (Almost) Identical Goats

וְנָתַן אַהֲרֹן עַל־שְׁנֵי הַשְּׂעִירִם גֹּרָלוֹת גּוֹרָל אֶחָד
לַה' וְגוֹרָל אֶחָד לַעֲזָאזֵל — *Aaron shall place lots on the two he-goats: one lot for Hashem and one lot for Azazel* (16:8).

he Talmud teaches that the two goats had to be identical to each other; only the lots would distinguish between the two. This brings to mind an event that occurred back in 1930.

In those days, various organizations would use a gimmick to promote contributions called "ribbon day." Solicitors would stand at street corners and busy sidewalks and give out, in return for a donation, a ribbon to be worn on the donor's lapel. These collection drives were held on designated "ribbon days." The major proponent of these "ribbon days" was the World Zionist Organization, which would distribute blue and white ribbons — corresponding to the colors of the Zionist flag — to all contributors.

In Charedi circles this method of raising funds was not employed, as it was seen as a form of imitation and emulation of the Zionists. Nevertheless, Poalei Agudas Yisrael (PAGI for short), the

Charedi workers' party, decided to hold a ribbon day on Lag Ba'omer, 5690 (1930), on the same day as a general Zionist ribbon day. They first sought and received the approval of Rav Moshe Blau, who allowed the practice, as long as the solicitations were separated according to the sexes — men were to approach men and women to approach women.

When Lag Ba'omer arrived, some people in the Charedi community were shocked that PAGI dared to imitate this Zionist tactic. Why, they were even using blue and white ribbons, just like the Zionists! Rav Jungreis came to Rav Blau to register his protest against the PAGI drive. Rav Blau tried to calm him down, and told him that in any event it was too late to stop what had already gotten under way. The PAGI organizers of the ribbon campaign, somewhat surprised at the depth of the offense taken by the Charedi public, quickly produced black ribbon to replace the blue and white ones, and distributed the substitute ribbons to all those who were soliciting contributions.

About an hour later, a messenger from Rav Yosef Chaim came to Rav Blau and told him that the Rav had asked to speak to him. Rav Blau set out to Rav Yosef Chaim's house, taking along Rav Jungreis and a member of the PAGI directorate. Having a representative from each side of the argument present ensured that Rav Yosef Chaim's ruling, whichever way it might lean, could be put into force immediately.

Rav Jungreis informed Rav Yosef Chaim about the Charedi public's concern over the "impropriety" that had been perpetrated by PAGI, and asked him to issue an order to have it stopped immediately. Rav Yosef Chaim turned to the PAGI representative and asked him if the ribbon business was raising money for their organization. He answered in the affirmative.

"If you are making money for your worthy cause with this campaign," Rav Yosef Chaim said, "I am afraid that it is your *opponents* rather than you who are acting like the Zionists — for they are embittered over the fact that you have found a way to tap a source of income that heretofore was utilized only by the Zionists!"

He then added, speaking directly to the PAGI representative,

"Don't stop the campaign! Continue to raise money. I am sure that these funds are badly needed by you!"

"But Rebbe!" protested Rav Jungreis. "At least they could postpone their collection drive to another day, so that it does not take place on the same day as the Zionist campaign!"

"No," responded Rav Yosef Chaim firmly. "It must go on today! If it is postponed at this point, it may end up being canceled altogether. Furthermore, many people worked hard to organize this event. Why should they be let down and see their efforts wasted?"

"Well, at least the Rav could tell them to change the color of their ribbon from blue and white," pleaded Rav Jungreis, unaware of the fact that the ribbon color had already been changed.

"No again!" declared Rav Yosef Chaim. "They must use the blue and white ribbon, just like the Zionists. Just as the Mishnah says about the two he-goats on Yom Kippur — they must be identical in height, value, appearance, etc. Except that one is for Hashem and the other for Azazel!"

That afternoon a couple of collectors knocked on Rav Yosef Chaim's door to solicit a donation. In return they extended to him the black ribbon they had been instructed to use. But Rav Yosef Chaim demurred. "I know you have leftover blue-and-white ribbons in your pockets! I want one of them!"

This story illustrates how level headed Rav Yosef Chaim was, always allowing rational consideration of the issues — rather than blind, emotionally laden slogans — lead him to form his opinions.

פרשת קדושים
PARASHAS KEDOSHIM

⋖§ Incongruous Approaches

לֹא־תִשְׂנָא אֶת־אָחִיךָ בִּלְבָבֶךָ — *You shall not hate your brother in your heart* (19:17).

In one of his dialogues with Moslem leaders, a certain sheikh turned to Rav Yosef Chaim and commented, "You know, you also oppose the Zionists. You too fight them. So we really have something in common! We both battle the Zionists!"

"It is true," answered Rav Yosef Chaim. "We both oppose the Zionists — but for opposite reasons! You hate them because of the Jewish elements of their ideology. *We* oppose them because of the Gentile elements of their ideology! And thus there is a very great difference between us indeed!"

⋖§ Reverence for the Temple — Today as Well

אֶת־שַׁבְּתֹתַי תִּשְׁמֹרוּ וּמִקְדָּשִׁי תִּירָאוּ — *My Sabbaths you shall observe and My Sanctuary you shall revere* (19:30).

The Gemara comments on this verse (*Yevamos* 6b): "Just as the observance of the Sabbath applies in all ages, so does the reverence of the Sanctuary (Temple) apply in all ages, even when it is no longer standing." All the laws that pertain to the reverence and awe shown to the Temple apply nowadays to the Temple site, even though there is no longer any physical sanctuary in that place. For this reason it is still forbidden for anyone who is ritually defiled (that is, every person in the world) to enter the Temple Mount, or at least large sections of that mountain.

The first British "high commissioner for Palestine" was Sir Herbert Samuel, who was himself a Jew. He respected Jewish religious tradition; he would walk by foot on Shabbos from his mansion on the Mount of Olives (Augusta Victoria) to the great "Churvah" synagogue in the Old City of Jerusalem.

Rav Yosef Chaim, as the representative of the old Orthodox community, met with Samuel on several occasions. At their first meeting, Rav Yosef Chaim presented him with a request that the government post signs at all the entrances to the Temple Mount stating that according to Jewish law it is forbidden for any Jew to enter the site.

The members of Rav Yosef Chaim's entourage were puzzled by his raising of this issue at this particular time. Surely there were more pressing matters for the Orthodox community to bring up with the commissioner! In any event, Jews generally did not dare to enter the Temple Mount in those days, out of fear of the violent reaction they might experience at the hands of the Moslems there.

Rav Yosef Chaim, however, explained that he was aware that there were more urgent issues at hand, but he was trying to make it known to Sir Herbert, in a polite manner, that he, too, was not allowed to enter the Temple Mount according to Jewish law.

Samuel asked Rav Yosef Chaim to submit his request in writing, which he did. The result of the Rav's efforts may be gathered from the following correspondence that took place between Rav Yosef Chaim and Rav Shimon Sofer of Erlau (known for his work, "*Hisorerus Teshuvah*").

On 4 Shevat 5695 (1935), Rav Sofer wrote:

Behold, by the grace of the Most High, He has given us a certain degree of freedom and has granted us favor in the eyes of kings, who allow everything to be conducted according to Torah law. Perhaps the "time of love" (time of Divine favor— *Ezekiel* 16:8) has arrived to grant us favor, to allow us to build an altar on which to offer sacrifices, as was done at the beginning of the Second Temple period (when sacrifices were brought on an altar even before the Temple itself was built — *Shevuos* 16a).

My great-grandfather, Rav Akiva Eiger, previously raised this issue and discussed it with my grandfather, the *Chasam Sofer*, and several other leading rabbis discussed it as well. If all the rabbis of *Eretz Yisrael* — or perhaps the rabbis of Jerusalem alone would suffice — would request this of the government, they would undoubtedly consent. Monetary expenses should not be a consideration, for every Jewish person would gladly give the half-shekel donation, which would add up to a very great sum. As far as the practical halachic questions about how to perform the sacrifices, how to select Kohanim, etc. — surely the great Torah scholars of *Eretz Yisrael* will be able to study these matters and issue decisions about them.

Rav Yosef Chaim's response, on 20 Shevat of the same year, was as follows:

Unfortunately, the information that has reached you is not correct — that great respect is accorded to the Jews by the government, allowing them complete ability to conduct themselves in accordance with the Torah's laws. As one example, a few years ago, when the British commissioner, a Jewish man, arrived here, I submitted a written request that the government give us permission to post signs notifying the public of the Torah prohibition against entry into the Temple Mount nowadays, a prohibition which is violated — in innocence and out of total ignorance of the matter — by many Jewish tourists from abroad. I informed the commissioner about the severity of this prohibition in Jewish law, but the request was unfortunately turned down, on the grounds that such a posted notice would give offense to the nonreligious Jews, the lawbreakers among our own people! (Since 1967, there have been signs at the entries to the Temple Mount informing visitors that Jewish law prohibits entry to the site — ed.)

Besides this, the entire Temple Mount is and has been in total control of the Arabs for a long time And false rumors about Jewish intentions to take over the site have already led to great Arab rage against the Jews. The situation would, of course, only be made worse if the Jews really do show intent to do this (to seek a stake on the Temple Mount for themselves) — for "Jacob would be delivered to plunder" (*Isaiah* 42:24). Therefore, we must wait for the salvation of God and pray to Him that he should send us the Messiah soon.

The Only True Acquisition

מִפְּנֵי שֵׂיבָה תָּקוּם וְהָדַרְתָּ פְּנֵי זָקֵן — *In the presence of an old person you shall rise, and you shall honor the presence of an elder* (19:32).

The Talmud (*Kiddushin* 32b) comments on this verse: The word שֵׂיבָה (*old person*) implies *any* old person. One might thus think that one must rise even in the presence of an old fool. Therefore the Torah elaborates: *You shall honor the presence of an elder*. The word *elder* (זָקֵן) refers only to someone who has acquired wisdom.

How does the Gemara know that זָקֵן refers only to "someone who has acquired wisdom"? The same root (ז ק נ) is, after all, used in other forms to indicate old age (see, e.g., *Bereishis* 18:13, 24:36, 27:2, etc.). Rashi explains that the Gemara interprets זקן to be a contraction of the words זֶה קָנָה (חָכְמָה) — "this person has acquired [wisdom]."

The problem with this explanation is that the word "wisdom" is in brackets. The main question, therefore, remains: Granted that זָקֵן stands for זֶה קָנָה (*this person has acquired*) — but how do we know that what he has acquired is "wisdom"? Instead of inserting "wisdom" in brackets as the acquired item we could just as well put "wealth," "power" — or, for that matter, "old age"!

Rav Yosef Chaim replied to this question based on a statement made by the Gemara elsewhere (*Nedarim* 41a):

In the West (*Eretz Yisrael*, which is west of Babylonia) they have a saying: "If he has this he has everything; if he doesn't have it, he has nothing. If he acquires this, he lacks nothing else; if he does not acquire it, he acquires nothing else."

The subject of the saying, as the Gemara makes clear, is *wisdom*. If a person has wisdom, he has everything. If he lacks wisdom, however, although he may have numerous possessions or other qualities, he is in truth bereft of anything worthwhile.

Thus, when the Torah speaks of "a person who has acquired" (זֶה קָנָה), without specifying what the acquisition is, it is self-evident that the item acquired is the ultimate acquisition, without which no other possession is meaningful.

פרשת אמור
PARASHAS EMOR

◆§ Avoiding Chillul Hashem at All Costs

וְלֹא יְחַלְּלוּ אֶת־שֵׁם קָדְשִׁי — *And they shall not desecrate My holy Name* (22:2).

he Sages caution against causing a "desecration of God's Name" (*chillul Hashem*) when a person who is regarded as a representative of Torah and Judaism is seen behaving improperly.

One time a certain figure involved in Charedi public affairs was accused of wrongdoing. Rav Yosef Chaim defended him and stood by his side despite all the rumors and accusations. When asked why he did so, he explained, "Whenever an offense is committed by such a person, there are always two aspects to his action — the wrongful act itself and the resultant *chillul Hashem* caused by the act, which is even worse than the sin *per se*. By standing by this man's side, at least I can minimize the *chillul Hashem* aspect of this unfortunate episode."

Rav Yosef Chaim revealed the same sensitivity toward this issue on other occasions as well. One time a *sefer Torah* was stolen from the synagogue in Battei Varsha (in Meah Shearim). The Torah had been donated by Reb Yisrael Isser Levy, who was one of the wealthiest and most prominent members of the Jerusalem community at that time. The Levy family conducted a private investigation of the theft, and they were able to establish with certainty the identity of the culprit. They intended to hand over the results of their findings to the Turkish police, so that they could arrest the thief. This man was someone who regularly appeared in many synagogues in town, and it certainly seemed that having the man arrested, and thus preventing him from acting again, was the proper and responsible thing to do. Reb Yisrael Isser, however, opposed taking this step without first seeking Rav Yosef Chaim's opinion on the matter.

After considering the details of the story carefully, Rav Yosef Chaim told the members of the family, "Let's calculate the pros and cons together. If we do not hand over the identity of the thief to the police, he will sell the *sefer Torah* to someone who is interested in using it, for he obviously has no other use for the scroll other than to sell it. The Torah will thus find its way into another synagogue, and it will probably be put to even more use than in Battei Varsha, where the synagogue already has many *sifrei Torah*. In other words, instead of sitting unused in the ark of Battei Varsha, it will be read on a regular basis in another synagogue. The *sefer Torah* itself, then, will not suffer any disgrace as a result of our refraining from having the thief arrested.

"However," he continued, "if you do give over the information to the police, a great *chillul Hashem* will emerge, for the enemies of the Jewish people — and we have plenty of them, both Jew and non-Jew! — will feast upon the news that a Jewish man steals *sifrei Torah* from synagogues. Furthermore, the Turkish police are known for their ruthlessness, and who knows if the man will ever get out of jail alive?

"As for your concerns that he if he gets away with this theft, he may be encouraged to steal other *sifrei Torah* from other synagogues — I suggest the following. Inform the thief, privately, that he has been discovered. This will surely deter him from ever trying to do this again!"

The Levys followed Rav Yosef Chaim's advice and sent a message to the culprit, informing him that his identity had become known. The man apparently was overcome with shame, for after a few weeks, the missing *sefer Torah* was found in its original place in the ark — and the entire affair was forgotten.

Rav Yosef Chaim would often bend over backwards in defense of those Jews who, owing to the difficulties of the times, had strayed from the path of Torah observance. He would always try to think of justifications and sources of merit for any Jewish person, no matter how irreligious he might be.

When some of his close confidants would sometimes express their wonderment over an expression that seemed to them to be overly sympathetic or tolerant toward such "wicked" Jews, Rav Yosef Chaim explained his attitude as follows. "When a person commits a sin, he should be pitied. The Sages teach that 'A person does not sin unless he is overcome by a spirit of madness' (*Sotah* 3a). There is no one so crazed as a person who ignores all the good that God does for him and intentionally rebels against His will! Now, when we come across a person who is suffering from mental illness, we show him kindness and sympathy. How much more so should we show compassion for someone who has abandoned the path of spiritual happiness and eternal life!

"This is all true on the individual level, for his actions do not have such a decisive effect on others in his surroundings. However, if a person's misdeeds do indeed involve *chillul Hashem*, in that they encourage others to follow his example and to reject the Torah life, we must tirelessly fight against this phenomenon with all our might. For any transgression that bears negative ramifications for the public's spiritual welfare can quickly lead to the most disastrous results, as we have seen so many times before."

✎§ Kamtza and Bar Kamtza in the Torah

וּמִיַּד בֶּן־נֵכָר לֹא תַקְרִיבוּ אֶת־לֶחֶם אֱלֹקֵיכֶם מִכָּל־ אֵלֶּה כִּי מָשְׁחָתָם בָּהֶם מוּם בָּם לֹא יֵרָצוּ לָכֶם —

From the hand of a foreigner you may not offer the food of your God from any of these. For their corruption is in them, a blemish is in them; they will not be accepted favorably for you (22:25).

As Rashi explains, this verse forbids us to accept from a non-Jew an animal that has one of the blemishes mentioned by the Torah previously. Although it is generally permissible for a non-Jew to sacrifice a blemished animal to

God, this is only when he does so on his own private altar. When he offers a sacrifice in the Mishkan or Temple, however, the animal must be unblemished.

What would happen if such a blemished animal would be offered by a non-Jew? The verse concludes: "They will not be accepted favorably for you." The words "for you" seem to be out of place. Since this verse is speaking about a non-Jew who presents a sacrifice in the Temple, it should have said, "They will not be accepted favorably for *them.*" When our verse says "you," it is addressing the Jewish people ("From the hand of a foreigner *you* may not offer"), not the non-Jews. In fact, the Torah never speaks directly to anybody but the Jews.

Rav Yosef Chaim answered this question by saying that the Torah's commandment is indeed addressed to us. If we accept a sacrifice from a non-Jew that has a blemish in it, we will be transgressing this command. This is what is meant by "They will not be accepted favorably for you." In offering these sacrifices for the non-Jew, *you* will be violating God's will, and these offerings will therefore not be a source of favor for *you.*

In a further insight into this verse, Rav Yosef Chaim saw an allusion to the famous Kamtza and Bar-Kamtza story in *Gittin* 55b ff. The basic outline of the narrative is this: There were two people in Jerusalem with very similar names, Kamtza and Bar-Kamtza (lit., *Son of Kamtza*). A third man was planning a feast, to which he invited many of the distinguished people of Jerusalem. One of the guests was to be Kamtza, his close friend. However, a messenger mistakenly delivered the invitation to Bar-Kamtza, who was the host's bitter enemy. When the day of the party arrived and Bar-Kamtza walked in, the host became enraged and ejected him unceremoniously, despite Bar-Kamtza's pleas to him to refrain from embarrassing him, including an offer of generous monetary compensation. Bar-Kamtza, who saw that the great rabbis of Jerusalem witnessed his humiliation and did nothing to defend him, was incensed, and decided to stir up some trouble for the entire Jewish religious establishment. He arranged an audience with the emperor of Rome, where he libeled the Jews, telling Caesar that they were planning a rebellion against him. To test their loyalty, he suggested that Caesar send a sacrifice to the Temple. If it would be accepted by the Jews, this would prove their innocence; if they rejected it, this would prove their hostility. The emperor complied and sent a beautiful calf to be offered in the Temple. Bar-Kamtza, who was the agent appointed to bring the animal to Jerusalem, made a blemish in the calf on the way, thus ensuring that the Kohanim would reject it.

An argument ensued among the Temple elders. Most rabbis were inclined to go ahead with the sacrifice despite its technical unacceptability, due to the extenuating circumstances. A certain Rabbi Zechariah ben Avkulas, however, objected to bending the rules, and it was his view that prevailed. The sacrifice was turned down, the emperor was infuriated — and the rest is history.

What exactly was behind the halachic argument between the Sages and Rabbi Zechariah? Rav Yosef Chaim analyzed the dispute as follows. Our verse allows for the acceptance of a sacrifice "from the hand of a foreigner," as long as it is unblemished. The sages of the Temple were well aware that it was Bar-Kamtza who had sabotaged the animal, said Rav Yosef Chaim. They thus knew that the calf was unblemished when it was originally sent by the emperor. They therefore ruled that such an instance did not constitute accepting a blemished offering "from the hand of a foreigner," for the animal was not yet blemished when it left "the hand of the foreigner (Caesar)."

Rabbi Zechariah, however, saw an allusion to this particular case in the words בֶּן נֵכָר. Aside from its meaning of "stranger" or "unfamiliar one" (or, as translated above, "foreigner"), the expression could also be rendered more literally, "the son (בֶּן) whose identity was obscured (נִתְנַכֵּר)." This entire incident had evolved from the fact that Bar-Kamtza ("Son of Kamtza") had been confused with Kamtza. It was thus precisely for such a case that the Torah commanded us, "From the hand of בֶּן נֵכָר (the Son [בַּר in Aramaic means son] whose identity was confused) you may not offer the food of your God from any of these." Despite the extenuating circumstances, and despite the other rabbis' derivation from the wording of the verse, he felt it would be disrespectful and sacrilegious to offer up a blemished animal on God's altar!

❧ Charity and Rosh Hashanah

וּבְקֻצְרְכֶם אֶת־קְצִיר אַרְצְכֶם לֹא־תְכַלֶּה פְּאַת
שָׂדְךָ בְּקֻצְרֶךָ וְלֶקֶט קְצִירְךָ לֹא תְלַקֵּט לֶעָנִי וְלַגֵּר
תַּעֲזֹב אֹתָם — *When you reap the harvest
of your land, you shall not finish the
corners of your field as you reap and
you shall not gather the gleanings of
your harvest; for the poor and the proselyte you shall leave them* (23:22).

The positioning of this commandment to leave over some of our crops for the poor is puzzling. Why is it inserted right in the middle of the Torah's discussion of the festival days, after Shavuos and before Rosh Hashanah?

Rav Yosef Chaim explained the reason for this juxtaposition as follows. Rosh Hashanah is the Day of Judgment, when "all of mankind passes before God like sheep of the flock" (*Rosh Hashanah* 16a). We pray that He judge us favorably and "inscribe us in the book" of life, health and prosperity. We know full well, however, that we are undeserving of such favorable treatment. Therefore we end our list of requests with the humble petition, "Our Father, our King: Show us grace and answer us, though we have no deeds (to warrant this). Act toward us with charity and compassion, and save us." But why should God show us compassion, and charitably grant us what we do not deserve?

The Talmud teaches that if someone shows forbearance toward others, God will do the same for him (*Rosh Hashanah* 17a). According to a homiletical interpretation, the verse "Hashem is your shelter (lit., *shade* or *shadow*)" (*Tehillim* 121:5) alludes to the fact that just as a person's shadow does exactly what he does, so does God behave toward a person exactly as he behaves toward others.

Now, consider the plight of the farmer. He toils and sweats for an entire season, plowing, sowing, and finally harvesting. What a sense of joy and satisfaction fills his heart as he literally reaps the benefits of his efforts. As he swings his sickle across a swath of grain, a stalk or two slips from his grasp. His natural inclination is to bend down and retrieve it. After all, he worked hard for it; it is his property, fair and square. But the Torah tells him, "Forget your selfish instincts. Forget even your sense of fairness and justice. *Leave them for the poor and the proselyte.*" Then, when the farmer, after much backbreaking labor, finally gets to the end of his field, all ready to celebrate with gratification the completion of his harvest, the Torah steps in again and says, "Don't go all the way to the end. *You shall not finish the corners of your field as you reap. Leave it for the poor and the proselyte.* They did not invest a stitch of work into this field. But they need it more than you do."

There are several endowments that a farmer must take off from his harvest and give to others — *Terumah* for the Kohen, First Tithe for the Levite, Poor Tithe for the poor, etc. But the beneficiaries of these gifts can at least be determined by the farmer himself. He can choose a Kohen of his liking to receive his *Terumah* — perhaps a friendly neighbor or a relative. The same goes for the other tithes and offerings. At least he gets some benefit out of these portions, in that he can dispose of them as he sees fit. When it comes to *pe'ah* (the unfinished edge of the field) and *leket* (dropped gleanings), however, they must be left for any and all poor people. It is forbidden for the farmer to give them to any particular poor person, or even to assist one poor person to get them over another. He has absolutely no benefit whatsoever from these portions of his crop; they are a total loss for him. But it is for this very reason that these offerings represent the most unselfish contribution to others that a farmer can make.

This, explains Rav Yosef Chaim, is why the Torah's command to leave *pe'ah* and *leket* for the poor is positioned just before its discussion of Rosh Hashanah. "If you expect God to go beyond the letter of the law for you, and grant you forgiveness and favor despite your unworthiness," the Torah tells us, "then you know what you must do first: Act toward others in a totally selfless and generous manner!"

⋖§ Rosh Hashanah — Day of Judgment

בַּחֹדֶשׁ הַשְּׁבִיעִי בְּאֶחָד לַחֹדֶשׁ יִהְיֶה לָכֶם שַׁבָּתוֹן
זִכְרוֹן תְּרוּעָה — *In the seventh month, on the first of the month, there shall be a rest day for you, a remembrance with shofar blasts (23:24).*

*R*osh Hashanah is known in rabbinic literature as the Day of Judgment, the first day of the ten days of repentance, culminating in Yom Kippur. Although this motif of Rosh Hashanah is not found explicitly in the Torah, various hints and allusions to it have been pointed out. To these, Rav Yosef Chaim added the following:

In *Iyov* (1:6) we read that "it happened on the day," the angels, with the Accuser (Satan) among them, assembled before God to discuss the affairs of mankind on earth. The Zohar comments that "the day" referred to was Rosh Hashanah. Similarly, the Zohar continues, when Elisha asked his Shunamite hostess "on the day" if he could intercede on her behalf before "the king," this was "the day" of Rosh Hashanah. We see, therefore, that often the word הַיּוֹם ("the day"), when it is left unspecified, is often used to refer to Rosh Hashanah. Thus, when it says in *Tehillim* (119:91), "They stand in judgment *on the day*, for they are all Your servants," we may assume that the verse refers to Rosh Hashanah as well. In fact, Rav Yosef Chaim noted, the numerical value of words of this verse (לְמִשְׁפָּטֶיךָ עָמְדוּ הַיּוֹם כִּי הַכֹּל עֲבָדֶיךָ) is exactly equal to that of the words Rosh Hashanah (רֹאשׁ הַשָּׁנָה) — 861!

(Rav Yosef Chaim also noted that the total number of words read from the Torah on the first and second days of Rosh Hashanah is 861 — the numerical value of רֹאשׁ הַשָּׁנָה.)

Rav Yosef Chaim offered another gematria allusion pertaining to Rosh Hashanah as well. In *Tehillim* 89:16 (the verse recited immediately after the blowing of the shofar in the synagogue), we read, "Happy is the nation that knows the shofar's blast." The word for "that knows" (יוֹדְעֵי) has the numerical value of 100, corresponding exactly to the number of shofar blasts customarily sounded on Rosh Hashanah.

One last curiosity discovered by Rav Yosef Chaim: The last word of the Torah reading on the second day of Rosh Hashanah is מַעֲכָה (*Ma'achah*), which can be seen as an acronym for מֶלֶךְ עַל כָּל הָאָרֶץ (*King over all the earth*), which is the central theme of the Rosh Hashanah prayers.

◆§ Preparations for Yom Kippur

אַךְ בֶּעָשׂוֹר לַחֹדֶשׁ הַשְּׁבִיעִי הַזֶּה יוֹם הַכִּפֻּרִים הוּא
— *But on the tenth day of this month it is the Day of Atonement* (23:27).

*Y*om Kippur itself is the Day of Atonement, but spiritual preparations for this great, holy day get under way ten days before that, on Rosh Hashanah. It is customary to precede even this date and begin with penitential prayers and deeds on *Rosh Chodesh* Elul, a month before Rosh Hashanah. Rav Yosef Chaim, however, went even further than that. He would begin preparing himself mentally for Yom Kippur on the second day of Sivan, which is traditionally known as *Yom Hameyuchas* ("the Distinguished Day"). Why it is called this is something of a mystery, but Rav Yosef Chaim found a special significance in this date: It is exactly eighteen weeks before Yom Kippur. He would announce in shul on *Yom Hameyuchas*, "Everyone should be aware that in eighteen more weeks we will be celebrating Yom Kippur, begging forgiveness for our sins. The time is short and the amount of work to be done (to mend our ways and rectify our sins) is great!" Thereafter he would count down the number of days left to Yom Kippur.

When the last week before Rosh Hashanah arrived, he would declare, "Today is the last Sunday (or Monday, etc.) of the year. Every person should rectify whatever wrongs he might have committed on all the Sundays of the foregoing year, by conducting himself with special holiness and repentance." (In this he was following a tradition ascribed to the Ari-*zal*.)

⧉ The Minimum Height for the Sukkah

בַּסֻּכֹּת תֵּשְׁבוּ שִׁבְעַת יָמִים — *You shall dwell in booths for a seven-day period* (23:42).

One of the first laws discussed in the Talmudic tractate that deal with Sukkos (*Sukkah* 2a) is that if a sukkah's *sechach* (thatched roof) is situated lower than ten *tefachim* (handbreadths) above the ground, it is invalid. One of the sources that the Gemara proposes for this law is the fact that God spoke to Moses from atop the Ark's lid (*Shemos* 25:22), which was exactly ten handbreadths above the ground. Since, as Rabbi Yosi said, "God's Presence has never descended further than ten handbreadths off the ground (the height of the Ark's lid)," this is the minimum height of the Sukkah's *sechach*.

What, we may ask, does the demarcation line below which the *Shechinah* does not descend have to do with the height of a sukkah? Rashi explains: This height is seen as a dividing line between the "lower domain," to which God's Presence does not descend, and the "upper domain," in which God does appear; this dividing line is hence used for the sukkah's height as well. Nevertheless, the connection between the two matters seems unclear.

Rav Yosef Chaim suggested an explanation for this, based on the words of the Zohar, which states (*Vayikra* 103) that when a person dwells in a sukkah during Sukkos, God's Presence, as it were, hovers over him, and the *sechach* represents God's sheltering wings. In light of this perspective, we can readily understand why the Gemara disqualifies a sukkah whose *sechach* is lower than ten handbreadths, on the grounds that the *Shechinah* does not descend to that level.

פרשת בהר
PARASHAS BEHAR

✑§ Sensitivity to Others

וְלֹא תוֹנוּ אִישׁ אֶת־עֲמִיתוֹ — *Do not mistreat one another* (25:17).

*A*s Rashi, quoting from *Sifra*, notes, our verse refers not to mistreating a person financially — for this prohibition is already mentioned just above (v. 14) — but to mistreating him personally (i.e., by insulting him or hurting his feelings). This prohibition is known as *ona'as devarim* ("mistreatment by words").

Rav Yosef Chaim, with his sterling character, was painstakingly meticulous in his observance of this precept. The following incidents exemplify the degree to which his sensitivity toward others extended.

A certain author of a Torah work wrote in his book, "Also in our day this phenomenon (of scorning Torah scholars and their scholarly works) exists. I myself recently encountered a wealthy businessman who was considered to be something of a *talmid chacham*, and asked him if he would help defray the extensive costs of the publication of my book with a donation. He was most uncooperative and heaped scorn and derision upon the Torah and its scholars. I departed from this encounter greatly aggravated."

When Rav Yosef Chaim saw this story in print, he wrote to the author, who was a colleague of his: "I was surprised that you printed the story about that wealthy man who spoke against Torah scholars. If that man regretted what he said — and we are supposed to give everyone the benefit of the doubt in this regard (*Kiddushin* 49b), particularly someone who is considered to be a *talmid chacham* (*Berachos* 19a) — and he repented, it is forbidden to remind him of his sinful utterances. Reminding a reformed person of his past misdeeds constitutes a transgression of the prohibition of *ona'as devarim*. And even though you did not mention the man's name in your book (!) — and it goes without saying that I myself have no idea who he is — that man, if he ever reads your book, will know that you are referring to him, and will feel distressed by the story."

Rav Yosef Chaim's door was open to all, and his house was always bustling with people coming to him to ask questions, to seek guidance, or just to pour out their hearts. This was all the more so over the holidays, when people from all over, great scholars and simple people alike, made it their business to go pay a visit to the renowned rabbi and be inspired by some of his Torah insights.

On one festival day, Rav Yosef Chaim greeted all those who came in to see him with his customary hearty "Good *Yom Tov*!" and added, somewhat mysteriously, "Oh, you are undoubtedly on your way back from (or on your way to) the *Kosel Hama'aravi*!"

Those who were close to Rav Yosef Chaim knew that this was not his usual greeting, and were quite puzzled by it. He understood that his behavior was causing some bewilderment, and explained himself to Rav Moshe Blau after everyone else had left. "You are probably wondering why I said that to all my visitors today! Well, you see, Rav Eliyahu Kletzkin, the Rav of Lublin, was sitting by my side the whole time, and I was afraid that his honor might be slighted when he saw that there were so many visitors coming to see me on the holiday. I therefore wanted to make it seem that all those people weren't really coming especially to see me, but were just passing through on their way to the nearby *Kosel*. That way I avoided making him feel uncomfortable!"

Rav Yosef Chaim was fond of pointing out that the numerical value of אִישׁ (*man*) is equal to that of לְרֵעֵהוּ (*to his fellow man*). This alludes to the fact that a person is not worthy of being called a human being unless he focuses his attention on caring for his fellow man.

One Purim he added to this thought the idea that *Mishloach Manos,* the practice of exchanging food portions on Purim, is described in the *Megillah* (9:19) as מִשְׁלוֹחַ מָנוֹת אִישׁ לְרֵעֵהוּ, "the sending of portions from each man to his fellow man." This practice, which is designed to promote feelings of brotherhood and fellowship among fellow Jews, is based on the fact that אִישׁ is equal to לְרֵעֵהוּ, said Rav Yosef Chaim. Most difficulties in interpersonal relationships, he said, arise from the fact that one person believes that he is more important in some way than his fellow. It is only when we recognize that אִישׁ (*man*) is exactly equivalent to לְרֵעֵהוּ (*his fellow man*) that these difficulties can be overcome.

✦§ Employees' Rights, Employers' Rights

> וּבְאַחֵיכֶם בְּנֵי־יִשְׂרָאֵל אִישׁ בְּאָחִיו לֹא־תִרְדֶּה בּוֹ בְּפָרֶךְ — *With your brethren, the Children of Israel — a man with his brother — you shall not subjugate him through hard labor* (25:46).

Rav Yosef Chaim often stressed the importance of employers showing fairness toward their workers, noting that there are a number of commandments in the Torah that call upon us to pay special attention to the rights of those who work for us.

On the other hand, he objected to the hateful, inciting anti-"capitalist" rhetoric of many workers in the socialist movements, which demonized all large-scale employers, and called for all power to be invested in the workers. Such attitudes, he said, were likely to damage only the workers themselves in the long run. Rather, each person must recognize his station in life and strive to fulfill his own role in good faith, with respect toward others who are in different positions, for each individual in society has a unique, important part to contribute toward the public welfare.

ספר במדבר
BAMIDBAR / NUMBERS

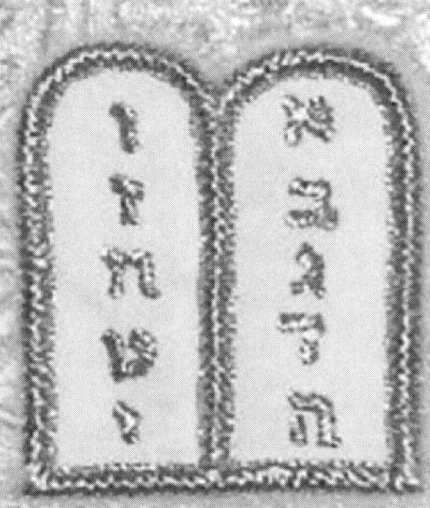

פרשת במדבר
PARASHAS BAMIDBAR

✒ Faulty Pedigree

וַיִּתְיַלְדוּ עַל־מִשְׁפְּחֹתָם לְבֵית אֲבֹתָם — *And they established their genealogy according to their families* (1:18).

(To understand the following anecdote, the reader should be aware that the Yiddish word for "grandson" is *einikel*, and the word for "great-grandson" — or any more distant descendant — is *uhr-einikel*.)

One time someone complained to Rav Yosef Chaim about the phenomenon in which people who are totally bereft of any true Jewish content come forth and brag, "You know, I am an *uhr-einikel* of the Taz (or the Maggid, the So-and-So Rebbe, etc.)."

Rav Yosef Chaim then quipped, "You know, *uhr* also means 'a watch.' Now, a watch that cannot tell you the time is not really a 'watch' at all, but just a piece of scrap! 'A broken *uhr* is not an *uhr* at all!' "

✒ Levites from the Midst of Israel

וַאֲנִי הִנֵּה לָקַחְתִּי אֶת־הַלְוִיִּם מִתּוֹךְ בְּנֵי יִשְׂרָאֵל — *I have hereby taken the Levites from among the Children of Israel* (3:12).

The Torah has numerous similar verses, such as "Take the Levites from among the Children of Israel and purify them" (below, 8:6); "They are given over, given over to

Me from among the Children of Israel" (8:16); see also 8:14, 8:19, 18:6. It is interesting to note that each time the concept of the selection of the Levites is recorded in the Torah, it is accompanied by the phrase "from among (מִתּוֹךְ, more literally, *from the midst of*) the Children of Israel." By doing so, said Rav Yosef Chaim, the Torah wishes to impart the message that the Levites should not come to regard themselves — nor should they be regarded by others — as a distinct, independent caste, separate from the rest of the people. Rather, they must be viewed as full-fledged members of the community of Israel.

Rav Yosef Chaim noted further that there is an allusion to this fact in the very word לְוִיִּם (*Levites*). The letters that spell Israel are י׳ ש׳ ר׳ א׳ ל׳, or, writing out the names of these letters in full, יוד שין ריש אלף למד. If we take the middle letter of each of these names, we will get ו י י ל מ, which are the very letters that make up the word לויים. This alludes to the fact that the Levites (לְוִיִּם) truly come "from the middle (midst) of Israel (יִשְׂרָאֵל)"!

פרשת נשא
PARASHAS NASO

◆§ Eighty Answers

> אִישׁ אִישׁ כִּי־תִשְׂטֶה אִשְׁתּוֹ... וְהֵבִיא אֶת־קָרְבָּנָהּ
> עָלֶיהָ — *Any man whose wife shall go*
> *astray... he shall bring her sacrifice for*
> *her* (5:12,15).

When the great Talmudic genius, Rav Yosef Engel, put out a book entitled גְּבוּרוֹת שְׁמוֹנִים (*The Strengths of Eighty*), in which he posited eighty learned answers to a single question dealing with a particular facet of the sacrifice brought by the *sotah* (unfaithful wife), my father remarked to his grandfather (Rav Yosef Chaim), "That's odd. Why did he choose to give precisely *eighty* answers? He surely could have provided more or less than this number!"

Rav Yosef Chaim shrugged and said to him, "Well, let's hear what *you* think!"

"I think it might be because the numerical value of *sotah* (סוֹטָה) is eighty!"

Rav Yosef Chaim was delighted with the answer, and said, "Yes, that's certainly the reason. I am only surprised that the author did not say so specifically in his introduction to the book!"

פרשת בהעלותך
PARASHAS BEHA'ALOS'CHA

Opening the Ark — Time for Prayer

וַיְהִי בִּנְסֹעַ הָאָרֹן וַיֹּאמֶר מֹשֶׁה קוּמָה ה' וְיָפֻצוּ
אֹיְבֶיךָ — *When the Ark would journey,
Moses said, "Arise, Hashem, and let
Your foes be scattered"* (10:35).

av Yosef Chaim, at an address delivered upon the occasion of the opening of the Sfas Emes Yeshivah in
Jerusalem, asked why it is that this verse is customarily recited as the ark is opened to take out a Torah scroll for
reading. He explained this custom as follows:

"The Zohar teaches that 'When the Torah is taken out to be read
in public, the gates of mercy in Heaven are opened as well. It is a
time when God's love is aroused, and a person should pray,
"Blessed be the Name of the Master of the Universe (בְּרִיךְ שְׁמֵיהּ
וכו')." May it be Your will that You open my heart to Your Torah.'

"It is apparent from the Zohar, then, that the opening of the ark
in the synagogue is an auspicious time during which to petition
God for assistance in achieving spiritual growth and advancement.
Now, it is known that whenever a window of spiritual accomplishment opens up for a person in his life, the powers of evil — those

that lurk within man and those that come from without — suddenly begin to put up resistance. The *yetzer hara* (the personification of man's evil impulses) cannot bear to see a person achieve spiritual growth, for this would constitute a significant defeat for him and his designs. We therefore pray immediately upon the onset of the potential for a spiritual spurt of growth, '*Arise, Hashem, and let Your foes be scattered! Let those who hate You flee from before You!* Let all the forces of evil depart, and allow us to take advantage of this opportunity without interference and distraction!'

"And, if God accepts our prayers and allows us to avail ourselves of the spiritual opportunity," Rav Yosef Chaim concluded, "we may hope to have fulfilled for us the verse that is recited immediately thereafter: 'כִּי מִצִּיּוֹן וכו, 'For out of Zion shall Torah emerge, and the word of Hashem from Jerusalem.' "

ⱻ§ The Lesson of the Manna

שָׁטוּ הָעָם וְלָקְטוּ — *The people would spread out and gather [the manna]* (11:8).

*R*av Yosef Chaim often stressed that a person should not dedicate all his energies to his pursuit of a livelihood. He should rather take the necessary steps to earn a living, and God will see to it that he is provided with whatever is necessary for him. This is the lesson we can learn from the manna, of which the Torah tells us that "The Children of Israel gathered [the manna], those who took more and those who took less. And they measured it in an Omer and found that those who took more had nothing extra and those who took less were not lacking; each person had gathered according to his eating needs" (*Shemos* 16:17-18).

Rav Yosef Chaim would also cite the comment of the Zohar on our verse, focusing on the word שָׁטוּ (*spread out*): "Those people of whom it says שָׁטוּ were truly שַׁטְיָא (*fools*)" — for sufficient manna was supplied to each person, without the need to stroll around and search for it, which was in any event a futile endeavor, as the aforementioned verse in *Shemos* clearly shows.

He would also mention a parable of the *Chafetz Chaim's* in this regard: A customer in a winemaker's shop once brought up a suggestion to the shopkeeper: "Why don't you put two spigots on each barrel instead of one? That way you could make twice as much money!" No matter how hard a person tries, the total amount of sustenance he is destined to receive is not increased one iota despite all his efforts!

On the other hand, one must not sit back and relax, with the attitude that "God will provide for me anyway, so why should I bother to exert myself?" The Torah writes, "so that God will bless you in all that you do" (*Devarim* 15:18). It is only when a person *does* and acts that he opens up the possibility for God to bring blessing to his work and provide for him. In fact, only when man must toil for his living does he develop a relationship with God as the Provider, for he recognizes that his success or failure is totally dependent on His grace.

Striving endlessly to earn more and more money, however, besides being futile and foolish, as explained above, is also likely to lead one to the dangerous delusion that "my strength and the might of my hand have brought this wealth to me" (*Devarim* 8:17). It is especially foolish for a person to cut down on the time he devotes to prayer and Torah study in order to work extra hours. For it is inconceivable that God should reward such spiritual decline by providing additional sustenance.

Rav Yosef Chaim himself exemplified this trait, as many stories told about him testify (see his biography, *Guardian of Jerusalem*). Even his apartment in Battei Machaseh, in which he lived for fifty-five years, came into his possession without any effort on his part. The home was originally built by the famous rabbi/business-man Rav Yaakov Ettlinger (known as "the *Aruch LaNer*," after his most well-known work, a commentary on several Talmud trac-tates), on the condition that Rav Avraham Shag — who was sup-posed to move to Jerusalem from Kubersdorf, Slovakia — would live in it. Rav Shag died in 1876, however, while still in Slovakia, some time before the apartment was finished. Years later, when

Rav Yosef Chaim, who was Rav Shag's most distinguished disciple, arrived in Jerusalem, people urged him to request of the "Kolel H.O.D. (short for 'Hollandischer und Deutscher')," who administered the property, that the apartment be granted to him. He adamantly refused, arguing, "How can I, such a simple person, dare to assume the mantle of my great rebbe and seek to 'inherit' the house that was intended for him?" After a few weeks, however, he received a letter from the "Kolel H.O.D." that the administrators of the kolel had decided to grant the home to him.

פרשת שלח
PARASHAS SHELACH

◁§ The Spies and Their Huge Fruits

בָּאנוּ אֶל־הָאָרֶץ אֲשֶׁר שְׁלַחְתָּנוּ וְגַם זָבַת חָלָב
וּדְבַשׁ הִוא וְזֶה־פִּרְיָהּ — *We arrived at the Land to which you sent us, and indeed it flows with milk and honey, and this is its fruit* (13:27).

The twelve spies (excluding Joshua and Caleb) who were sent by Moses to *Eretz Yisrael* are described as "those who spread an evil report about the Land" (14:37). They had done their research and compiled their report, the conclusion of which was essentially: "Grave danger ahead. Abort mission! Head back to Egypt immediately!"

One wonders, therefore, why they bothered to admit that the Land was "indeed flowing with milk and honey." Their evil designs would certainly have been better served had they given a negative report about the produce of the Land. Rashi addresses this issue, and explains that even a scoundrel or a liar knows that he must introduce some elements of truth into his story in order to gain his audience's credibility. Nevertheless, we would have expected them to express their main point — that a conquest of *Eretz Yisrael* was an impossibility — first, and only then to inject their token element of truth, rather than vice versa. Even more puzzling is the fact that the first thing the spies did upon returning from their mission was to "show them the (extraordinary) fruit of the Land" (v. 26).

Let us raise one more difficulty before returning to resolve all the questions. When Moses was giving instructions to the spies, he gave them a list of approximately seven items to check out in *Eretz Yisrael*: Do the people live in open areas or in fortified cities? Is it a fertile or lean land? Etc. (vv. 18-20). Concerning the item, "Are there trees in it or not?" (v. 20), Rashi explains that the question was really a metaphor for something else entirely. What Moses really wanted to know was if there were any righteous people living among the Canaanites, who could "shelter them in their shade" — that is, supply them with a source of merit that might impede the Israelite conquest of the Land.

In the Covenant Between the Parts (*Bereishis* 15), God told Abraham, "The fourth generation will return here, [but not before that,] because the sin of the Amorites is not complete as yet." As long as the Canaanite and Amorite inhabitants of *Eretz Yisrael* were not sinful enough to warrant being driven out of the Land, Abraham's descendants would be unable to dislodge and supplant them. This is why Moses instructed the spies to ascertain if there were any righteous people in *Eretz Yisrael* to protect its inhabitants, for if there were, it was not yet time for the Israelites to conquer the Land.

But how was a band of twelve spies, who were totally unfamiliar with the Land and its inhabitants, supposed to ascertain whether or not there were some righteous people mingled among the notoriously depraved Canaanite populace (see *Vayikra* 18:3, 18:24ff.)?

My grandfather, Rav Yaakov Meir Sonnenfeld, Rav Yosef Chaim's son, proposed the following answer to these questions. He began by citing a passage from the Gemara (*Kesubos* 112a):

Rabbi Yehoshua ben Levi once passed by Gavla (a place in *Eretz Yisrael*). He saw a grapevine that was bearing huge clusters, as big as calves. He thereupon declared, "O Land! O Land! For whom are you producing such fruits? For these Arabs who, because of our sins, have displaced us?!"

Rabbi Yehoshua ben Levi's question seems strange. Did he really expect the Land to cease bringing forth its produce just because the Jews had been driven out of it? The yield of a parcel of land is determined by natural factors, such as quality of soil, weather conditions, etc., not by the relative merit of its inhabitants! Are there no fruits growing in the lands of the non-Jews?!

The lesson we learn from this passage, explained my grandfather, is that *Eretz Yisrael* is different from all other lands. In this Land there is indeed a direct relationship between the actions of its inhabitants and the ability of the ground to bring forth its produce. The Torah itself says as much: "If you follow my laws the land will yield its produce and the trees of the field will yield their fruit" (*Vayikra* 26:3-4), and conversely (ibid., v. 20). This motif appears in numerous other places throughout the *Tanach* as well. Thus, it was quite understandable why Rabbi Yehoshua ben Levi was so shocked when he saw the remarkable produce growing in *Eretz Yisrael* though the Jewish inhabitants had been exiled from the Land.

But how could the spies know if there were righteous people among the Canaanites? They could reveal this information from the kind of produce grown in the Land, for, as we established above, *Eretz Yisrael*'s unique quality is that its produce always corresponds with the relative merit of its inhabitants. If the fruits were large and plentiful, this would be an indication that there were people of merit among the Canaanites; if not, it would prove the opposite conclusion. Thus, just before telling the spies to see if there were any "trees" in the Land (a metaphor for righteous individuals, as mentioned above), Moses told them to ascertain if the land was "fertile or lean" — for the two matters are directly dependent on each other.

Now we can understand why the spies so hastily and eagerly showed the tremendous fruits of the land to Moses and the people. By exhibiting the excellent quality of the land's produce, they were essentially proving that there were indeed people of merit in Canaan, and that it would therefore be impossible to defeat them.

Bearing this interpretation in mind, we can better understand Joshua and Caleb's refutation of the other spies' words as well. "If Hashem desires us, He will bring us to this Land and give it to us, a Land that flows with milk and honey" (*Bamidbar* 14:8). What they meant to say was, "The fact that the produce is so exceptional is not necessarily a proof that there are righteous people among the Canaanites. It is for *our* sake that God has made the Land so fertile — in order to bring *us* into a Land flowing with milk and honey. You surely didn't expect Him to bring us to a Land languishing under famine and drought!" Then they continued, "Do not fear the people of the Land, for they are our food" (14:9). The traditional explanation of the difficult phrase "they are our food" is that "We will devour them [the inhabitants] like food" (see Rashi). But according to our interpretation, we can explain it on a much simpler level: "They [the fruits that you see] are *our* food. They have grown in *our* merit, in expectation of *our* arrival, for *us* to eat as food." Then they concluded, "Their protection has departed from them. Do not fear them." As Rashi explains, "their protection has departed" means that any righteous people who may have lived among them, and who may have provided a source of protection through their merit, have already departed and died off. These were Joshua's and Caleb's closing words to the people, for, as we have shown, the entire argument between them and the other spies revolved around this exact issue — whether or not there were men of merit among the Canaanite inhabitants.

◆§ Exercising Eye Control

וְלֹא־תָתוּרוּ אַחֲרֵי לְבַבְכֶם וְאַחֲרֵי עֵינֵיכֶם —
And you shall not go astray after your heart and after your eyes (15:39).

The Gemara (*Berachos* 12b) interprets what is meant by "straying after one's heart and eyes": "Straying after the heart" refers to entertaining heretical thoughts, and "straying after the eyes" alludes to allowing lewd thoughts to enter the mind. The Torah thus commands us here to distance ourselves from such sinful contemplations, and provides us with *tzitzis* as a reminder of our obligation to exercise care in avoiding these pitfalls.

Rav Shlomo Zalman Auerbach related that during one of his visits to Rav Yosef Chaim, a question was asked by someone whether or not it was permissible to visit the Abarbanel library. (This library was founded by Maskilim and contained many "Maskilish" books — that is, books expressing unorthodox and heretical ideas — but also had many rare Torah books that were unavailable elsewhere.)

Rav Yosef Chaim answered the question most emphatically in the negative. The prophet Isaiah (33:15), he noted, speaks out in praise of one who "closes his eyes [preventing them] from seeing evil." The Talmud (*Bava Basra* 57b) comments: "This refers to someone who averts his glance when he encounters women bending over their laundry (who are slightly exposed)." Then the Gemara goes on to ask, "What is the case? If there is an alternative path to his destination (which does not pass by these women at all), then he is not praiseworthy, but wicked for choosing this path!" The Gemara thus considers a person to be "wicked" if he can avoid passing by a sight that might lead him to sinful thoughts — even if he is careful to close or avert his eyes from the problematic sight! Apparently the fact that a person allows himself to enter a situation in which he could be exposed to temptation if he *would* open his eyes brands him as "evil" even if he does not in fact open them. The same is true with the Abarbanel library, he concluded. Even if a person is sure that he will not be tempted to look into any of the heretical books found in the library, but will direct his attention only to the Torah books, he must avoid putting himself into the situation of temptation altogether.

Rav Yosef Chaim saw an allusion to the concept of "guarding one's eyes" in the story of Kamtza and Bar Kamtza, related in *Gittin* 55b. (See above, on *Vayikra* 22:25, for a synopsis of the story.) We are told that Bar Kamtza inflicted a blemish on the calf that Caesar had sent to be offered in the Temple. He made a slit in the eyelid of the animal, which, the Gemara tells us, is "considered a blemish by us (Jews), but is not considered a blemish by them (the non-Jews)." (He chose this particular type of blemish to evade detection by Caesar and his officers.)

Rav Yosef Chaim interpreted this statement allegorically. The flaw in the eye represented a person's lack of control over what his eyes glance at. Such carelessness is considered "a blemish" — a fault of character — by the Jews, but the non-Jewish nations see nothing wrong at all with it; they consider it to be completely normal to allow the eye to wander and see whatever is in view.

According to another version of the story presented by the Gemara, the blemish inflicted by Bar Kamtza was a slit in the animal's *lip*. It was this defect, according to this version, that is "considered a blemish by us, but is not considered a blemish by them." This too, said Rav Yosef Chaim, can be explained figuratively. A Jew is expected to guard his lips from uttering obscene expressions or statements. If he does not do so, it is considered to be a fault, a blemish in his character. The Gemara goes so far as to say that using one's mouth to issue a disgusting utterance causes even a sealed Heavenly decree of seventy years of good fortune to be annulled (*Shabbos* 33a). Among the non-Jewish nations, however, such lack of restraint in one's mode of speech is not considered to be a flaw at all.

פרשת קרח
PARASHAS KORACH

◈§ The Sober Rabbi

הִבָּדְלוּ מִתּוֹךְ הָעֵדָה הַזֹּאת — *Separate yourself from amid this assembly.* (16:21).

*R*av Yechiel Mordechai Gordon, the *Rosh Yeshivah* of the yeshivah in Lomza, Poland (and subsequently *Rosh Yeshivah* of the Lomza Yeshivah of Petach Tikvah), visited *Eretz Yisrael* in 1927. At that time the Charedi public was divided between two disparate philosophical schools of thought. Some people were drawn after the teachings of Rav Kook, who preached cooperation and harmony with the secular Zionist establishment, while others identified with the "Eidah Chareidis" and its more conservative, rejectionist outlook, represented by Rav Yosef Chaim.

Rav Gordon, as a well-known Torah personality who was respected by all circles, decided that he would try his hand where others had failed — in an attempt at some form of reconciliation or dialogue between the two camps, for the sake of harmony in the Orthodox community and the resultant consolidation of their energies to achieve their common goals. Toward that end, he met with both Rav Kook and Rav Yosef Chaim. He later recounted part of the dialogue that took place between himself and Rav Yosef Chaim:

As a man well versed in the style of *musar*-lectures of the Lithuanian yeshivos, I explained to Rav Yosef Chaim the tremendous advantages that could be gained if only the Charedi camp could be united into one front. By doing so they would surely have more success in hampering the secular Zionists' progress in their efforts to "de-Judaize" the Jewish people by abandoning their religious heritage and transform them into a "modern" nation like all other nations. I mentioned, among other things, the idea that what was happening with the Jewish community in *Eretz Yisrael* was of great historic import for our people, a miraculous process of ingathering of Jewish exiles to their homeland, with the support and approval of the community of nations, in the wake of the Balfour Declaration.

When I finished my speech, the elderly rabbi did not try to engage me in matters of dogma and philosophy, though he was well known for his skill in presenting his case and for his powers of persuasion. He said to me, simply, "I would like you to know that in fact I am not the rabbi of the 'Eidah Chareidis' at all. Despite the great solemnity and implications of this title that was bestowed upon me against my will, I am in actuality nothing more than a 'Purim Rav.' "

I had never heard of a Purim Rav, and was puzzled by what Rav Yosef Chaim was getting at. The rabbi went on to explain.

"In Pressburg, under my rebbe the *Ksav Sofer* — and, before him, under his father the *Chasam Sofer* — every year a person was appointed as 'Purim Rav.' What was the function of this Rav? Since everyone — rabbis included — drinks a bit on Purim, as is required, and it is forbidden to render a halachic decision even after a small drink, the following problem arose: What if an urgent halachic question arose on Purim, and there would be no one capable of issuing a decision? For this reason a knowledgeable member of town, someone familiar with the basic *halachos* that arise in day-to-day matters, was chosen to act as Purim Rav. His job was to abstain from alcohol completely and handle all halachic queries for the day.

"This is how I see my function here today," the Rav continued. "When the Balfour Declaration was issued, and control over all matters of the Jewish community of *Eretz Yisrael* began to be consolidated under the Zionist Organization, a sense of euphoria "intoxicated" many people in the community, including many prominent rabbis, and blurred their minds. The people's desperation and their age-old longing for redemption hypnotized them into seeing the institution of political Zionism as a beginning of the ultimate redemption process. Temporarily blinded by these sensations, they were not able to see the dangers for the Jewish people that lurked within this phenomenon.

"Thanks to the One Who grants man wisdom, however, I have managed to remain sober and lucid while others have lost their sense of reality. And it is quite clear to me that there has never in our entire history existed a threat to our existence as a people so great as the danger posed by Zionism, which seeks to uproot our ancient heritage that has been our legacy since Sinai, and to detach the Jewish people from everything that connects it to its glorious past. Someone who joined forces with the Zionists once asked me why I am not filled with joy over the Balfour Declaration. I answered him, 'The drunk also wonders why everyone else isn't joining him as he frolics in drunken revelry.' I am not drunk, and therefore I cannot rejoice."

פרשת חוקת
PARASHAS CHUKAS

~§ A True Disciple of Aaron

וַיִּבְכּוּ אֶת־אַהֲרֹן שְׁלֹשִׁים יוֹם כֹּל בֵּית יִשְׂרָאֵל —
*And the entire House of Israel wept for
Aaron thirty days* (20:29).

he Torah tells us that "the entire House of Israel" wept
for Aaron, though when Moses died it was only "the
Sons of Israel" (*Devarim* 34:8) who mourned him. Rashi
explains the difference: Aaron was beloved to *all* the people —
men and women, sophisticated and simple — on a personal level,
because he dedicated himself to settling disputes between friends
and to restoring harmony between man and wife when domestic
quarrels arose. Aaron is in fact the symbol of the peacemaker, as
we are taught in *Pirkei Avos* (1:13): "Be a disciple of Aaron — be
a lover of peace, a pursuer of peace and a lover of human
beings."

Rav Yosef Chaim personified these admirable traits in his own
life. Whenever he became aware of a dispute among neighbors or
between a married couple, he would get involve in his famous
peacemaking efforts, not resting until peace and tranquility were
restored.

It was not infrequently that he would personally visit one of the parties to the quarrel in his home. A knock would be heard at the door. "The Rav is here! He wants to speak to you," someone would call out to the father of the house. Rav Yosef Chaim would not hesitate to get someone out of bed for this purpose, either! The man would throw on a robe and come hurrying into the living room, awed and perhaps overwhelmed by the personal visit of the great Rav. He would already be on the defensive, and after the Rav would raised the issue over which he had come, and issue a compelling lecture on the evils of senseless strife, it would not take long to elicit a capitulation or at least a compromise on the issue at hand. The two of them would then make their way over to the house of the other disputant, where the matter would be brought to a final conclusion, and peace and harmony would be restored between the two parties.

His family members would sometimes ask him, "Is it really befitting for such a prominent rabbi as yourself to go 'schlepping' to the houses of such simple people to beg them to mend their differences? Wouldn't it be more appropriate for you to summon these parties to see you here in your house?"

But Rav Yosef Chaim would hear of no such thing. "I have two responses for you," he told them. "First, am I a more prominent rabbi than Aaron the Kohen, who would go from tent to tent to make peace between neighbors and between spouses? Second, I know the members of my community. If I summon them, they will procrastinate and put off the appointment. In the meantime, the quarrel will only become exacerbated. For, as the Sages teach (*Sanhedrin* 7a), contention is like a crack in a dam — each moment it is allowed to linger, the wider and more irreparable the gap becomes. Furthermore, if they come to my house it is easier for them to evade my attempts at reconciliation than when I 'put them on the spot' by taking the trouble to call on them personally."

The same approach was used for marital disputes. If it was only a matter of minor domestic discord, he would try to determine the underlying problem. If he felt the husband was being unfair toward his wife, he would call him in and reprimand him for being insensitive to the importance of the woman's role in the home. What would his house look like without her faithful execution of the endless list of chores involved in its upkeep? How could one put a price on the work involved in bringing up one's children and caring for their every need?

If the wife demanded that the husband bring home more money, Rav Yosef Chaim would tell him, "She's not looking for a life of luxury, you know. She's only looking out for the benefit of the house and the children — *your* house and *your* children! Why the arguments? You know that God's blessing is found in a household only by the merit of the woman of the house!"

And if the problem was in the house of one of the full-time Torah students, whose meager livelihood was based on the scant stipend he received from his yeshivah, he would give the wife a pep talk about the great merit of living in the household of a *talmid chacham* who devotes all his energies to Torah study. Why, the daughters of Israel in the past would have given anything for such a privilege! Would she prefer that her husband and sons were *talmidei chachamim* and her daughters the children of a Torah scholar, or that the husband should go out to earn a few more dollars and forget all his learning? The Gemara (*Berachos* 17a) teaches, after all, that a woman's place in the Next World is determined by the extent with which she enabled and encouraged her husband and sons to devote themselves to Torah study! Before long, the woman would begin to look at her husband from a different perspective, and marital harmony would be restored. When the husband returned from his studies at night, he would detect a shift in attitude on the part of his wife. He did not have to ask too many questions as to what had precipitated the change; it was quite clear that Rav Yosef Chaim had been involved here!

<h1 style="text-align:center">פרשת בלק
PARASHAS BALAK</h1>

~§ Moab's Fear

וַיָּגָר מוֹאָב מִפְּנֵי הָעָם מְאֹד כִּי רַב־הוּא —
Moab became very frightened of the people, because it was numerous (22:3).

*W*hy were the Moabites afraid of the Israelites? After all, the Jews had been commanded concerning the Moabites, "Do not provoke war with them" (*Devarim* 2:9); they seemingly had nothing to worry about! Rashi (ad loc.) supplies the answer: Unlike the Ammonites, whom the Israelites were commanded "not to provoke" *at all* (*Devarim* 2:19), the Moabites were off limits to the Israelites only as far as "provoking war" with them. They were permitted, however, to vex them, intimidate them, take spoils, etc. This was the cause of Moab's concern. They were not afraid for their lives, for they knew the Israelites would not fight a war against them; they feared only the destruction of their property and tranquility.

This, then, was what the Moabite king Balak meant when he declared, "Now the congregation will lick up our entire surroundings, as an ox licks up the greenery of the field" (*Bamidbar* 22:4). It was not death or destruction that he dreaded, but a "licking" — i.e., exploitation.

Now, why was Moab so concerned? The Torah tells us that it was "because it (Israel) was numerous." This is, at any rate, the traditional understanding of the phrase כִּי רַב־הוּא. However, it is possible to suggest another interpretation as well, based on the words of Rashi in *Bereishis* 19:37. Both of Lot's daughters became pregnant by him. The older daughter gave birth first, and called her son "Moab," from the word מֵאָב, "[He came] from my father." The younger daughter also memorialized her son's incestuous origins, but more discreetly so, calling him Ben Ami (the ancestor of the Ben Ammonites, or more simply, the Ammonites), meaning "the son of my people." The younger daughter, Rashi writes, was rewarded for her more chaste choice of a name years later, when her descendants, the Ammonites, were granted greater protection from the Israelites than were the Moabites (as explained above). Thus, we may interpret the phrase כִּי רַב־הוּא as "because it (Moab) was the older one" (רַב, as in וְרַב יַעֲבֹד צָעִיר, *the older one will serve the younger one* — *Bereishis* 25:23). The fear of the Moabites was based on the fact that they were descended from the older grandson/son of Lot, Moab, and, due to their ancestress's choice of name for her son, they were fated to be exposed to the hostility of the Israelites.

✥ Balaam's Plan of Attack

וַיִּשְׁלַח מַלְאָכִים אֶל־בִּלְעָם... לֵאמֹר, הִנֵּה עַם יָצָא מִמִּצְרַיִם הִנֵּה כִסָּה אֶת־עֵין הָאָרֶץ וְהוּא יֹשֵׁב מִמֻּלִי — *He sent messengers to Balaam... saying, "Behold, a people has come out of Egypt; behold, it has covered the surface of the earth, and it is situated opposite me"* (22:5).

ashi, noting that the word מִמֻּלִי (*opposite me*) is spelled missing a ו (it should have been spelled מִמּוּלִי), explains that Balak was alluding to a secondary meaning of the word, from the root מל (meaning *to cut down*, or *to demolish*, as in אֲמִילַם [*Tehillim* 118:10]): "Come and help me, for the Israelites are threatening to demolish me!"

Rav Yosef Chaim suggested that Rashi's approach might be used to show yet another shade of meaning to Balak's choice of expression, for the word מַל can also mean *to circumcise*. We know that the Israelites did not perform circumcision on their children all during their forty years of wandering in the desert (*Yehoshua* 5:5). Although the Gemara (*Yevamos* 72a) explains that this was due to health considerations and was unavoidable, it was nevertheless a sign that the Jews had fallen out of favor with God, Who could have provided the necessary conditions to allow circumcision (*Tosafos*, citing *Sifrei*). Balak was thus alluding to a flaw he had noticed among the Jews — that they had not fulfilled the commandment of circumcision.

In *Michah* 6:5 we read, "My people, recall, if you will, what Balak, king of Moab, schemed, and what Balaam son of Beor answered him, [and all the events] from Shittim to Gilgal — in order to recognize the mercy of Hashem." The Gemara (*Berachos* 7a) explains that Balaam had the supernatural ability to determine the moment of the day during which God's wrath burns, and was thus theoretically capable of destroying Israel by uttering a curse at that moment. By *the mercy of Hashem*, however, God refrained from becoming angry during those days in which Balaam uttered his curses against Israel. How exactly Balaam sought to ignite God's wrath against the Jews we are not told, but Rav Yosef Chaim suggested that it was by pointing out their lack of adherence to the mitzvah of circumcision. This fact, he added, is alluded to in one of Balaam's declarations: "For from the top of mountains I see them [Israel], and from hilltops I view them" (23:9). The word צֻרִים, translated here as "mountains," is also used to describe the knives that the Israelites used to circumcise themselves upon their arrival in *Eretz Yisrael* (*Yehoshua* 5:2-3), in a place called Gilgal, which was named to commemorate the mass circumcision ceremony (ibid., 5:9). The place was also called גִּבְעַת הָעֲרָלוֹת, the Hilltop of the Foreskins. Hence, what Balaam was saying to Balak was essentially: "You called me to curse Israel through calling attention to their lack of circumcision. But in fact I see ahead in the future that the moment they arrive at their destination, at the very first opportunity that will present itself, they will perform this circumcision. *For from beforehand* (מֵרֹאשׁ) *sharp knives* (צֻרִים) *I see for them* (אֶרְאֶנּוּ), *and from the vantage point of hilltops* (וּמִגְּבָעוֹת) — the Hilltop of Foreskins — *I view them.*" The fact that they did not delay for even one moment the fulfillment of this mitzvah proves conclusively that their lack of fulfillment of circumcision in the desert was not due to any sort of neglect or laxity on their part, but solely and genuinely out of health considerations that were beyond their control. Their not being circumcised, then, could not be used as a source for a curse against them.

With this idea in mind we can better understand the verse from *Michah* which we cited above as well: "My people, recall what Balak, king of Moab, schemed, and what Balaam son of Beor answered him, [and all the events] from Shittim to Gilgal — in order to recognize the mercy of Hashem." Why, one might ask, does the verse bring in Balak's role in the affair? And why is Gilgal, of all places, mentioned in connection with Balaam and his attempted curse? In light of what we have explained above, of course, the answers to these questions become obvious. It was Balak who came up with the idea to call attention to the Israelites' lack of circumcision as a possible means of stirring Divine anger against them. And it was in Gilgal that they removed the "shame" (*Yehoshua* 5:9) of being uncircumcised from themselves, proving that it was their desire to fulfill this mitzvah all along.

◆§ What Pinchas Saw

וַיַּרְא פִּינְחָס בֶּן־אֶלְעָזָר בֶּן־אַהֲרֹן הַכֹּהֵן וַיָּקָם מִתּוֹךְ הָעֵדָה וַיִּקַּח רֹמַח בְּיָדוֹ... וַיִּדְקֹר אֶת־שְׁנֵיהֶם אֵת אִישׁ יִשְׂרָאֵל וְאֶת־הָאִשָּׁה אֶל־קֳבָתָהּ וַתֵּעָצַר הַמַּגֵּפָה מֵעַל בְּנֵי יִשְׂרָאֵל — *Pinchas son of Elazar son of Aaron the Kohen saw, and he arose from amid the assembly and took a spear in his hand... and he pierced them both — the Israelite man and the woman in her stomach. And the plague was halted from the Children of Israel (25:7-8).*

The following remarks were made by Rav Eliyahu Meir Bloch, *Rosh Yeshivah* of Telshe, in his eulogy for Rav Yosef Chaim:

"The Midrash relates:

The man (Zimri) showed respect neither toward God nor toward his other men.

She (the Midianite woman) told him, "I will listen only to Moses."

He said, "I am just as great as he is!"

He took her to Moses and said, "Son of Amram, is this Midianite woman permitted or forbidden to me?"

When Moses told him she was forbidden, he asked him, "And isn't your own wife a Midianite?"

At that point Moses' hands became weakened (he was paralyzed with astonishment), and the halachah (for such cases) escaped him.

"*Pinchas saw*" — and everyone else did not see? Doesn't it say, "[Zimri] brought over a Midianite woman to his brothers, in the sight of Moses and in the sight of the entire assembly"? Rather, it means, "He saw what was happening and remembered the halachah [i.e., that such sinners are to be stricken down by zealots]."

"The Midrash's answer leaves us puzzled. We still do not understand what caused Pinchas to 'see' something that Moses and the rest of the assembly did not. Why did the halachah escape Moses' and everyone else's mind, but not that of Pinchas?

"I heard an explanation of this matter from my master and rebbe. He noted that the Midrash does not say that Moses 'forgot' the halachah, but that 'it escaped him' (נִתְעַלְמָה)). There are times in a man's life when the halachah becomes clouded by the heavy burdens created in times of distress or calamity. He is aware of the halachic imperatives in a given situation, but it becomes obfuscated by all the other factors involved. A person's nature is to see each individual action in the context of the general situation at hand. He is incapable of evaluating the matter as an isolated incident — especially at a time of great upheaval, at a time when all the ordinary priorities and rules seem to be cast aside. Such was the situation here. Suddenly there was no Torah and no *derech eretz* (decent conduct), no Moses and no Aaron, no sense of embarrassment or modesty; a prince of Israel marches in and performs his abhorrent sin in broad daylight! When Moses and Aaron saw this act, when they pondered the depths of the scandal and the dreadful destruction that would inevitably come in its wake, they did not see a simple, isolated act to which the halachah applied, but a general rebellion against God. It did not occur to them that they could bring the matter to a swift close by putting into practice the general and straightforward halachah that 'When a man has relations with a non-Jewish woman, zealots may strike him down.' Pinchas, however, did not succumb to the overwhelmingly shocking background of the situation. He was able to 'see' the act that was taking place for what it was, an isolated incident. He realized that the halachah, which represents the will of God, is unalterable, and applies in all times, in every situation. This is what is meant by *Pinchas saw* — he saw the act that was associated with the halachah of 'zealots may strike him down,' and acted in accordance with what he saw.

"Rav Yosef Chaim excelled in this trait as well. The battle surrounded him from all sides, he was always in situations of intense pressure. Every step he took was set up for criticism and opposition from this camp or the other. Yet, despite all these daunting obstacles, he did not flinch or compromise on anything. He *saw* each particular, individual issue for what it was, and acted in accordance with the strict dictates of the halachah."

פרשת פינחס
PARASHAS PINCHAS

Zimri's "Noble" Intentions

וְהִנֵּה אִישׁ מִבְּנֵי יִשְׂרָאֵל בָּא וַיַּקְרֵב אֶל־אֶחָיו אֶת־
הַמִּדְיָנִית לְעֵינֵי מֹשֶׁה וּלְעֵינֵי כָּל־עֲדַת בְּנֵי־יִשְׂרָאֵל...
וְשֵׁם אִישׁ יִשְׂרָאֵל הַמֻּכֶּה אֲשֶׁר הֻכָּה אֶת־הַמִּדְיָנִית
זִמְרִי בֶּן־סָלוּא נְשִׂיא בֵית־אָב לַשִּׁמְעֹנִי — *Then,*
a man of the Children of Israel came and
brought the Midianite woman next to his
brothers in the sight of Moses and in the
sight of the entire assembly of the Chil-
dren of Israel... The name of the slain
Israelite man, who was slain with the
Midianite woman, was Zimri son of Salu,
leader of a father's house of the Simeon-
ites (25:6,14).

Zimri's conduct seems to be most inappropriate, especially for a distinguished tribal leader. As a nobleman,
he should have exemplified better character traits than
to indulge in such immoral behavior. Even if he found himself
swept away by uncontrollable passion, he should at least have
committed his indecent act in private. What was his point in
passing the woman right under Moses' nose, and in plain view of
the entire assembly?

To answer this question, Rav Yosef Chaim said, we must first
understand why the Israelite men's straying after the Midianite

women was so problematic in the first place. As the Torah tells us (v. 2; see Rashi), there was much more at stake here than a "mere" case of rampant promiscuity. For the Midianite women used their encounters with the men to lure them into worshiping their gods.

Zimri, explained Rav Yosef Chaim, as a leader in Israel, was concerned about the idolatrous worship that was taking root through this tactic of the Midianites. For the good of the nation, he knew something had to be done about this problem. He therefore came up with the following idea: If we cannot stop the young men from lusting after the Midianite women, at least we can prevent this sin from leading to the further sin of idolatry! Instead of the Jewish men going to the Midianite homes to indulge their desires, which results in their practicing idolatry, let us bring the Midianite women into the Israelite camp. There they will at least not be able to ensnare the Jewish men into worshiping their gods; perhaps they might even be persuaded to join us in worshiping the true God. We should strive to "bring them near" to us and our religion.

It was against this "deal with the devil" that Pinchas rose up. He realized that such a compromise was even worse than the original situation that it was intended to replace, for in this manner the sacred "camp of God" of the Israelites would become desecrated. Let those who cannot control their passions go to the Midianites and sin there, but the Camp of Israel must retain its purity and sanctity!

The Gemara (Sanhedrin 82b) relates that the Israelites were not impressed with Pinchas's show of zealousness in killing Zimri. Who did this rabble-rouser think he was, anyway? "Do you see?" they said to one another. "This fellow's grandfather (Yisro) used to fatten up calves to sacrifice to idols, and now he goes and kills a prince in Israel!" The Torah therefore reminded the people of Pinchas's lineage on his father's side — he was a grandson of Aaron.

Exactly what point were the people trying to make by recalling the idolatrous background of one of Pinchas's ancestors? And what was the Torah's message in stressing his paternal lineage? Everyone knew quite well that Pinchas was descended from both of these grandfathers! Rav Yosef Chaim explained that the people's argument was as follows: "Since Pinchas has an idolatrous priest in his family, this explains why he was so opposed to Zimri's plan to minimize idolatry in the Israelite camp. That's why he killed him!" The Torah therefore refuted this contention by providing genealogy on his father's side, as if to say: "You people are mistaken. In striking down Zimri, Pinchas was guided by considerations of service to God, which he inherited from Aaron, and not from any negative spiritual flaw he may have inherited from his idol-worshiping side."

Rav Yosef Chaim's own convictions exemplified the attitude of Pinchas as explained in this interpretation. He fought bitterly against those who sought to make compromises in principles in order to foster better relations with those who rejected the Torah. The possible advantages to such plans, he argued, were at best meager, while the losses were definite and severe.

On the other hand, Rav Yosef Chaim was no fanatic either. One time, in the course of an argument over an important communal manner, a zealot by the name of Rav Nota Maggid (Weiss) accused Rav Yosef Chaim, "The Rav used to be a real zealot once, when his rebbe, Rav Yehoshua Leib Diskin, was alive! But now it seems he has mellowed!"

"I was never a zealot," countered Rav Yosef Chaim in his gentle, soft-spoken voice. "I was only following the dictates of my rebbe. And today I still follow those same dictates with the same determination!"

There was a group of disciples of Rav Yehoshua Leib who were known for their great devotion to their rebbe — and for their uncompromising zealousness on all religious issues.

One of them, Rav Leib Levine, decided to disassociate himself from the group after Rav Yehoshua Leib's death. "Zealousness," he explained, "is like a sharp needle. If it has a head, you can use it, but if the head is taken away it is too dangerous a tool to use!"

פרשת מטות
PARASHAS MATTOS

◆§ Reuben's and Gad's Proposition

> וַיֹּאמְרוּ אִם־מָצָאנוּ חֵן בְּעֵינֶיךָ יֻתַּן אֶת־הָאָרֶץ
> הַזֹּאת לַעֲבָדֶיךָ לַאֲחֻזָּה — *They said, "If we have found favor in your eyes, let this land be given to your servants as a portion"* (32:5).

*M*oses' reaction to the Reubenites' and Gadites' request to be allotted the land of Gilead was quite harsh: "Why do you dishearten the Children of Israel? Behold, you have risen up in place of your fathers, a society of sinful people, to add more to the wrath of Hashem against Israel!" (vv. 6, 14).

The two tribes thereupon came up with an alternative idea. They would join their brothers in war, building fortified settlements for their wives and possessions, to which they would ultimately return (vv. 16-19). Moses accepted this offer (vv. 20-22), but once again offered a stern rebuke in the event the Reubenites and Gadites would not keep their side of the deal (v. 23): "If you do not do so, behold, you will have sinned to Hashem. Know your sin that will encounter you!"

The Reubenites and Gadites assured Moses that they would do as they had said. "Your servants will do as my lord commands. Our small children, our wives, our livestock will be there in the cities of the Gilead, and your servants will cross over, every armed person of the army to do battle, as my lord has spoken" (vv. 25-27).

This narrative presents several difficulties. First, why did Moses see fit to rebuke the Reubenites and Gadites once again, *after* they had already agreed to join their brethren in the conquest of *Eretz Yisrael*? Second, why did the men of these two tribes restate their plan all over again in vv. 25-27? They had already laid out the exact same idea earlier, in vv. 16-19! Even more puzzling is the fact that now, when repeating the plan a second time, they referred to it (*twice!*) as Moses' idea — "as my lord commands" (v. 25); "as my lord has spoken" (v. 27) — when it fact it was *they* who had proposed the plan in the first place!

I would like to suggest the following approach, which will supply solutions to all these problems.

When the Reubenites and Gadites first laid out their compromise plan, by which they would join forces with their brethren, but leave their families behind, they said, "We will build flock enclosures for our livestock here and we will arm ourselves swiftly in the vanguard of the Children of Israel until we will bring them to their place" (vv. 16-17). Everything they said revolved around "we." *We* will make war alongside the Children of Israel; *we* will bring them to their place.

Moses accepted their offer, but rebuked them for their attitude. The taking of *Eretz Yisrael* was not going to consist of ordinary, natural wars of conquest, with one army battling the other until the stronger or more determined one prevailed. Rather, it was a series of supernatural battles, with God providing victory to Israel, beginning with the spectacular toppling of the walls of Jericho. He therefore said to them, when restating the terms of the agreement, "If you do this thing, if you arm yourselves and cross the Jordan *before Hashem* and the Land shall be conquered *before Hashem*" (vv. 20-22). "You must realize," he admonished them, "that the battle you are offering to join is to be fought *before Hashem*, through His guidance." If they did not understand this message, however, and if they would continue to view the conquest and settling of *Eretz Yisrael* as an ordinary, natural phenomenon, they would have "sinned to Hashem" (v. 23).

The Reubenites and Gadites understood the message loud and clear. They therefore recapitulated the agreement, with some alterations: "Your servants will cross over, every armed person of the army, *before Hashem*, to do battle." Attributing this revision of the deal to its true author, they added, "as my lord has spoken."

◆§ Propriety in the Eyes of Both Hashem and Israel

וְהִיִיתֶם נְקִיִם מה' וּמִיִּשְׂרָאֵל — *And you will be vindicated from Hashem and from Israel* (32:22).

The Talmud (*Yoma* 38a) praises the Garmo family, who were the bakers of the "showbread" (לֶחֶם הַפָּנִים) in the Temple, because of the fact that "there was never found any high-quality bread among the sons of that family, to prevent people saying, 'They are helping themselves to the Temple's showbread,' to fulfill what is written in the Torah, 'you will be vindicated from Hashem and from Israel.' " It is not enough to avoid actual sin; one must be careful not to give the *appearance* that he is sinning either.

Rav Yosef Chaim was famous for personifying this trait to the fullest. He never took advantage — for himself or for family members — of any of the numerous funds that were sent to him to help support the Orthodox Jewish community of Jerusalem.

One time his own granddaughter, who had been orphaned at a young age, was about to be married to a poor student of the Torah. She came before Rav Yosef Chaim with tears in her eyes, arguing, "Why should I be worse off than any other orphan, whose grandparents assist them financially to meet the costs of setting up their households? Of all the money that goes through your hands, entrusted to you to 'dispose of as you see fit,' why should I be less entitled to a grant than anyone else? Even disregarding the fact that I am your granddaughter, I should be given some assistance as an ordinary Jewish poverty-stricken orphan!"

Rav Yosef Chaim was touched by her plea, and his eyes too began to well up with tears. But he could not fulfill her request. "Do not continue to press me in this manner, my dear granddaughter," he implored. "Would you like it if because of you I would break my strict rules of conduct with charity money? For my entire life I have strictly refrained from endowing any one of my children from charity funds that are entrusted to me. The Sages teach (*Pesachim* 13a): 'Those in charge of charity money may give change (from the fund's coins) to others, but not take change for themselves. Those in charge of food distribution to the poor may sell unused food to others (and return the money to charity), but not to themselves. For it says, *You will be vindicated from Hashem and from Israel.*' I am willing to sell my bed and pillow and give you the proceeds — but I cannot give you anything from the charity funds entrusted to me. I know better than anyone how much you have suffered throughout your life since your mother died. But now, leave this matter alone. Go in peace, and may God, in His great mercy, provide you with such great happiness in your lot that all the richest girls in town will be jealous of you!"

As it happened, Rav Yosef Chaim's words of blessing materialized. This young woman went on to become the matriarch of a family whose sons were among the most illustrious *talmidei chachamim* of Jerusalem, and they were indeed a source of tremendous pride and comfort for her.

ספר דברים
DEVARIM / DEUTERONOMY

פרשת ואתחנן
PARASHAS VA'ESCHANAN

❧ See for Yourself

עֲלֵה רֹאשׁ הַפִּסְגָּה וְשָׂא עֵינֶיךָ יָמָּה וְצָפֹנָה וְתֵימָנָה
וּמִזְרָחָה וּרְאֵה בְעֵינֶיךָ כִּי־לֹא תַעֲבֹר אֶת־הַיַּרְדֵּן
הַזֶּה — *Ascend to the top of the peak and raise your eyes westward, northward, southward and eastward and see with your eyes, for you shall not cross this Jordan (3:27).*

The words "and see with your eyes" seem superfluous. Moses was already told to "raise his eyes" toward all the directions; of course this was to be done in order to see what was there!

Rav Yosef Chaim suggested an alternative reading of this verse, which eliminates this difficulty. The word כִּי, translated here as "for [you shall not]," can also mean the relative pronoun "that." Substituting this meaning of the word כִּי, the verse would now read: "Ascend to the top of the peak and raise your eyes westward and see with your eyes that you cannot cross this Jordan." The explanation of this statement is as follows.

The Sages tell us that if Moses had been allowed to cross the Jordan and enter *Eretz Yisrael*, it would have been rendered impossible for the land to ever be destroyed at the hands of Israel's enemies. Now, the Midrash (*Eichah Rabbasi*; see Rashi on *Kiddushin* 31b), commenting on *Eichah* 4:11, explains that when God "poured out His wrath and set fire to Zion," this was actually good news for the Jewish people. Instead of destroying the Jewish people themselves, as they deserved, God "vented" his anger on the wood and stones of the buildings in Zion, sparing the lives of His people. Thus, if Moses had entered *Eretz Yisrael*, thereby preventing the destruction of the land by Israel's enemies, this would have indirectly led to an even worse fate being visited upon them — their own physical destruction. Therefore, God told Moses to take a good look at the beauty of *Eretz Yisrael* and understand "that you cannot cross this Jordan," for Israel's own good.

⋘ God's Compassion and Torah Learning

פֶּן־תִּשְׁכַּח אֶת־הַדְּבָרִים אֲשֶׁר־רָאוּ עֵינֶיךָ... וְהוֹדַעְתָּם לְבָנֶיךָ וְלִבְנֵי בָנֶיךָ. יוֹם אֲשֶׁר עָמַדְתָּ לִפְנֵי ה׳ אֱלֹקֶיךָ בְּחֹרֵב — *Do not forget the things that your eyes beheld ... and make them known to your children and your children's children — the day that you stood before Hashem, your God, at Horeb* (4:9-10).

T he morning prayers, just before the *Shema*, contain the following passionate prayer:

You have loved us with abundant love, and You have shown compassion to us with great and exceeding compassion. Our Father, our King, for the sake of our forefathers who trusted in You and whom You taught the decrees of life, may You be equally gracious toward us and teach us. Our Father, merciful Father, Who acts mercifully, have mercy upon us and instill in our hearts the ability to understand and elucidate, to listen, learn, teach the words of Your Torah's teaching. Enlighten our eyes with Your Torah so that we shall not be ashamed for eternity.

There are several passages in this prayer that require explanation. First, what is meant by "so that we shall not be ashamed for eternity"? Is this the only reason we seek to be blessed with the ability to study and understand the words of the Torah — so that we should not suffer shame? The Torah is our very "life and the length of our days" (*Devarim* 30:20). It "restores the soul, provides wisdom to the foolish, gladdens the heart, etc." (*Tehillim* 19). As a single mitzvah the study of Torah outweighs all others (*Pe'ah* 1:1). It seems to be an understatement of the value of Torah knowledge to seek it only to avoid embarrassment!

Another question is: Why is there such a continuous emphasis on "compassion" and "mercy" in this prayer? What is the unique role of compassion in our request for Torah wisdom, more than in other prayers?

Last: Why do we base our request for Torah knowledge on "the sake of our forefathers"? When we pray for good health and prosperity, for instance, we do beseech God to grant us these requests "for the sake of our forefathers"!

Rav Yosef Chaim explained these difficulties based on a comment made by the Gemara (*Kiddushin* 30a) concerning our verse: "When someone teaches his grandson Torah, it is considered as if he (the grandson) had received it from Mount Sinai, as it says, *'Make them [the words of the Torah] known to your children's children — the day that you stood before Hashem, your God, at Horeb.'* "

The obvious question that arises in connection with this dictum is: Why is learning Torah from one's grandfather considered tantamount to receiving the Torah at Mount Sinai, more than learning from one's father — or from any other teacher, for that matter?

The answer given to this question is based on the well-known principle of "decline of the generations," a doctrine that is obvious to all students of the Torah. This rule declares that each successive generation becomes weaker than its predecessor in terms of its capabilities of mastering the depths of Torah knowledge. The reason for this is self-evident: The further removed one gets from the source, the weaker the influence of the power emanating from that source becomes. This is true in general, and certainly for the teachings of the Torah, which are "longer than the land in measurement and wider than the sea" (*Iyov* 11:9); each generation that passes becomes, by definition, more distant from the original source of Torah, when Moses first received it at Mount Sinai. When one learns Torah directly from his grandfather, he helps to bridge this gap somewhat, by skipping backwards an extra generation. He is one step closer to Sinai than he would have been had he learned from his father. This is why the Gemara compares his learning to "receiving the Torah at Sinai."

Now let us return to the passage from the morning liturgy cited above. Our request in this prayer is not simply to be granted insight into the Torah, but to gain Torah knowledge *on the level of our fathers* of previous generations. This is what is meant by the words, "for the sake of our forefathers whom You taught the decrees of life, may You be equally gracious toward us and teach us." We beseech God to be *gracious* to us and allow us to gain an understanding of the Torah that is comparable to that of our forebears, despite the fact that such a phenomenon would stand in contradiction to the principle of "decline of the generations," and is thus contrary to the natural order. For such an extraordinary request, it is indeed befitting to invoke God's *mercy* and *compassion*.

The question that now arises is: Why indeed do we pray for something that is so exceptional? Why should we not suffice with achieving Torah knowledge that is befitting for our own generation, deficient though it may be in comparison with previous eras? The answer is that when the time comes for us to leave this world, and our souls go on to the Next World, we will come into contact with our fathers and forebears. How inadequate we will feel in their presence! How our own meager spiritual accomplishments will pale in comparison with theirs! We therefore state the reason for our far-reaching request: it is so that we not be ashamed "for eternity" — in the World of Eternity, when we will be reunited with our learned and spiritually superior ancestors.

⋘ Amazing Sight

> הֲנִהְיָה כַּדָּבָר הַגָּדוֹל הַזֶּה אוֹ הֲנִשְׁמַע כָּמֹהוּ —
> *Has there ever been anything like this great thing or has anything like it been heard?* (4:32).

av Yosef Chaim was never very impressed with the various inventions and discoveries that were so common in the beginning of the 20th century. He used to say that the ancient sages already knew the basic principles behind these inventions, but that the time was not right for their actual production and introduction into use.

When a German zeppelin appeared over the skies of Jerusalem in 1927, all the residents — men, women and children alike — ran up to the rooftops to gaze at the flying marvel. But Rav Yosef Chaim did not get up from his chair and interrupt his studies for even one second. He just declared to himself, "How great are Your works, Hashem; You have made all of them with wisdom" (*Tehillim* 104:24).

On the other hand, he did not hesitate to show how greatly impressed or excited he was when he heard an interesting Torah insight or a new approach to a question, or when he saw a Torah book he had not seen before.

☙ Fear of God —Man's Essence

מִי־יִתֵּן וְהָיָה לְבָבָם זֶה לָהֶם לְיִרְאָה אֹתִי וְלִשְׁמֹר אֶת־כָּל־מִצְוֹתַי כָּל־הַיָּמִים — *If only this heart they have to fear Me and to observe all My commandments would remain with them all the days* (5:26).

Fear of God is of central importance to man's very being. The Book of *Koheles* echoes this sentiment in its penultimate verse: "The sum of the matter, when all has been considered, is: Fear God and keep His commandments, for that is man's whole essence."

Rav Yosef Chaim suggested an interesting interpretation for this verse of *Koheles*. Each person is blessed with certain unique talents and strengths that others do not have. These are gifts from God. One cannot take credit for possessing them, nor can a person be taken to task for *not* having them. We do not look down on an average person for not being an accomplished artist or musician if he happens not to be talented in these areas. But each individual is expected to take advantage of whatever talents he does have and utilize them to the fullest. As the rebbe Reb Zushe used to say, "In heaven they will not admonish me by saying, 'Why did you not become a great Torah genius?' But they *will* say, 'Why didn't you become Zushe?'" The more talent a person has, the greater is his responsibility to develop his gifts to the fullest. The Sages expressed this concept with the maxim: "According to the camel is the size of the load" (*Kesubos* 67a).

This is true for all of man's qualities, except for one — fear of God. In this area, no man is more or less predisposed to be God-fearing than any other individual. Each person is capable — if he has the desire and is willing to put in the effort — of achieving the highest possible levels of spirituality. "Everything is in God's hands except for fearing God," the Sages teach (*Berachos* 33b). Unlike other character traits or natural talents, then, the potential to fear God is the one thing that all men have in common. This, suggested Rav Yosef Chaim, is what Koheles meant when he said, "Fear God and observe His commandments, *for this is for every man*" (כִּי־זֶה כָּל־הָאָדָם — translated above as, "for that is man's whole essence"). This is the challenge that *every man* faces equally.

Rav Yosef Chaim offered another interpretation for this phrase as well. The main theme of *Koheles* is expressed in its opening verse: "Futility of futilities; all is futility!" There is no worth to anything a person strives for in the world; everything is pointless. The natural reaction to hearing twelve chapters' worth of such declarations pronouncing the futility of all of life's endeavors would be despair: "Why should I bother to do anything with my life if all is so meaningless?" For this reason *Koheles* ends off with an important "disclaimer": When we speak of the futility of life, we refer only to a person whose life is devoid of fear of God and of following His commandments. If a person works hard his whole life to earn a livelihood or to achieve some other accomplishment, it is all meaningless — unless he devotes his money or accomplishment to the service of God, such as giving charity, doing good deeds for the benefit of others, etc. In that case, his toil and efforts have attained true, lasting purpose. Fear of God, then, lends meaning to all of the facets of man's activity, and to all his life's accomplishments; it is what makes "the entire man" worthwhile (כִּי־זֶה כָּל־הָאָדָם).

✒ "With All Your Money"

וְאָהַבְתָּ אֵת ה׳ אֱלֹקֶיךָ בְּכָל־לְבָבְךָ וּבְכָל־נַפְשְׁךָ וּבְכָל־מְאֹדֶךָ — *You shall love Hashem your God, with all your heart, with all your soul and with all your might (6:5).*

When Rav Yosef Chaim heard the story (related in אנשים של צורה [*Men of Stature*], pp. 159—169) of Rav Yosef Levi Hagiz, who was prepared to lose all his possessions rather than transgress the rabbinical prohibition of requesting a non-Jew to do a *melachah* (an act forbidden on Shabbos) for him, he responded with great enthusiasm. On that occasion he shared the following insight into our verse.

It is interesting to note that in the first passage of the *Shema* we recite, "You shall love God with all your heart, with all your soul and with all your might," while in the second passage it states, "If you hearken to My commandments to love Hashem, your God, and to serve Him with all your heart and with all your soul, then I shall provide" (below, 11:13—14). The third phrase, "with all your might," is omitted in this passage. What is the significance of this change in expression between the two paragraphs?

In order to answer this question, we must bear in mind that the Sages' interpretation of the word מְאֹדֶךָ (translated here as "your might") is "your money" (*Berachos* 54a): We must love God even if this involves a loss of money. Another fact that must be borne in mind is that although modern English does not differentiate between singular "you" and plural "you," the Hebrew of the first paragraph of the *Shema* is written in the singular: "You (the individual) shall love God with all your heart, etc." The second paragraph, on the other hand, is in the plural: "If you (the entire congregation) hearken... to love God with all your heart, etc."

The Torah commands us to love God with all our heart and with our very lives (*souls*). This concept applies on both a communal and individual level, and therefore appears in both passages. However, the ability to love God with all one's possessions and to make great financial sacrifices for His sake is something that only certain unique individuals are capable of doing. It is for this reason that this phrase is omitted in the second passage, which is addressed to the community as a whole.

◆§ Torah and Luxury Don't Mix

וְדִבַּרְתָּ בָּם — *And you shall speak of them* (6:7).

In the Gemara's discussion (*Kiddushin* 29b) of the question as to whether it is better to marry before or after studying the Torah, Rav Yochanan declares, "With a millstone around his neck, can one study Torah?" Burdened with the responsibility of earning a livelihood and feeding his family, it is impossible for a married person to devote sufficient attention and time to Torah study.

Rav Yosef Chaim adopted Rav Yochanan's saying, in a slightly altered form: "If one seeks to 'live the good life' (רָאֶה חַיִּים, a play on the word רֵיחַיִם, *a millstone*), can he study Torah?" Torah study requires toil and effort, and someone who leads a lifestyle in which he pursues comfort and luxury cannot hope to achieve greatness in Torah. In the words of the Sages, "The Torah is not preserved except in someone who kills himself over it" (*Berachos* 63b).

◆§ True Love of God

וְאָהַבְתָּ אֵת ה' אֱלֹקֶיךָ בְּכָל־לְבָבְךָ... וְשִׁנַּנְתָּם לְבָנֶיךָ — *You shall love Hashem, your God, with all your heart ... and you shall teach [the words of Torah] to your children* (6:5-7).

The juxtaposition of these verses is significant, wrote Rav Yosef Chaim in a letter to Rav Yissachar Dov Teichtal. The Torah commands us to love God with all our heart and soul. But how can this love of God be expressed in actuality? The answer is given by the Torah itself: "you shall teach [the words of Torah] to your children." By raising our children to study the Torah — this is how we show our own true love for God.

פרשת עקב

PARASHAS EIKEV

◄§ Keeping Perspective in Misfortune

כִּי כַּאֲשֶׁר יְיַסֵּר אִישׁ אֶת־בְּנוֹ ה' אֱלֹקֶיךָ מְיַסְּרֶךָ —

For just as a man chastises a son, Hashem, your God, chastises you (8:5).

Rav Yosef Chaim experienced more than his share of "chastisement" (the Hebrew יִסּוּרִים also indicates "suffering") in his life. Eight of his eleven children died in his lifetime, most of them in the prime of their youth or middle age. He was remarkable in the strength of character shown in dealing with these personal tragedies, never uttering so much as a sigh of complaint or anger over his fate. Whatever misfortune befell him, he managed to see in it the greatness of God and His wondrous ways. Typical are the sentiments expressed in these lines, written to his brother during the difficult years of famine and illness of World War I, after having recently lost two sons, a son-in-law and a grandson:

> Dear Brother,
>
> I received your precious letter. It is difficult for me to write. Our Father in Heaven has taken away from me to the World of Truth my dear son Shmuel Binyamin, who had lain ill from typhus for fourteen days. He was a man at the height of his accomplishment, and we had expected great things of him. The ways of God are hidden, but we believe

with complete faith that everything that appears to us now as incomprehensible — like the mystery of the world in its entirety — will have an explanation in the future, when it will become clear that it was all for the good. This is actually the meaning of our Kaddish prayer.

Rav Yosef Chaim was fond of relating the story of a chasid who went to his rebbe and asked, "How is it humanly possible to fulfill the Sages' dictum that one must 'bless God when misfortune occurs just [as wholeheartedly] as when good fortune occurs' (*Berachos* 54a)?"

"Go to the house of my disciple So-and-so, and you will understand," the rebbe answered.

The chasid did as he was instructed. When he arrived at the man's run-down house where he clearly lived in great poverty, the chasid told him, "The rebbe sent me to you to find out an answer to my question: How can a person possibly be expected to praise God wholeheartedly and joyfully when misfortune occurs?"

The rebbe's disciple cast a puzzled glance at his visitor, and said to him apologetically, "I'm afraid there must be some mistake here! I have never experienced misfortune in my entire life! I don't even know what 'misfortune' is!"

In *Tehillim* 19:10 it is stated, "The laws (or *judgments*) of Hashem are true; they are altogether just." What is meant by "altogether just"? Rav Yosef Chaim explained that God does not mete out punishment to an individual until He takes into account the effect that this sentence will have on others. For instance, if a person is deemed to be deserving of death, but such a decree would cause hardship for his wife and children, God will not bring this punishment upon him, out of consideration for those who would survive him — unless they, too, are deserving of such suffering. Thus, while the verdicts rendered by a mortal court system may be just and fair, it is only the judgments of Hashem that are "altogether just." When tragedy strikes in a family, casting a pall of grief over the family members, they must realize that somehow, by God's infinite wisdom, they were deemed worthy of experiencing this anguish. Mortal man is often incapable of understanding the reasons for God's judgments — especially when he himself is the victim — but this is only an indication of his own imperfect comprehension. It is comparable to a situation in which a fool sees a carpenter cutting perfectly smoothed boards into little pieces and wonders why the artisan is destroying such fine pieces of wood, not realizing that in the long run the carpenter's actions will serve a constructive purpose in a finished product.

Rav Yosef Chaim's son, Reb Shmuel Binyamin, passed away from typhus late on a Friday afternoon. The Rav, who had remained by his bedside day and night reciting *Tehillim*, left the hospital, and arrived home just before Shabbos. When the members of his household inquired about Reb Shmuel Binyamin's condition, he said only, "May God have mercy!"

He put on his Shabbos frock, bid his wife and children "Good Shabbos," and went upstairs to the *beis midrash* where he normally prayed. And so, throughout the entire Shabbos, his demeanor and the special Shabbos countenance that always graced his face betrayed no indication to those who saw him and spoke to him that tragedy had struck. Immediately after *Ma'ariv* on Saturday night, however, he began to feel the pain of this seventh loss of a child in all its intensity, and, overcome by grief, he fainted.

The funeral was held a few hours later. As Rav Yosef Chaim and the other mourners made their way through the twisting alleyways of the Old City, dimly lit by an occasional kerosene lamp, he encountered one of the local secular rabble-rousers, a man known for his vitriolic hatred of the Charedim and anything even remotely related to religion. "*Nu*, Reb Chaim," the man said with shocking insolence, "it looks like you are being punished from On High for waging such a bitter war against us!"

Rav Yosef Chaim and the others were stunned at the despicable impropriety and impudence of the man's remark. But the Rav maintained his composure and responded, "Yes, you are right. I *am* being punished from On High — for not fighting hard enough to counter the influence of those who violate God's covenant and forsake the Torah, and for having started too late with too little resolve! I hereby accept upon myself from now on to dedicate myself more intensively to the battle against those who seek to uproot the Torah from the Jewish people!"

⋙ The Importance of Prayer

> לְאַהֲבָה אֶת־ה' אֱלֹקֵיכֶם וּלְעָבְדוֹ בְּכָל־לְבַבְכֶם וּבְכָל־נַפְשְׁכֶם — *To love Hashem, your God, and to serve Him with all your heart and with all your soul* (11:13).

The Gemara (*Ta'anis* 2a) comments on this verse: "What is meant by 'service of God with one's heart'? This refers to prayer."

"Turning constantly in prayer to the One Who is able to answer prayers," Rav Yosef Chaim used to say, "is one of the greatest forms of perfection a person can achieve — if only he can manage to do this." He wrote to a grandson living in America, "The main thing is to strengthen yourself in prayer every day before our Father in Heaven, with a pure heart, for this is the 'service of the heart' that remains for us today, and through it we will merit to have the service of Hashem in the Temple restored."

פרשת ראה
PARASHAS RE'EH

⮩ Trust in God —
an Imperative for One and All

כִּי מְנַסֶּה ה' אֱלֹקֵיכֶם אֶתְכֶם לָדַעַת הֲיִשְׁכֶם אֹהֲבִים אֶת־ה' אֱלֹקֵיכֶם בְּכָל־לְבַבְכֶם וּבְכָל־נַפְשְׁכֶם — *For Hashem, your God, is testing you, to know whether you love Hashem, your God, with all your heart and with all your soul* (13:4).

*R*av Yosef Chaim never held other people to the same strict standards of piety that he set for himself. When it came to matters of faith in God, however, he did not hesitate to exhort people to strengthen themselves in this regard. With his pleasant, congenial manner and his own rock-solid convictions, he usually had no problem conveying his message and obtaining results.

A certain well-known farmer from Petach Tikvah once asked Rav Yosef Chaim what he should do during the *Shemitah* (Sabbatical) year. How could he possibly keep the laws of *Shemitah*, refraining from working his land, when his financial situation was so desperate, and this was his only source of livelihood?

Rav Yosef Chaim took a copy of the Book of *Jeremiah* from the shelf and opened it up to the verse, "Cursed be the man who trusts in people and turns his heart away from Hashem" (17:5). He showed the farmer Rashi's comments on the verse: *"Cursed be the man who trusts in people* — by plowing and reaping, saying, 'I will sow crops during *Shemitah*, and I will have what to eat.' By doing so, he *turns his heart away from Hashem*, Who promised in the Torah, 'I will ordain My blessing for you [for the seventh year]' (*Vayikra* 25:21)."

The farmer had no response or arguments. From that year on he strictly observed all the laws of *Shemitah*.

In another incident, a certain businessman was suing a debtor through the British mandatory court system. Rav Yosef Chaim called the man in and asked him how he could do such a thing, when there was a fully qualified *beis din* (a court that rules according to Jewish law) available to him.

"But Rebbe," the man protested, "the suit involves (a very considerable sum)! I cannot risk taking this case to the *beis din*, because they do not have sufficient power to enforce their decision, even if they do find the defendant liable."

Rav Yosef Chaim opened up a *Chumash* to the verse (*Shemos* 21:1), "These are the [monetary] laws that you shall place before them." He pointed out to the businessman Rashi's comment on the verse: "*Before them* — but not before a non-Jewish court. For one who brings a case involving Jewish litigants to a non-Jewish court desecrates Hashem's Name, and gives glory and honor to their gods."

"Now," Rav Yosef Chaim continued, "the Sages say (*Yoma* 86a) that the sin of desecrating God's Name (*chilul Hashem*) cannot be atoned for through repentance or physical suffering, nor through the atonement of Yom Kippur. Only through death can one obtain forgiveness for this most serious of sins!"

The businessman heeded Rav Yosef Chaim's advice and withdrew his claim, taking his case to *beis din* instead.

"There are still some people around who fulfill the commandment (*Devarim* 6:5) to 'love Hashem with all your might' (*money*; *Berachos* 54a)," Rav Yosef Chaim commented when he heard that the man had decided to drop the case in the secular court. "I believe with complete faith that such people do not come out losing any money in the end!"

Putting one's trust in God is a good thing when it is applied to oneself, Rav Yosef Chaim used to say, but not when it comes to other people's situations. The *yetzer hara*, he remarked, is even willing to instill an intense feeling of "trust in God" in a person's heart, if this can be exploited as an excuse to avoid extending a helping hand to someone in need!

He explained that this is the message of the verse in *Yirmiyahu* that says, "Blessed is the man who trusts in Hashem, and makes Hashem his refuge" (17:7). The second half of the sentence seems to be completely redundant. What does "makes Hashem his refuge" add to "trusts in Hashem"? The answer is that while it is an important trait to trust in Hashem, this is only when he "makes Hashem *his* refuge" — not the refuge of someone else!

Whoever had a problem or needed assistance knew that he could find a sympathetic ear in Rav Yosef Chaim's house. Whether it was arranging a loan or a contribution for a person in need, issuing a recommendation on someone's behalf, arranging medical care for an indigent patient — no sooner was the request voiced than Rav Yosef Chaim's hat and coat were on, as he prepared himself to go out and help in whatever manner possible. He was especially involved in Shaarei Tzedek Hospital, which catered extensively to the impoverished Charedi community. Whenever someone needed assistance in having a hospital bill reduced — or canceled — the address to turn to was Rav Yosef Chaim, who had a very close relationship with Dr. Moshe Wallach, founder and administrator of Shaarei Tzedek.

The following typical story — one of many — serves to illustrate the extent of Rav Yosef Chaim's selfless dedication to the needs of others. Rav Menachem Mendel Sheinin relates:

"It was the day before *Rosh Chodesh* Nisan, 5688 (1928). I prayed *Minchah* and *Ma'ariv* with the Rav in the Battei Machaseh shul, and after the prayers I accompanied him home. I tried to grasp his arm as he descended the steps to his house beneath the shul, for I knew that he had fasted that day, as was his custom on *erev Rosh Chodesh* (and Rav Yosef Chaim was 80 years old at the time — ed.). The Rav refused my help, however, informing me that 'If I can do something on my own, by the grace of God, I don't like to lean on others!'

"As soon as we entered the house, a man rushed in in a panic. Panting, with his voice breaking, he told the Rav that his wife was having difficulty in childbirth and needed to be admitted to Shaarei Tzedek at once. But he could not secure her admission without the Rav's personal recommendation.

"Rav Yosef Chaim grabbed his frock and flung it over his shoulders — not even taking the time to put his arms into the sleeves — and hastened out the door with the man.

"Just then the Rebbetzin appeared with a cup of coffee and a piece of cake, for the Rav had not yet broken his fast. 'Where did the Rabbi go?' she asked me.

"When I told her what had happened, she ran out the door to find her husband, so that he should eat something and not collapse from hunger on the way. After a few moments, however, she returned empty—handed.

"'It's no use,' she said. 'I overheard the two of them in a heated argument. The man wanted to wait for a cab at the entrance to Battei Machaseh, but my husband insisted that it would be faster for them to run up to *Sha'ar Yafo* and get a cab there, where the traffic was much busier. When I heard that, I knew that there was nothing that could stop him until he had finished his mission and seen to the admission of the woman to the hospital!'"

⋙ Cleaving to God — Through Kindness

וְאֹתוֹ תַעֲבֹדוּ וּבוֹ תִדְבָּקוּן — *And you shall serve Him and cleave to Him* (13:5).

"How is it possible to 'cleave' to God?" asks the Talmud (*Sotah* 14a), "when God is described as 'a consuming fire' (*Devarim* 4:24)?" The answer the Gemara gives is that the Torah here commands us to cleave to God's *ways*: "Just as He supplies clothes for the naked, visits to the sick, comforts mourners and buries the dead, so should you supply clothes for the naked, etc." Rav Yosef Chaim was exemplary in his application of these principles to his own life.

He became a *gabai* (official) of the *Chevrah Kaddisha* (burial society) already in his younger years, and before long he was appointed head of the *Chevrah*. He fought energetically and faithfully to preserve the burial traditions of the Jerusalem community, despite efforts from various sources that sought to implement changes in the system.

One time, during World War I, it became known to him that the Turkish government had decided to change burial regulations, in a manner that would have compromised the customary interment procedure. He immediately set out to speak to Rav Nissim Danon, the "Hacham Bashi" (the Chief Rabbi officially appointed by the Turkish government to represent the Jewish community), to intercede with the relevant government officials. The problem was that at the time, the Hacham was staying in the village of Motza, which was several miles from Jerusalem. Nearly all the coaches had been pressed into service for the Turkish army, and those few that remained were known to be disease ridden, owing to the rampant epidemics that plagued the country during this difficult time. Rav Yosef Chaim felt that he had to see Rav Nissim immediately, however. So, despite the fact that it was the 17th of Tammuz (a fast day), he set out *on foot* from the Old City to Motza. The meeting was successful, and the Hacham was able to deal with the emergency effectively.

Though he was at the head of the *Chevrah Kaddisha*, he did not see this office as a ceremonial position of honor and prestige; he continued to personally participate in burials — especially when the deceased was a *talmid chacham*.

One time, when Rav Yosef Chaim was quite old, he was participating in a funeral of a Torah scholar on a Friday afternoon. As the funeral cortege approached "Yad Avshalom" (an ancient landmark in the Kidron Valley, on the road to the Mount of Olives, where the cemetery was), they noticed a large group of Arabs in a procession known as "Nebi Musa." The procession would soon be coming down the road, making it impossible for the funeral to pass by for quite some time — and it was already almost Shabbos. The *Chevrah Kaddisha* members told Rav Yosef Chaim to turn back to the Old City while they would make a dash for the Mount of Olives with the body, to head off the Arab procession. "What's wrong?" he replied. "Do you think I can't run? Am I not just as obligated as anyone else to pay my respects to a *talmid chacham* by accompanying him to his final resting place?" And before anyone had a chance to respond, he raced up the road, overtaking the pall—bearers as they too ran to pass ahead of the Arab procession.

In one of the small, vaulted alleyways of the Old City was a hospice for the terminally ill. The miserable, emaciated patients had no reprieve from their unremitting pain and despondency; even their relatives found visits to this institution too emotionally draining to bear. The only solace these pitiful souls experienced was a visit from Rav Yosef Chaim, who made it his business to frequent the hospice and sit by the bedside of each and every patient, providing some much-appreciated words of comfort and encouragement. For a few moments a week they were able to feel that they were more than wretched, abandoned pariahs. In this, Rav Yosef Chaim followed in the footsteps of the Amora Rabbi Yehoshua ben Levi, who went to teach Torah to people afflicted with *ra'asan*, a disease so horrendous and contagious that those who suffered from it were completely shunned by all — except Rabbi Yehoshua ben Levi (*Kesubos* 87b).

⋽ Inappropriate Curse

וּבִעַרְתָּ הָרָע מִקִּרְבֶּךְ — *And you shall destroy the evil from your midst* (13:6).

*R*av Noach Gad Weintraub, in his book *Bishishim Chochmah*, recounts that he was having a conversation with Rav Yosef Chaim, in which they were discussing the new generation of youth which was growing up without any exposure to Torah and religion. At one point Rav Weintraub referred to a leader of one of the antireligious movements with the epithet *yimach shemo* — "may his name be blotted out." Rav Yosef Chaim interrupted him immediately and objected, "Heaven forbid! One must not wish upon a Jewish person that his 'name be obliterated'!"

"But aren't you yourself engaged in a fierce battle against them, seeking their total eradication?" he asked.

"In this world," Rav Yosef Chaim explained, "we are obligated to try with all our might to fight against and obliterate those who reject the Torah, as it says, 'Those who hate You, Hashem, I hate, and I contend with those who rise up against You' (*Tehillim* 139:21). But we dare not pray that their name should be obliterated — which means that they should have no place in the Next World either. Instead, you should pray that they see the light and repent, like I do!

"We are commanded, 'You shall destroy the evil from your midst.' We are therefore obligated to fight against those who seek to undermine the Torah and its authority. But when it comes to matters that are beyond our grasp and hidden from us, we should not meddle. David forgave Shimi ben Gera for sedition and did not execute him, though he deserved this punishment, because he foresaw through his *ruach hakodesh* (prophetic inspiration) that a great *tzaddik* (Mordechai) would descend from him (see *Megillah* 13a). All the more so must we, who have no way of knowing what hidden merits a person might have, watch our tongues from uttering such curses. It is only Amalek about which the Torah says, 'I will utterly blot out the remembrance of Amalek' — and all the enemies of Israel who seek its destruction are included in that category. But for our fellow Jews, we must pray for their spiritual regeneration rather than for their eternal obliteration."

Another, similar story was related by my father:

"I was walking in the new city with my grandfather (Rav Yosef Chaim), along with the Maggid, Rav Nota Weiss. When we reached Ben Yehudah Street — which had recently been named after Eliezer ben Yehudah, the secularist who is credited with the restoration and modernization of the Hebrew language — Rav Nota was overcome with a spirit of zealousness and exclaimed, 'May his name and remembrance be obliterated!'

"Grandfather cast an angry look at him and said, 'I never use this epithet about him. In this world we are obligated to fight with all our might against the influence of such people, to try to contain and eliminate the damage that they do for the Jewish people by undermining their religion. But when they have already gone on to the Next World, we have nothing more to do with them. It is not for us to get involved in God's business! I do not approve of those who say about any Jew, 'May his name be obliterated.' On the contrary, I hope and pray that their souls find the proper rectification to achieve eternity in the Next World!'"

◄§ Charity for Dubious Recipients

כִּי־יִהְיֶה בְךָ אֶבְיוֹן מֵאַחַד אַחֶיךָ... לֹא תְאַמֵּץ אֶת־
לְבָבְךָ וְלֹא תִקְפֹּץ אֶת־יָדְךָ מֵאָחִיךָ הָאֶבְיוֹן. כִּי־פָתֹחַ
תִּפְתַּח אֶת־יָדְךָ לוֹ... הִשָּׁמֶר לְךָ פֶּן־יִהְיֶה דָבָר עִם־
לְבָבְךָ בְלִיַּעַל... וְרָעָה עֵינְךָ בְּאָחִיךָ הָאֶבְיוֹן וְלֹא תִתֵּן
לוֹ וְקָרָא עָלֶיךָ אֶל־ה' וְהָיָה בְךָ חֵטְא. נָתוֹן תִּתֵּן לוֹ
וְלֹא־יֵרַע לְבָבְךָ בְּתִתְּךָ לוֹ כִּי בִּגְלַל הַדָּבָר הַזֶּה
יְבָרֶכְךָ ה' אֱלֹקֶיךָ בְּכָל־מַעֲשֶׂךָ וּבְכֹל מִשְׁלַח יָדֶךָ —

If there be a poor person among you, from among your brethren... you shall not harden your heart or close your hand against your poor brother. Rather, you shall open your hand to him... Beware lest there be a base thought in your heart... and you look with malice upon your poor brother and refuse to give him; then if he calls out against you to Hashem, it will be a sin for you. You shall surely give him, and let your heart not feel bad when you give him, for because of this matter Hashem your God will bless you in all your deeds and in all your undertakings (15:7—10).

*I*n 1923 a group of beneficiaries of *Kolel Shomrei Hachomos* (a charity organization that distributes money to Jerusalem families) expressed their disapproval over the *kolel's* system of distribution of funds, by which money was distributed to all those on the roster, without ascertaining whether the recipient was needy or not. At one point this party wrote a letter to the directorate of the *kolel* in America, seeking the intervention of the chairman of the board in this matter. They took the liberty of declaring that they spoke for the entire membership of the *kolel*, including its president, Rav Yosef Chaim Sonnenfeld.

The truth was, however, that Rav Yosef Chaim was in total disagreement with the goals of the group, as he wrote in this letter:

> I state unequivocally that I am opposed to any change in the system of administration of the funds of the *kolel*, for the great rabbis and *tzaddikim* who founded the *kolel*, the pillars of Israel who established it with their great integrity, decided, in their prophetic wisdom, that it was specifically in this manner that the settlement in the Holy Land would become established.
>
> By the grace of God, I have had the privilege of living here in Jerusalem for fifty years, and I have never seen any one of the members of our *kolel* who had any wealth to bequeath upon his death. Almost all of those who were considered by others to be "well-to-do" left behind them nothing but debts.
>
> The Tannaim have already established the punishment for people who take money from charity when they do not need it. (*Pe'ah* 8:9: "Whoever is not entitled to take [charity] and takes it anyway shall not pass from this world before he indeed becomes dependent upon others.") Let us leave such people to the fate determined for them by our Sages, and not implement a new system of distribution.

The group of complainers had also claimed that when donors give money to the *kolel* they undoubtedly do so with the specific intent that their money be given only to those in dire need. To this Rav Yosef Chaim replied at length, providing in the process a novel interpretation for our verse.

When the Torah says, *Beware lest there be a base thought* (lit., "a thought of baseness") *in your heart*, he said, it does not mean to say that the thought of the potential donor itself is base, but that he portrays the *supplicant* who has asked him for money as a base person. "Perhaps this guy isn't as poor as he claims. Maybe he's a base person, a faker." This is the "thought of baseness" that the Torah warns us not to entertain. For "*if you look with malice upon your poor brother* (judging him unfavorably or suspiciously in this manner), then you will, of course, *refuse to give him.*

There is obviously nothing wrong with refusing to give charity to a nondeserving person, or even to someone who legitimately raises suspicion. The Talmud (*Kesubos* 68a) goes so far as to say, "We owe a debt of gratitude to charlatans, for if not for them (providing us with the excuse not to give charity to everybody who asks for it), we would be committing sins every day. For it says, 'if he calls out against you to Hashem, it will be a sin for you.'" If someone refrains from giving charity to a person because he genuinely appears to be of questionable character, he is not technically considered to have violated the Torah's positive command of *You shall open your hand to him*, nor the negative command of *you shall not harden you heart or close your hand against your poor brother.* Nevertheless, although one is perfectly justified in exercising caution over giving money to people without being sure of their deservedness, the Torah warns us against utilizing this justification. For if it just so happens that the person you turn away is genuinely poor, and, in his bitterness *he calls out against you to Hashem*, then it will not help you that you were technically within your rights. The cry of the poor never goes unheeded, *and it will be a sin for you.* The better course of action, the Torah assures us, is, *You shall surely give him* — take the chance and give him, even if you have your doubts. And don't think that you are being taken for a fool because you might be giving money to an undeserving person: *Let your heart not feel bad when you give him.* Don't be concerned about that, *for because of this matter Hashem your God will bless you in all your deeds and in all your undertakings.* God will see to it that ultimately you will suffer no monetary loss for having given charity, no matter what the circumstances.

פרשת שופטים
PARASHAS SHOFTIM

❧ No Favoritism

> שֹׁפְטִים וְשֹׁטְרִים תִּתֶּן־לְךָ בְּכָל־שְׁעָרֶיךָ... וְשָׁפְטוּ אֶת־הָעָם מִשְׁפַּט־צֶדֶק. לֹא־תַטֶּה מִשְׁפָּט לֹא תַכִּיר פָּנִים — *Judges and officers shall you appoint in all your cities... and they shall judge the people with righteous judgment. You shall not pervert judgment, you shall not show favoritism* (16:18-19).

*M*y father relates the following story about "righteous judgment":

Rav Yitzchak Yerucham Diskin, son of the chief *dayan* of Jerusalem, Rav Yehoshua Leib Diskin, was in the lumber business. One time he had a business dispute with another merchant, and they wanted to bring their case before a *beis din* for adjudication. The other merchant told Rav Yitzchak Yerucham that he wanted to have his father, Rav Yehoshua Leib, act as arbitrator in the matter. Although he was the father of one of the litigants, and thus technically disqualified to act as judge, the halachah is that a relative may judge a case as long as both parties agree to this arrangement.

The two of them approached Rav Yehoshua Leib and told him

that they had decided to accept him to hear their case and render a decision. The rabbi refused to become involved, however, remarking, "Even if the *Shulchan Aruch* explicitly says 'liable' in a given case, if someone has a personal interest in the matter he will somehow see the word 'exempt' written there!"

✺§ Beis Din's "Divine Judgment"

*M*y father also relates that he heard the following story about "rabbinical judgment" when it was related to Rav Yosef Chaim by Rav Eliyahu Kletzkin, the Rav of Lublin, on a visit to Jerusalem. He heard it from Rav Yitzchak Elchanan Spektor, the rav of Kovna, Lithuania, when the latter was examining him for *semichah* (rabbinical ordination).

"One time I was traveling in a coach from Kovno to another city to take care of an important community matter. Along the way I began to feel very tired, and I asked the wagon driver to pull into one of the tiny villages that were scattered off the main road. He obliged my request and we rode into town, looking for the rabbi's house, which we soon found. He was shocked to see the Kovno Rav knocking at his door, and became very nervous. I calmed him down, explaining that I just happened to be passing near his town and needed a place to rest for an hour or two. The rabbi was not the most learned Torah scholar, to put it politely, but he was very hospitable, and directed me to a bed in a side room of the house.

"No sooner had my head hit the pillow than a knock was heard at the door. Two simple Jewish farmers had come to talk to the rabbi. 'Rebbe,' they announced, 'we have a *din Torah* (litigation) for you!'

" 'Well, you are in luck, then,' the rabbi informed them. 'You'll never believe who is here in my house! The Kovno Rav! He came here to rest for a while. I'll go see if he is still awake.'

"The rabbi tiptoed over to my room and peeked in to see if I was available. I was totally exhausted and did not want to be bothered, so I pretended to be sleeping. He went back and forth to my room a few times. He apparently preferred not to get involved in the case if he could pass the matter on to a big-city, expert *rav*."

" 'I'm afraid the Rav is sleeping,' he finally told his callers.

" 'It doesn't matter,' they said, growing impatient. 'Anyway, you are our *rav*, not some rabbi from Kovno! Please hear our case and give us your decision!'

"I overheard the two men presenting their arguments to the rabbi. But then I fell asleep. When I woke up, the rabbi told me what had happened. 'Just after you went to sleep, two men came and asked me to arbitrate a monetary dispute for them. I tried to get them to wait and present their case to you, but they were impatient, so I had to handle the matter myself.'

" 'And what was the nature of the case?' I asked. The rabbi reviewed the statements of the two litigants, which I had, of course, already heard. Then he told me how he ruled in the matter. I was flabbergasted. It was an uncommon and somewhat complicated case, yet the rabbi's decision was exactly on the mark, in accordance with the words of the *poskim* (halachic authorities). How, I wondered, did this unlearned rabbi come to such an erudite conclusion?

" 'That's a fine ruling!' I congratulated him. 'Can you please show me the source upon which you based this decision?'

"The rabbi pulled a *Shulchan Aruch* off the shelf, opened it up, and pointed to a comment made by *Ba'er Hetev* (one of the commentators). 'That's where I got it from!' he told me.

"I looked at the passage he showed me, and was flabbergasted once again. The rabbi had completely misread the *Ba'er Hetev*, whose comment had absolutely nothing to do with the case at hand!"

The message of the story is clear. When a rabbi has to *pasken* (render a halachic decision), he is not acting alone. He is blessed with a certain measure of Divine assistance to ensure that the proper ruling emerges, even if it emerges through "error."

The Chief Rabbinate

av Yosef Chaim referred to this "Divine assistance" aspect of halachic rulings on another occasion.

In 1919, the office of the Chief Rabbi of Palestine was

created. This Chief Rabbi was to be under the auspices of the World Zionist Organization, and was to be its official halachic authority. There was considerable opposition to this post in Charedi circles, and a protest rally was held, in which Rav Yosef Chaim played a dominant role.

In his speech to the assembly, Rav Yosef Chaim brought up the story of the baby Moses being found by Pharaoh's daughter. "Shall I go and summon for you a wet nurse from the Hebrew women? (*Shemos* 2:7)," offered Miriam, who had been watching over the child. "Why did Moses need a *Hebrew* woman to nurse him?" ask the Sages (*Sotah* 12b). Were there no women servants in Pharaoh's palace who were capable of nursing a baby? The answer, the Sages tells us, is that indeed Pharaoh's daughter tried to give the baby to her servants, but he refused to nurse from any of these non-Jewish women, thinking to himself, "Shall the mouth that is destined to speak with the *Shechinah* (God's Presence) take milk from nonkosher women (women who eat nonkosher food)?!" This is why Miriam had to offer the services of specifically a *Hebrew* woman. Although it is perfectly permissible for a child to nurse at the breast of a non-Jewish woman (see *Yoreh De'ah* 155:1), explained Rav Yosef Chaim, when it comes to "the mouth that speaks with the *Shechinah*," extra caution must be taken, and a higher standard must be adhered to.

"If this is so," concluded Rav Yosef Chaim, "then how much more so must it be applied to a rabbinical body, of whom it is said (*Tehillim* 82:1), 'God stands in the Divine assembly; in the midst of the judges He judges' (see *Berachos* 6a). Such a group of rabbis and judges are dependent upon the constant influence of Divine assistance and inspiration in their discussions and decisions. How, then, can they 'nurse' — receive their authority and legitimacy — from an antireligious body, which seeks to supplant the Torah altogether? Such a situation poses a grave danger to the independence and integrity of the institution of the rabbinate in Judaism!"

✺ Avoiding Bias

לֹא תַכִּיר פָּנִים — *You shall not show favoritism* (16:19).

In 1905, a dispute erupted between the residents of Baron Rothschild's settlements (Ekron, Rishon LeTziyon, Zichron Yaakov, etc.) and the baron himself, about the settlers' rights over the land that they had toiled to develop. The argument was brought before a *beis din* for adjudication. Rav Yosef Chaim was one of the three judges of this *beis din*.

After the ruling was issued, the baron paid a wage of 50 napoleons (gold coins) to each of the rabbis who had worked on the case, which had taken up a considerable amount of the rabbis' time. Rav Yosef Chaim refused to accept this grant, explaining that as soon as he had consented to act as an arbiter he had resolved not to accept any payment whatsoever, as he felt that this might affect his ability to view the case impartially.

✺ Greased Palms

וְלֹא־תִקַּח שֹׁחַד — *And do not take a bribe* (16:19).

Dr. Chaim Weizmann (the leader of the Zionists, who ultimately became the first president of Israel) used to say, "I have ample access to the most sought-after commodity in the world — money! But it is available only for those who fall into line!"

Rav Yosef Chaim remarked to him, "Do you know why the back of the hand is hairy, but the palm is totally smooth? It is to teach the lesson that one's palms (i.e., the money he receives) must remain totally clean and smooth of any taint of dishonesty!"

◆§ Herod — an Outsider

שׂוֹם תָּשִׂים עָלֶיךָ מֶלֶךְ... מִקֶּרֶב אַחֶיךָ תָּשִׂים עָלֶיךָ מֶלֶךְ — לֹא תוּכַל לָתֵת עָלֶיךָ אִישׁ נָכְרִי — *You shall surely set over yourself a king... from among your brethren you shall set a king over yourself; you cannot place over yourself a foreign man* (17:15).

My father pointed out to Rav Yosef Chaim — who expressed his approval — that the numerical value of נָכְרִי (*foreign*) is the same (281, עִם הַכּוֹלֵל) as that of הוֹרְדוֹס (*Herod*), an allusion to the fact that King Herod, although he considered himself a Jew, was in fact a foreigner (see *Bava Basra* 3b).

It is interesting to note another interesting *gematria* that the Baal HaTurim points out: מִקֶּרֶב אַחֶיךָ (*from among your brethren*) has the same numeral value (381) as מִשֵּׁבֶט יְהוּדָה (from the tribe of Judah), alluding to the fact that the king of the Jews must come from the tribe of Judah (see *Bereishis* 49:10).

In Faith, Don't Begin with Questions

תָּמִים תִּהְיֶה עִם ה' אֱלֹקֶיךָ — *You shall be innocent with Hashem your God* (18:13).

The question is asked concerning the אֵין כֵּאלֹקֵינוּ prayer said at the end of *Shacharis* on Shabbos (and, according to the Sephardic and the universal *Eretz-Yisrael* custom, every day): After declaring "There is none like our God, there is none like our Lord, etc." in the first stanza, how can the second stanza of the poem go on to ask, "Who is like our God? Who is like our Lord? etc." It makes no sense to ask a question after it has already been answered! It would have been more logical had the order been reversed (as it indeed is in some ancient versions — ed.), thus: "Who is like our God? There is no one like our God!" etc.

Rav Yosef Chaim answered this question by referring to a parable. A man has to enter a long, dark, winding cave, and he has no torch to see by. If he is smart, he will not go any further into the cave than where he is absolutely sure he will be able to retrace his steps back to the cave's opening. If he is even cleverer, he could enter even further into the cave, by laying a rope down as he goes. As long as he keeps grasping the rope, he will be able to find his way back, by following its course back to the beginning.

The world of philosophical speculation is no less perilous than a dark, twisted cave, concluded Rav Yosef Chaim. Before entering the subject too deeply, one must take care to ensure that he has secured a dependable way to get out of the "cave." Thus, it is first necessary to anchor oneself by declaring unequivocally that "there is no one like our God." Once this point is made, it is possible to proceed further, with questions such as "Who is like our God?" Only after the answer is secured is it possible to go on to the question!

פרשת כי תצא
PARASHAS KI SEITZEI

⋑ Taking Undue Advantage

כִּי יִקָּרֵא קַן־צִפּוֹר לְפָנֶיךָ בַּדֶּרֶךְ בְּכָל־עֵץ אוֹ עַל־הָאָרֶץ אֶפְרֹחִים אוֹ בֵיצִים וְהָאֵם רֹבֶצֶת עַל־הָאֶפְרֹחִים אוֹ עַל־הַבֵּיצִים לֹא־תִקַּח הָאֵם עַל־הַבָּנִים. שַׁלֵּחַ תְּשַׁלַּח אֶת־הָאֵם וְאֶת־הַבָּנִים תִּקַּח־לָךְ — *If you encounter a bird's nest on the road, on any tree or on the ground, [with] young birds or eggs, and the mother is roosting on the young birds or on the eggs, you shall not take the mother with the young. You shall surely send away the mother and take the young for yourself* (22:6-7).

What is the rationale behind this mitzvah? If it is to spare pain to the mother bird, it would make more sense to forbid taking the young altogether. Surely the mother will be anguished when she returns to the nest after a few moments and finds her chicks missing!

The real reason for the Torah's commandment, explained Rav Yosef Chaim, is to impart an important ethical lesson: It is forbidden to take advantage of a mother bird's instinctive love for her children in order to catch her more easily. Under normal conditions a bird flies away as soon as a predator — including a human — approaches. However, if she has eggs or chicks in her nest, her survival instinct is overridden by her motherly love, and she prefers remaining in the nest in defense of her young to flying away to her own safety. It is this motherly instinct that we are commanded to respect, and not to use it to our advantage by making an "easy catch" of the devoted mother bird. The reward for obeying this command is "so that it will be good for you, and you will prolong your days" — for when someone shows benevolence and mercy toward other creatures, God does the same for him.

A support for this explanation of the mitzvah may be found in the words of the Rambam (*Hil. Shechitah* 13:7): "If a person sent away the mother, but she came back, and after this he took her, this is permitted. The Torah forbids only catching a mother bird when she is incapable of flying away because of her young, over whom she hovers to prevent them from being taken."

Rav Yosef Chaim applied a similar line of reasoning to explain another matter as well. The Mishnah (*Yoma* 85b) teaches: "If someone says, 'I will sin now, and later I will repent,' he is not granted the opportunity to repent. If he says, 'I will sin now, and when Yom Kippur comes it will atone for the sin,' Yom Kippur does not atone for that sin." Why should such people be denied the basic privilege of mending their ways and repenting of their sins?

To explain this mishnah, Rav Yosef Chaim cited a passage from the *Talmud Yerushalmi* (*Makkos* 2:6):

They asked Wisdom, "What should happen to one who sins?" She replied, "Evil shall pursue sinners" (*Mishlei* 13:21).

They asked Prophecy, "What should happen to one who sins?" She replied, "The soul that sins shall die" (*Ezekiel* 18:4).

They asked God, "What should happen to one who sins?" He replied, "Let him repent, and his sins will be atoned for."

What emerges from this passage is that logically speaking (Wisdom) and ethically speaking (Prophecy), it is a basic truth that when one sins he must bear the bitter consequences. The existence of the option of repentance as a means of eradicating the sinful act as if it had never occurred runs counter to both logic and morality; it is only by the grace of God that it is made possible.

The person described in the mishnah cited above (who says, "I will sin now, and later I will repent") would, as indicated by his own declaration, not ordinarily entertain the thought of sinning and bearing the bitter consequences of his actions. It is only because he is aware that the opportunity of repentance (or Yom Kippur) is open to him that he decides to commit the sin. By doing so, he is taking God's gracious gift of repentance, which is designed to improve man's spiritual life, and taking advantage of it, using it as a tool against God's will. This is why the availability of this option is withdrawn from him.

✑§ Modest Dress

וְהָיָה מַחֲנֶיךָ קָדוֹשׁ וְלֹא־יִרְאֶה בְךָ עֶרְוַת דָּבָר — *Your camp shall be holy, so that [God] should not see any unseemly thing among you* (23:15).

The Gemara (*Berachos* 20a) relates the following story in regard to people who wear immodest, unseemly clothing.

Rav Pappa asked Abaye, "Why is it that the earlier generations experienced miracles, whereas we nowadays do not experience miracles?"

Abaye responded, "It is because the people of the previous generations performed acts of self-sacrifice (מָסְרוּ נַפְשָׁם) for the glory of God. For instance, Rav Adda bar Ahavah once saw a non-Jewish woman wearing a *carbalta* (a provocative red cape, considered immodest dress) in the marketplace and, thinking she was a Jewess, tore it off her. When it was discovered that she was not Jewish (and not bound by the customary Jewish codes of decency in dress), the *beis din* fined him 400 zuzim [for embarrassing the woman in public].

"Rav Adda asked her, 'What is your name?'

"'Mathun,' she replied.

"Whereupon he said, 'Mathun, Mathun is equal to 400 zuzim!'" (Rashi: "*Mathun* (מאתן) in Aramaic means '200,' so *Mathun* and *Mathun* adds up to 400. He meant to say, 'Your very name alludes to this incident!'")

Several questions present themselves in this story related by Abaye. Firstly, from the fact that Abaye included the detail of the 400-zuz fine — and indeed this detail seems to constitute the punch line of the story — it seems that it is this monetary loss that is supposed to illustrate the great self-sacrifice of Rav Adda. But according to the story, Rav Adda did not even know that the woman was a non-Jew and that he would thus be fined for removing the garment! Where, then, is the great sacrifice in his actions?

Another question is: Why did Rav Adda ask the woman her name? Furthermore, after hearing her answer, what was his point in making the pun on her name and noting that it bore an allusion to this event? Why was this incidental quip recorded for posterity altogether?

Rav Yosef Chaim addressed all these issues, explaining the story as follows. The self-sacrifice of Rav Adda lay not in the fact that he incurred a considerable financial loss, for, as noted above, he did not enter into this loss deliberately. Rather, it was the act of removing the *carbalta* that illustrated Rav Adda's great sacrifice for the glory of God.

When it emerged that the woman was not Jewish and Rav Adda was fined, however, he wondered, "How is it that I have been 'rewarded' for my efforts in doing what I honestly thought was a great mitzvah by suffering such a loss? It does not seem fair that God should punish me for acting zealously!" Searching for a reason that might lie behind God's judgment, he thought that perhaps the woman's name might contain a clue to the mystery.

He indeed found the answer to his question. The women in town would undoubtedly relate and discuss the story of the *carbalta* among themselves. During the course of the conversation, the name of the non-Jewish woman would be brought up — *Mathun*. Once this name would be mentioned, the women would be reminded of the fact that Rav Adda was fined 400 zuzim for what he did. "That's quite a bit of money!" they would surely marvel to one another. "Obviously the *beis din* felt that it was a very harsh embarrassment that the woman underwent. And yet Rav Adda did not hesitate to treat her in this manner — all because of the seriousness of the sin of dressing improperly!" The added drama of the fine would serve to publicize even more the critical message of the importance of modest dress.

"If this is the case," Rav Adda remarked, "Mathun, Mathun is worth (שָׁוְיָא, translated above as 'is equal to') four hundred zuzim to me! I do not mind the loss of this money, for it, too, will contribute to the glorification of God's Name through the strengthening of the observance of the rules of modesty."

◆§ Good Advice

כִּי־יִקַּח אִישׁ אִשָּׁה וּבְעָלָהּ וְהָיָה אִם־לֹא תִמְצָא־חֵן בְּעֵינָיו כִּי־מָצָא בָהּ עֶרְוַת דָּבָר, וְכָתַב לָהּ סֵפֶר כְּרִיתֻת וְנָתַן בְּיָדָהּ וְשִׁלְּחָהּ מִבֵּיתוֹ — *If a man marries a woman and lives with her, it shall be that if she does not find favor in his eyes, for he found in her a matter of immorality, he shall write for her a bill of divorce and send her from his house* (24:1).

*T*he Mishnah records a dispute as to what grounds might justify a divorce. "Beis Shammai says: A man should not divorce his wife unless he 'finds in her a matter of immorality' (i.e., she committed adultery). Beis Hillel says: Even if she burned his food [he may divorce her, if he wishes]."

My mother once posed the question to Rav Yosef Chaim (her grandfather-in-law), "How is it possible that such a trivial matter like burning the food should provide grounds for such a weighty and tragic step as divorce? Why should a women suffer so for the rest of her life because of such a simple mishap?"

Rav Yosef Chaim answered her, "If the husband is such a mean person that as soon as the food burns he begins to entertain thoughts of divorce, then this woman is much better off getting away from him, and the sooner the better!"

◆§ Administering a *Get* — an Overwhelming Responsibility

וְכָתַב לָהּ סֵפֶר כְּרִיתֻת — *He shall write for her a bill of divorce* (24:1).

*R*av Yosef Chaim was a master at relating events that he witnessed under his mentors, toward whom he felt a palpable, almost contagious, feeling of awe. One time he recounted how a *get* (bill of divorce) was administered by his rabbi, the *Ksav Sofer*: He turned to the members of his *beis din* and, overcome with emotion, declared, "Let us all now say *Vidui* (confession of sins) before we undertake the responsibility of releasing this married woman from her status of 'woman prohibited to others by the Torah' and allowing her to remarry another man." A great aura of solemnity gripped the other rabbis, and they, too, began to weep, as they said *Vidui*.

✄§ Amalek Today

> תִּמְחֶה אֶת־זֵכֶר עֲמָלֵק — *You shall blot out the memory of Amalek* (25:19).

*I*n 1898, Kaiser Wilhelm II, emperor of the German Empire, paid an official visit to Jerusalem. The Jewish community — along with everyone else in Jerusalem — welcomed him with great homage, and built a special ornamental archway in his honor, under which he was greeted by the rabbis of the community, headed by Rav Shmuel Salant.

Every single Jew who lived in Jerusalem — man, woman and child — came out to witness the historic sight and to pronounce the rare blessing recited when seeing a monarch: "Blessed are You... Who has imparted of His glory to mortal men."

The only one who stayed home that day was Rav Yosef Chaim. His reason for boycotting the event, he explained, was, "I have a tradition from my mentor and rabbi, Rav Yehoshua Leib Diskin, that the Germans are the modern-day descendants of Amalek. It is not possible to go out and recite a blessing over a king who is a descendant of Amalek, whose memory we are supposed to blot out!" (This was more than forty years before the Holocaust — ed.)

(See *Megillah* 6a, where "Germania" is identified as a country descended from Esau. Amalek was Esau's grandson.)

פרשת כי תבוא
PARASHAS KI SAVO

The Challenge of Wealth

הַשְׁקִיפָה מִמְּעוֹן קָדְשְׁךָ מִן־הַשָּׁמַיִם וּבָרֵךְ אֶת־
עַמְּךָ אֶת־יִשְׂרָאֵל — *Look down from Your holy abode, from the heavens, and bless Your people, Israel* (26:15).

The word הַשְׁקִיפָה (translated here as *look down*), the Midrash tells us, always has negative connotations — to "cast a hostile eye" on someone or something. Our verse, which voices the prayer recited after successfully dispensing the required tithes from the produce of the field, is the sole exception to this rule, for here it is used to express God's looking down at us to *bless* us. The Midrash expresses it as follows: "Giving *tzedakah* (charity) is so great that it can even transform [God's] Attribute of Strict Justice into His Attribute of Mercy. For הַשְׁקָפָה always has an evil insinuation, while here, where the people do as they were commanded (to give their tithes to the Levites and the poor), it is transformed into a pleasant word."

Why, asks the *Ksav Sofer* in the name of his father, the *Chasam Sofer*, does the Torah use a negative-sounding word here in the first place, only to "correct" it into a positive meaning by adding the words, "and bless Your people"? It would have been much simpler to just use the word הַבִּיטָה (*look*), which has no negative overtones at all, at the outset!

The *Ksav Sofer* answers that prosperity and material blessing can in fact have a negative influence on a person's life. For one thing, the more a person receives material reward for his deeds in this world, the less the spiritual reward that will remain for him in the Next World. Furthermore, wealth often leads its beneficiaries to a lack of fear of God, and consequently to sin, as the Torah itself testifies: "Jeshurun (Israel) grew fat and kicked... and it deserted God, its maker" (*Devarim* 32:15). And: "Take care.. lest you eat and be satisfied, and build good houses and occupy them, and your cattle and flocks increase, and you amass silver and gold ... and your heart becomes haughty and you forget Hashem ... and you say in your heart, 'My own strength and the power of my hands earned me all this wealth!'" (ibid., 8:11-17). Since the true, ultimate purpose of life is to serve God faithfully and to achieve eternal life in the World to Come, it follows that material blessing is in fact *not* good for a person. It is only when one uses his money and resources for the service of God — through giving charity, supporting Torah study, helping the needy, etc. — that his wealth can be a source of true, eternal blessing in the form of spiritual merit.

This, he explains, is why the Torah uses the word הַשְׁקִיפָה, for material prosperity often bears out the negative connotations of this word. But through the giving of *tzedakah* and tithes, the negative aspects of wealth are transformed into positive sources of merit.

פרשת נצבים
PARASHAS NITZAVIM

✌§ Stubborn Resistance

> וְהָיָה בְּשָׁמְעוֹ אֶת־דִּבְרֵי הָאָלָה הַזֹּאת וְהִתְבָּרֵךְ בִּלְבָבוֹ לֵאמֹר שָׁלוֹם יִהְיֶה־לִּי כִּי בִּשְׁרִרוּת לִבִּי אֵלֵךְ — *And it will be that when he hears the words of this curse he will reassure himself in his heart, saying, "I will have peace if I follow the desires of my heart"* (29:18).

*I*t is a testimony to the incredibly stubborn and hedonistic nature of the human soul that a person could still think, after hearing all the horrific curses of the *Tochechah* (*Devarim* 28), that "I will have peace if I follow the desires of my heart"!

A similar sentiment is expressed in *Tehillim* 49:5-7: "I will open my ears to a parable; I will present my allegory with my harp. Why should I fear during days of evil? The sins that I tread upon surround me! Those who rely on their possessions, and boast of their great wealth..."

The verse announces its intention to tell us a "parable and allegory," but there seems to be no parable in sight in the subsequent verses! Rav Yosef Chaim explained that the Psalmist seeks to portray the ludicrousness of those who put their faith and trust in their wealth. Such people may be compared to someone who says, "I have nothing to fear when the 'evil times' come. After all, I am surrounded and protected by my numerous sins, upon which I constantly tread!" This statement, of course, is the height of absurdity — expecting one's sins, of all things, to shield him during times of misfortune! This is the parable that the Psalmist refers to. It is patently obvious that those who trust in their sins for protection are foolish, for sins constitute a source of Divine wrath, not refuge! So, too, it is clear that one cannot put his trust in his wealth, for monetary possessions are often more likely to be sources of spiritual decline, rather than of merit (see previous piece).

◆§ The *Mashiach's* Arrival

וְשָׁב ה' אֱלֹקֶיךָ אֶת־שְׁבוּתְךָ וְרִחֲמֶךָ — *And Hashem, your God, will return your captivity and have mercy on you* (30:3).

his verse forms the basis of our belief in the coming of *Mashiach*, as elaborated subsequently by the prophets (Rambam, *Hil. Melachim* 11:1).

Rav Yosef Chaim used to sign off his letters with, "awaiting the [Messianic] salvation soon," as opposed to the formula, "*looking forward* to the [Messianic] salvation soon," used by others. He elaborated on the difference between the two terms: "Awaiting" (מְחַכֶּה) expresses a situation in which a person waits for his friend to meet him at an certain place, at an appointed time, expecting his imminent arrival. "Looking forward" (מְצַפֶּה), however, suggests a more distant expectation, a hope that something will eventually — not imminently — happen. "I use the former term," he explained, "because I eagerly *await* the coming of the *Mashiach*, every moment of the day, expecting the deliverer to appear and bring eternal salvation!"

Rav Yosef Chaim was once asked by someone attending one of his *shiurim*: "The Gemara says 'The *Mashiach* will only come when [Israel] is unmindful of him (i.e., not thinking about him).' How can such a situation ever be possible, when we mention our desire for the advent of the Messianic era several times a day in our prayers, and recite *Ani Ma'amin* ('I believe with complete faith in the coming of the Messiah') each day?"

"Let me explain to you what 'unmindful' means," responded Rav Yosef Chaim. "If someone would run into shul from the street now and shout, 'Mashiach is here! He is standing right here on Street of the Jews!' — our automatic, instinctive reaction would be to dismiss the report as a delusion. This shows how 'unmindful' we really are of the imminence of Mashiach's arrival!"

On another occasion Rav Yosef Chaim remarked that the arrival of the Mashiach is facilitated through our study of Torah. This fact is alluded to in the verse "Zion will be redeemed through justice, and those who return to her [will be redeemed] through righteousness" (Isaiah 1:27). Zion will be redeemed through justice (צִיּוֹן בְּמִשְׁפָּט תִּפָּדֶה) has the same numerical value as Talmud Yerushalmi (1076), and and those who return to her through righteousness (וְשָׁבֶיהָ בִּצְדָקָה) is equivalent to Talmud Bavli (524)!

The Czech consul in Jerusalem, who maintained a friendly relationship with Rav Yosef Chaim, once asked him, "Why is it that the Jews refer to the Messiah as 'the righteous redeemer' (גּוֹאֵל צֶדֶק, lit., the redeemer of righteousness)?"

"Nowadays," he answered, "all the world leaders and politicians throw words like 'righteousness' and 'justice' around with complete hypocrisy and distortion. The Jewish people pray for the day when the Mashiach will come and act as the 'redeemer of righteousness' — redeeming the word 'righteousness' from its corrupted misusage!"

✑§ An Abode for Hashem

אֲשֶׁר אָנֹכִי מְצַוְּךָ הַיּוֹם לְאַהֲבָה אֶת־ה׳ אֱלֹקֶיךָ לָלֶכֶת בִּדְרָכָיו — *That which I command you today, to love Hashem, your God, to walk in His ways* (30:16).

Rav Yosef Chaim liked to quote the verse, "I will not allow sleep to my eyes nor slumber to my eyelids, before I find a place for Hashem, an abode for the Strong One of Jacob" (Tehillim 132:4-5). Although David was talking about his vow to build a Temple to God without delay, Rav Yosef Chaim saw a different interpretation for the verse as well:

"Each night, before I allow sleep into my eyes, I undergo soul-searching, asking myself: 'What did I do this day to *find a place for Hashem*? Did I find room for God in my busy schedule? Have I contributed to the glory of God today? Have I, through my deeds, made the abode of God's Presence on earth greater than it was previously?' Only after pondering these matters and making the necessary calculations do I deliver my soul into God's hands, so that He might return it to me refreshed the following morning, ready to serve Him and perform His will once again."

Rav Yosef Chaim never kept a list of boys he had circumcised, for he thought it unfavorable to dwell on one's past achievements. Instead, one should concentrate on what he has not yet achieved, on those things that remain to be done.

As an allusion to this idea, he cited the prayer in the *Ma'ariv* service: "Remove Satan (spiritual disruption) from in front of us and from behind us." The *yetzer hara* (man's drive to do what is wrong) tries to dissuade us when a mitzvah opportunity presents itself, saying, "That's not significant enough to bother with. You have more important things to do!" Then, if this approach has failed, and the person did the mitzvah anyway, the *yetzer hara* tries once again to ensnare him in sin by telling him, "Look what a tremendous deed you have done! Now you may congratulate yourself and rest on your laurels. You may also brag to others about your great deeds!" This is why we pray that these enticements — before the deed and after the deed — not deter us from serving Hashem properly and not lull us into a sense of complacency.

‹§ Faithful Soldiers

כִּי הוּא חַיֶּיךָ וְאֹרֶךְ יָמֶיךָ לָשֶׁבֶת עַל־הָאֲדָמָה אֲשֶׁר נִשְׁבַּע ה' לַאֲבֹתֶיךָ — *For it is your life and the length of your days, to dwell upon the land that Hashem swore to your forefathers* (30:20).

*D*uring one of the discussions that Rav Yosef Chaim had with Dr. Chaim Weizmann, he was asked: "What exactly is the contribution of the 'yeshivah man' to our society?"

Rav Yosef Chaim explained that the role of a yeshivah student is similar to that of a soldier. A soldier does not fight wars each moment of the day. It is possible that during all the days of his life he will participate in one actual battle, and many soldiers do not even do that. Nevertheless, the soldier plays an important — indeed, an indispensable — part in the defense of the country by his very existence, because a country can have no security at all without an army.

"The yeshivah student also," continued Rav Yosef Chaim, "by his very existence forms a protective shield for the nation, for 'the Torah protects and saves' (*Sotah* 21a) the Jewish nation from both physical and spiritual dangers. It is a known, established fact that those places in the world that were centers of yeshivos and Torah study preserved their Jewishness, and life in the community at large in these places was led on a higher spiritual and ethical plane."

⋅⋗ A Blessing for the Wicked

כִּי הוּא חַיֶּיךָ וְאֹרֶךְ יָמֶיךָ לָשֶׁבֶת עַל־הָאֲדָמָה אֲשֶׁר נִשְׁבַּע ה' לַאֲבֹתֶיךָ — *For it is your life and the length of your days, to dwell upon the land that Hashem swore to your forefathers* (30:20).

"Fear of God," Rav Yosef Chaim used to say, "is the greatest feeling of happiness and contentment that a person can experience. Nevertheless, I wish this happiness and bliss upon all the sinners of Israel!"

Similarly, he would remark, "Koheles speaks of 'the days of evil'(12:1), referring to a person's old age (see *Shabbos* 151b). Nevertheless, I do not wish this particular form of evil (i.e., longevity) upon any of the enemies of Israel!"

פרשת וילך
PARASHAS VAYEILECH

ও§ The World Will Manage!

וַיִּכְתֹּב מֹשֶׁה אֶת־הַתּוֹרָה הַזֹּאת וַיִּתְּנָהּ אֶל־
הַכֹּהֲנִים בְּנֵי לֵוִי — *Moses wrote this Torah and gave it to the Kohanim, the sons of Levi* (31:9).

av Yosef Chaim kept up a correspondence with the members of his family that he left behind in Czechoslovakia. One of his relatives once asked him what he did for a living, to which he replied that his permanent vocation was the study of Torah.

The relative then posed the question to him: "How could the world survive if everyone would just sit and learn Torah?"

"It is a well-known fact," responded Rav Yosef Chaim, "that the desire to make money and amass wealth is an integral part of all the civilized world, outside of the 'Torah world.' We could ask them the same question you asked me: 'If everyone would become rich, who would take care of the everyday, menial jobs that must be done in order for society to function? Society needs poor people!' Yet, for some reason, everyone still seeks economic advancement and wealth. No one says, 'If, God forbid, everyone becomes rich, who will bake the bread? Who will sew clothing and make shoes?' Somehow there will always be enough poor people to go around. In fact, the Torah guarantees it: 'Poor people will not cease to exist in the land' (*Devarim* 15:11)! The gap between the 'haves' and the 'have-nots' will always be with us, though it would be better for all if it could be narrowed!

"I feel the same way about learning Torah. I am not concerned over the problem that you raise. In fact, it would be the best thing if everyone would devote themselves to Torah study, for then we would all benefit from the blessings and serenity that the Torah promises for those who devote themselves to it!"

◄§ Moses' *Kal Vachomer*

הֵן בְּעוֹדֶנִּי חַי עִמָּכֶם הַיּוֹם מַמְרִים הֱיִתֶם עִם־ה׳, וְאַף כִּי־אַחֲרֵי מוֹתִי — *Behold, even while I am still alive with you today, you have been rebellious against Hashem, so much more so after my death!* (31:27).

This is one of the ten "*kal vachomers*" found in the Torah (*Bereishis Rabbah* 92). A *kal vachomer* is a kind of logical deduction (*a fortiori*), based on the argument, "If something applies in a weaker case, then it certainly applies in a stronger case." The argument Moses presents here is, "If you rebel against God when I am living among you (the weaker case), then certainly there is a danger that you will rebel when I am no longer living (the stronger case)." But the logic of this argument seems to be flawed, taking into consideration the following story from the Talmud (*Sanhedrin* 37a):

There were some troublemakers in Rav Zera's neighborhood, whom he used to befriend in order to try to persuade them to change their ways. The [other] rabbis objected [to Rav Zera's approach]. After Rav Zera died, these troublemakers said, "When Rav Zera was alive he used to pray for us; now that he is gone there is no one to pray for us!" They took the matter to heart, and repented.

In this story we see that the death of their mentor caused these troublemakers to come to the sudden realization that they had no choice but to shape up and become more accountable for their own actions. In the case of Moses, then, the argument that the people would be *more* likely to act rebelliously after his death was not necessarily true!

Rav Yosef Chaim answered this question as follows: When Moses said, "While I am still alive with you today you have been rebellious against Hashem," he was referring specifically to the incident of the Golden Calf, the epitome of rebellion against God. Now, in that incident, the Sages tell us, the people had fallen under the mistaken impression that Moses had died, and therefore did not return at the prescribed time (see Rashi on *Shemos* 32:1). Moses' argument was thus indeed sound: "If you rebelled against God when you only *thought* that I was dead, then certainly you have the capacity to do so when I am *actually* dead!"

פרשת האזינו
PARASHAS HA'AZINU

⊷§ Looking at Future Generations

וַיַּרְא ה׳ וַיִּנְאָץ מִכַּעַס בָּנָיו וּבְנֹתָיו. וַיֹּאמֶר אַסְתִּירָה פָנַי מֵהֶם אֶרְאֶה מָה אַחֲרִיתָם כִּי דוֹר תַּהְפֻּכֹת הֵמָּה בָּנִים לֹא־אֵמֻן בָּם — *Hashem will see and grow angry from the provocation of His sons and daughters. He will say, "I shall hide My face from them and see what their end will be; for they are a generation of capriciousness, children without trust"* (32:19-20).

ne night Rav Yosef Chaim was walking down one of the alleyways of the old city when he was approached by a certain Zionist leader by the name of Ben Hillel, who had been raised as an Orthodox Jew before he became "secularized" and rejected religion, and who now served as chairman of the Zionist National Council. He greeted the Rav and said to him condescendingly, "Rav Chaim, you are known to be a wise man, full of understanding and keen insight. Can't you see, with all your wisdom, that the future belongs to the new, modern generation, who have turned away from all those outdated, obsolete laws and traditions? Anyone who looks at matters objectively can see that this trend of modernization and enlightenment is a process that cannot be stopped by any force in the world! In another twenty or thirty years your kind of people, with their old-fashioned views, will disappear completely. Is it worth it for you to wage such a passionate, tireless battle against your fellow Jews over those few more years that your kind will survive? Do you really delude yourself into thinking that your grandchildren will follow in your path? They, too, will have to attend regular schools, if they don't want to lag behind!"

Rav Yosef Chaim was taken aback by the man's chutzpah, but did not hesitate with his response, uttered with equal conviction and confidence. "And are *you* so sure that your children will follow in *your* ways? On the contrary, I am quite certain that your grandchildren will end up going to yeshivos and rejecting all your barren, false ideologies! I tell you that your descendants will one day open their eyes and realize the hollowness and shallowness of your new, 'modern' beliefs that you have invented. They will cry out, 'Indeed, it was all falsehood that our ancestors inherited; futility that has no purpose' (*Jeremiah* 16:19)."

"And what makes you so sure of *that* unlikely prediction?" Ben Hillel asked him.

"It is stated clearly in the Torah," answered the Rav. " 'Hashem will see and grow angry from the provocation of His sons and daughters.' Why, it is asked, does the verse use the Name of God 'Hashem,' which indicates God's Attribute of Mercy, when speaking of His anger and His becoming provoked? It would have been more fitting to use 'Elokim,' the Name used to indicate His Attribute of Strict Justice! The answer is that although God will be angered by the Jews' adopting new, invented ideologies (v. 17), He will not lash out at them and destroy them. Rather, employing his Attribute of Mercy, He will grant them a reprieve, during which time He will stand by: 'I shall hide My face from them and see what their end will be.' The reason for this is that it is clear to Him that this lapse in His people's faith will not last long: 'For they are a generation of capriciousness (or *reverses*).' By the time the next generation comes around, they will reverse the disastrous course of their ancestors. They are 'children without trust' — a new generation, that gives no credence to the spurious beliefs of their parents! They will realize the emptiness of these new doctrines and will search for something more meaningful — a search that will ultimately lead them back to the rich, fulfilling lifestyle of their forefathers. They will realize that man is no better than beast if his life has no spiritual content with which to elevate himself above the basic instincts and drives that are common to them."

Ben Hillel had nothing further to say and, somewhat chastened by Rav Yosef Chaim's admonishment, he went on his way. The Rav's grandson — my father — who was accompanying him at the time, turned to him after Ben Hillel's departure and said, "Grandfather, in light of the precipitous decline in observance and mass defections to the Torah that we see going on day after day, do you really believe what you told that man? Do you really think his grandchildren will return to Jewish tradition?"

Rav Yosef Chaim cast a piercing, determined glance at him and answered, "Of course! And you will live to see it!"

And of course, he did live to see the reversal of the process — the advent of the *teshuvah* movement, when rejection of all things Jewish ceased to be stylish and the return of the masses to the tradition of their forefathers became a prominent phenomenon.

פרשת וזאת הברכה
PARASHAS VEZOS HABERACHAH

◈§ No Compromise Possible in Torah

וְלֹא־קָם נָבִיא עוֹד בְּיִשְׂרָאֵל כְּמֹשֶׁה... לְכָל־הָאֹתֹת וְהַמּוֹפְתִים אֲשֶׁר שְׁלָחוֹ ה' לַעֲשׂוֹת בְּאֶרֶץ מִצְרָיִם... וּלְכֹל הַיָּד הַחֲזָקָה וּלְכֹל הַמּוֹרָא הַגָּדוֹל אֲשֶׁר עָשָׂה מֹשֶׁה לְעֵינֵי כָּל־יִשְׂרָאֵל — *Never again has there arisen in Israel a prophet like Moses... with all the signs and wonders that Hashem sent him to perform in the land of Egypt... and with all the strong hand and great, awesome deeds that Moses performed before the eyes of all Israel. (34:10-12).*

Rashi, commenting on the words "before the eyes of all Israel," writes (based on *Sifrei*): "This refers to the fact that he was moved to shatter the Tablets *before their eyes*, an act that God ultimately approved of (see *Shabbos* 87a)." Why did the Sages see fit to interpret this phrase as a reference to the breaking of the Tablets, and not, as suggested by the simple reading of the words, as a reference to the great miracles that Moses performed *before their eyes*? What was so great about Moses' shattering of the Tablets that would justify including this act on the list of the greatest achievements of his phenomenal career as leader and redeemer of the Jewish people?

The conclusion we must draw from this is that indeed the breaking of the Tablets was one of the most significant feats Moses ever performed. For it imparted an important lesson, one which serves as a source of guidance to the Jewish people throughout the ages. If a time should come when certain leaders seek to "save the Torah" by compromising it through the admixture of other ideologies and branches of wisdom — as happened in the previous generations before our time — the Torah leaders of the generation must rise up and emulate Moses, who declared, upon seeing the Golden Calf, "Whoever is for Hashem, come to me!" (*Shemos* 32:26), and who did not hesitate to shatter the Tablets that had been given to him by God Himself. The Tablets of the Covenant could not coexist side by side with the dancing and merrymaking of Calf-worship. By doing this, Moses laid the foundations of "the strong hand and the great, awesome deeds" upon which the preservation of the Torah throughout the generations would rest. The Torah must be preserved in its pure, unadulterated form, or it cannot exist at all.

In Rav Yosef Chaim's lifetime, many people could not understand or appreciate his harsh, unyielding stance in opposition to any compromise on the purity of unadulterated Jewish tradition and dedication to the Torah. In hindsight, however, it is plain for all to see that it was through his steadfast inflexibility that Torah-true Judaism managed to hold its ground, and in fact went on to prosper and flourish.

מגילת אסתר
MEGILLAS ESTHER

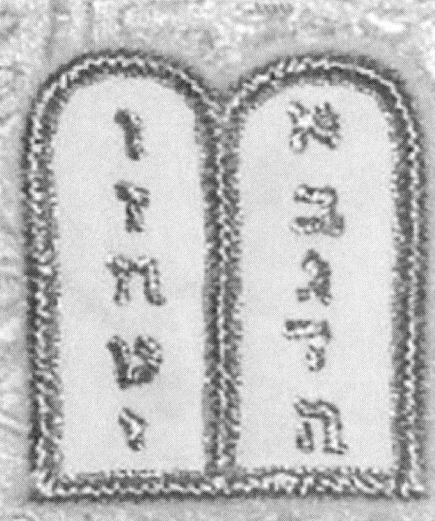

מגילת אסתר
MEGILLAS ESTHER

◆§ Why Mordechai Would not Bow to Haman

וְכָל־עַבְדֵי הַמֶּלֶךְ... כֹּרְעִים וּמִשְׁתַּחֲוִים לְהָמָן... וּמָרְדֳּכַי
לֹא יִכְרַע וְלֹא יִשְׁתַּחֲוֶה. וַיֹּאמְרוּ עַבְדֵי הַמֶּלֶךְ... לְמָרְדֳּכָי
מַדּוּעַ אַתָּה עוֹבֵר אֵת מִצְוַת הַמֶּלֶךְ? וַיְהִי כְּאָמְרָם אֵלָיו
יוֹם וָיוֹם וְלֹא שָׁמַע אֲלֵיהֶם, וַיַּגִּידוּ לְהָמָן לִרְאוֹת הֲיַעַמְדוּ
דִּבְרֵי מָרְדֳּכַי, כִּי־הִגִּיד לָהֶם אֲשֶׁר הוּא יְהוּדִי. וַיַּרְא הָמָן
— כִּי־אֵין מָרְדֳּכַי כֹּרֵעַ וּמִשְׁתַּחֲוֶה לוֹ, וַיִּמָּלֵא הָמָן חֵמָה.
All the king's servants... bowed and prostrated themselves to Haman... but Mordechai did not bow or prostrate himself. So the king's servants said... to Mordechai, "Why are you disobeying the king's command?" Now it happened when they said this to him day after day and he did not heed them, that they told Haman, to see whether Mordechai's words would prevail, for he had told them that he was a Jew. When Haman saw that Mordechai did not bow and prostrate himself to him, Haman was filled with rage (Esther 3:2-5).

There are several obvious difficulties with the narrative related in the above four verses:
(1) The Megillah does not tell us what Mordechai

answered to the king's servants' question, "Why are you disobeying, etc.?"

(2) "Now it happened...that they told Haman." Why did the servants have to tell Haman that Mordechai was not bowing down to him? Why couldn't he see it for himself? Furthermore, below, in 5:13, Haman makes it quite clear that he himself regularly saw Mordechai refusing to bow to him.

(3) What is meant by "to see whether Mordechai's words would prevail"? What words did Mordechai say? The Megillah does not quote a single utterance of Mordechai's until the next chapter! A further question is: What does the following phrase — "for he had told them that he was a Jew" — have to do with what precedes this phrase, i.e., the mysterious "Mordechai's words"?

(4) In what sense did the servants want to see "whether Mordechai's words would prevail"? Did they really have any doubt as to who would win a contest of strength between "Mordechai's words" (whatever they were) and the king's explicit edict to bow to Haman?

Rav Yosef Chaim suggested the following theory to alleviate all these difficulties. First, it is important to note that according to *Targum*, Haman held an idolatrous image in his bosom, so that the edict to bow down to him was in effect a decree involving bowing to an idol. This explains why Mordechai was so adamant about refusing to bow to Haman, for otherwise there does not seem to be any great matter of principle at stake in showing obeisance to a senior government minister. Ibn Ezra, in his commentary on this passage, agrees that Haman carried an idol with him, and attributes this interpretation to the Sages.

Now, it stands to reason that when the king issued his edict to bow to Haman, he did not intend for this requirement to force anyone to violate his religious beliefs. If Haman was wearing or holding an idolatrous image, and this would cause problems for someone, on religious grounds, to uphold the king's ruling, then this would probably be seen as a valid excuse to be exempted from the edict. This, then, is what Mordechai told the king's servants — that, due to his religious convictions as a Jew, he was unable to bow to Haman as long as he had the idol in his hand.

This is why Haman, when he at first saw that Mordechai did not bow to him, did not think much of the matter.

The king's servants, however, decided to put Mordechai's intentions to the test. They advised Haman to remove the idolatrous image once, and pass before Mordechai. If he was telling the truth about his reasons for refraining from bowing, he would have to bow to Haman once he had discarded the idol. In this manner, they wanted "to see whether Mordechai's words would prevail" — whether his story was really true, or was just an excuse for something deeper.

Haman followed the servants' advice, and arrived at the palace the next day without his idol. Yet, he saw that still "Mordechai did not bow and prostrate himself to him." It is interesting to note that in v. 2, it says, "Mordechai did not bow or prostrate himself," while here, in v. 5, it states, "Mordechai did not bow and prostrate himself *to him*," meaning to Haman. Now, unlike previously, the only object of the bowing was Haman, for the idol was no longer present, and nevertheless, Mordechai did not bow, even *to him*. This is why Haman suddenly became "filled with rage," although he had already known previously that Mordechai did not bow to him. This time he realized that Mordechai's behavior was intended as a personal affront to him, and was not due to religious conviction.

≈§ Blood Money

וַיַּגֶּד־לוֹ מָרְדְּכַי אֵת כָּל־אֲשֶׁר קָרָהוּ, וְאֵת פָּרָשַׁת הַכֶּסֶף אֲשֶׁר אָמַר הָמָן לִשְׁקוֹל עַל־גִּנְזֵי הַמֶּלֶךְ בַּיְּהוּדִים לְאַבְּדָם. — *Mordechai told him of all that had happened to him, and the account of the money that Haman had promised to pay to the royal treasuries for the annihilation of the Jews (Esther 4:7).*

The question has been asked: Why did Mordechai see fit to mention the "account of the money"? Was this not a trivial detail when the lives of thousands — perhaps millions — of Jewish lives were at stake? Furthermore, Haman's offer to line the king's coffers with 10,000 silver shekels was actually refused by the king, who told him, "Keep the money for yourself, and do whatever you want with the people anyway" (3:11). This being the case, the "account of the money" — which in fact never materialized — was certainly an irrelevant point to relate to Esther!

Before dealing with this question, let us consider a number of other difficulties. When Esther told Ahasuerus that someone had passed a decree to kill her people, he responded by asking incredulously, "Who is this, and which one is it, who dared to do this?" Ahasuerus knew perfectly well who came up with the idea of exterminating the Jews; he himself had endorsed the plan!

And one more question: Why did Esther tell Ahasuerus, "We have been sold, I and my people, to be destroyed, to be slain and to be exterminated"? As noted above, Haman's offer to pay for the "privilege" of killing the Jews was rejected. The Jews were thus not "sold" in any sense of the word; they were rather "given over" for mass murder.

In order to answer these questions, it is important to bear in mind that according to the Midrash, the greedy Haman was not content to be viceroy; he had his sights set on the ultimate prize — the crown. Eventually he would find a way to get rid of Ahasuerus and usurp the throne from him. (Ahasuerus himself later suspected Haman of subterfuge, as the Megillah records in 7:8.) Rav Yosef Chaim therefore submitted that Haman's offering to pay Ahasuerus for the "privilege" of killing the Jews was part of Haman's plan to oust Ahasuerus. As emperor over 127 countries, and probably hundreds of smaller ethnic groups, agreeing to annihilate a nation for monetary reward was a sure recipe for discontent and rebellion on the part of Ahasuerus's subjects. Which member of an ethnic group would trust a ruler who sells his citizens' life to the highest bidder? Haman therefore sought to undermine Ahasuerus by portraying him as a purveyor of genocide — and publishing this fact to all the nations within the text of the royal edict. This is why Ahasuerus rejected Haman's offer of 10,000 shekels — it was not due to Ahasuerus's disdain for money, to be sure, but out of purely tactical considerations.

Haman, however, double-crossed Ahasuerus, and when the text of the royal edict was drawn up "in accordance to everything that Haman commanded" (3:12), he included the "fact" that the royal treasury was to receive a handsome profit from the operation — although it was not true.

Mordechai found out "all that had been done" by Haman (4:1). As Rashi comments on this verse, Mordechai came by this knowledge through Divine inspiration, for the edict itself had not yet been delivered and was as yet unknown to the public. If he was apprised of the decree of annihilation that had been issued against the Jews, it is logical to assume that he was informed also about the detail of Ahasuerus's supposed monetary prize that was recorded in the edict as well. Thus, when he told Esther about the impending cataclysm that was to befall the Jews, and instructed her to use her influence with Ahasuerus to annul the decree, he also informed her about the crucial fact that Haman had included in the edict the fact that Ahasuerus was receiving payment for the extermination of the Jews. Mordechai knew that Ahasuerus himself would not have given instructions to publicize this fact — even if it might be true — and he realized that the inclusion of this information must have been Haman's diabolical deed. Esther needed to know about this "account of the money," for this would enable her to expose Haman's insidious plot to the king and provoke his rage against him.

This is why Esther told the king, "We have been sold," for according to the information that had been sent out for public knowledge this is exactly what had happened. Now we can understand as well why the king burst out with incredulous outrage, "Who is this, and which one is it, who dared to do this?" He was not referring to the edict involving the mass murder of the Jews, for he knew quite well who was the author of that order. Rather, he wanted to know who inserted the "account of the money" — which was in fact a complete fabrication — into the text of the edict. To this question came Esther's reply, "A man who is an adversary and an enemy! This wicked Haman!" — a response that sealed Haman's fate, and saved the Jewish people.

הגדה של פסח
THE PASSOVER HAGGADAH

הגדה של פסח
THE PASSOVER HAGGADAH

❧ The Splitting of the Sea in the Seder

קַדֵּשׁ וּרְחַץ וכו' — *Recite Kiddush, Wash, etc.*

Some Haggadah commentators ask why it is that the miracle of the Splitting of the Red Sea is not given more prominence in the observances of the Seder. In the formal order of the Seder (קַדֵּשׁ וּרְחַץ וכו'), there is not a single item that even indirectly alludes to this most phenomenal event!

Rav Yosef Chaim pointed out that in fact one of the steps of the Seder does indeed bear an allusion to this miracle. The word כַּרְפַּס (*karpas*, the piece of celery or other vegetable eaten right after Kiddush) is an anagram of an acronym for the phrase כָּל־ סוּס רֶכֶב פַּרְעֹה *all the horses of the chariots of Pharaoh* (*Shemos* 14:9). By dipping the *karpas* into salt water, as is customary, we are commemorating the fact that "all the horses of Pharaoh's chariots" were submerged into the salty waters of the Red Sea!

❧ Paying Guests

כָּל דִּצְרִיךְ יֵיתֵי וְיִפְסַח — *Anyone who needs, let him come and celebrate Pesach (with us).*

One year, the night before Pesach, after having finished his search for *chametz*, Rav Yosef Chaim received an unexpected visit from a group of distinguished visitors from the Budapest Jewish community. At the end of their discussions, the four men expressed their fervent desire to be able to join Rav Yosef Chaim for his Seder the following night.

Realizing the awkwardness and difficulty that their last-minute "self-invitation" might cause, they offered to pay the Rav in advance for all the expenses that might be incurred They were quite surprised when Rav Yosef Chaim immediately, without even a pretense of hesitation, accepted their offer — especially since they had been told in advance by those who knew the Rav that he would never accept money for hosting company. One of the men took out a respectable sum of money from his wallet and handed it to Rav Yosef Chaim.

As the men were about to leave, Rav Yosef Chaim turned to his wife and punned, "Tomorrow, you will have 'four' within your borders!" quoting from *Shemos* 10:4, but substituting אַרְבֶּה (*arbeh* — "locusts") with אַרְבַּע (*arba* — "four").

The men arrived the following night for the Seder as planned. As one of the guests related later, it was the greatest spiritual experience of his life to witness Rav Yosef Chaim's moving perfor-mance of the Seder and its mitzvos.

The morning after the festival day, on the first day of *Chol Hamoed* (the intermediate days of the holiday), Rav Yosef Chaim went to visit the four men in their hotel room. Being residents of Hungary, the four were celebrating *Yom Tov Sheni*, the second day of the holiday that is observed in all lands "outside Israel." The men were quite honored that the Rav had come to spend time with them, and were in fact a bit puzzled as to why he had come. Rav Yosef Chaim and the men chatted a while, and then, as he was taking his leave, he took an envelope out of his pocket and placed it on the table of their room. It contained the money that the four had given him as payment for participating in his Seder meal. Since it was *Yom Tov* (a festival day) for them, they were not permitted to touch the money, and were powerless to force it back upon Rav Yosef Chaim.

The men were now more puzzled than ever. Why had Rav Yosef Chaim taken the money in the first place, only to return it afterwards?

The Rav explained his actions to his bewildered guests. "Pesach is the 'Feast of Freedom,' is it not? What kind of feeling of free-dom can one have when he feels he is imposing on his hosts, by having come to the meal uninvited, and at the last minute? In order to avoid causing you these awkward feelings, and so that you should not hesitate to help yourself to as much food as you might want, I accepted your offer of payment for the meal. However, I did not for a moment consider actually keeping the money. Now, here is the money back. You cannot refuse it now! Take it, and have a good *Yom Tov*!"

✺ Who Administered the Last Plague?

וַיּוֹצִיאֵנוּ ה' מִמִּצְרַיִם – לֹא עַל יְדֵי מַלְאָךְ, וְלֹא עַל יְדֵי שָׂרָף, וְלֹא עַל יְדֵי שָׁלִיחַ, אֶלָּא הַקָּדוֹשׁ בָּרוּךְ הוּא בִּכְבוֹדוֹ וּבְעַצְמוֹ. שֶׁנֶּאֱמַר, וְעָבַרְתִּי בְאֶרֶץ מִצְרַיִם בַּלַּיְלָה הַזֶּה וְהִכֵּיתִי כָל בְּכוֹר בְּאֶרֶץ מִצְרַיִם —

"And Hashem took us out of Egypt" — not through an angel, not through a seraph and not through an agent, but the Holy one, Blessed is he, in His glory, by Himself, as it is said, "And I shall pass through the land of Egypt on this night, and I shall smite every firstborn in the land of Egypt."

*T*he Plague of the Firstborn, the Haggadah tells us here, was administered directly by God, without the use of any sort of intermediary force. This assertion seems to stand in contradiction to an explicit verse in the Torah (*Shemos* 12:23): "Hashem will pass through to strike Egypt, and He will see the blood on the lintel and He will not allow the Destroyer to enter your houses to strike." There was, then, a "Destroyer" — the Angel of Death, presumably — who was involved in administering this plague! How can this be reconciled with the Haggadah's statement that it was carried out by God personally? Indeed, why was it necessary for the Israelites to smear the blood of the Pesach offering on their doorways, if the Plague was meted by God Himself — Who surely did not need any help in identifying the Jewish houses? This powerful question is posed by virtually every Haggadah commentator.

Another question is sometimes raised, pertaining to the Torah's commandment to redeem our firstborn sons (*Shemos* 13:2, 13:15, 22:28, 34:20). This practice is supposed to be a commemoration of the fact that the Israelite firstborn were spared when God struck down all those of the Egyptians (*Shemos* 13:15). The following difficulty thus presents itself: The group of Egyptians killed in the Plague of the Firstborn — and thus the Israelites who were spared from that plague — consisted of both those who were firstborn to their fathers *and* those who were firstborn to their mothers. Yet when it comes to the commandment to redeem the firstborn male child, it applies only to the one "who opens the womb," i.e., the first boy born to his *mother*. How can we account for the discrepancy between the group of people who were the beneficiaries of God's protection on the night of the Plague and the group who are required to undergo the process of "redemption of the firstborn"?

The key to answering these questions, said Rav Yosef Chaim, lies in a passage in the Talmud (*Bava Metzia* 61b):

Why does the Torah mention the Exodus from Egypt when it speaks of not loaning with interest (*I am Hashem, your God, Who took you out of the land of Egypt* — *Vayikra* 25:38), honest weights (ibid., 19:36) and *tzitzis* (*Bamidbar* 15:41)? God is telling us: "I am the One Who discerned between the first issue of the fathers of Egypt (during the Plague of the Firstborn), and am also the One Who will mete out punishment to those who use non-Jewish front-men to lend their own money on interest, to those who store their weights in salt (to increase their weight) and to those who wear *tzitzis* dyed with indigo (rather than real *techeles*)."

Rashi comments on the words, "I am the One Who discerned," that the Gemara refers to a case in which a single Egyptian woman had consorted with several Egyptian men, and had a child by each of them. All these children grew up in their mother's house, but no one — not even the child, and possibly not even his mother, not to mention others outside the family — knew who each child's father was. This was hidden information, much like the knowledge of who is cheating in business or in his religious observances. It was thus only God Who was capable of discerning which Egyptian males were actually firstborn to their fathers, and those who did fit this classification were struck down during the Plague of the Firstborn. No human being — nor even an angel — could have performed this task in place of God.

This is why, as the Haggadah relates, the Plague of the Firstborn was administered directly by God Himself, and not through any intermediary. The use of an agent in this case was impossible, for he would not be able to identify which males were to be stricken. The identity of those males who were firstborn to their *mothers*, however, was certainly known to them, and was common knowledge among all the family's acquaintances as well. Being easily identifiable, it was possible for God to entrust the execution of this Plague to an intermediary, as is His usual manner.

Thus, the Plague of the Firstborn consisted of two distinct components: the smiting of those who were firstborn to their mothers, which was carried out by an intermediary — the "Destroyer" — and the killing of those who were firstborn to their fathers, which was administered by God Himself. This accounts for the apparent contradiction between the Haggadah's assertion that it was "God in His glory by Himself" Who carried out the Plague of the Firstborn, and the Torah's mention of a "Destroyer" who executed the task.

The commandment to commemorate the Plague of the Firstborn by redeeming all male firstborn children relates only to the part of the Plague that was described in *Shemos* 12:23, in which the Destroyer went from house to house, skipping over the houses of the Israelites who had smeared the blood of the paschal lamb over their lintels — and thus relates only to those who are firstborn to their mothers, as explained above.

תפילה
PRAYER

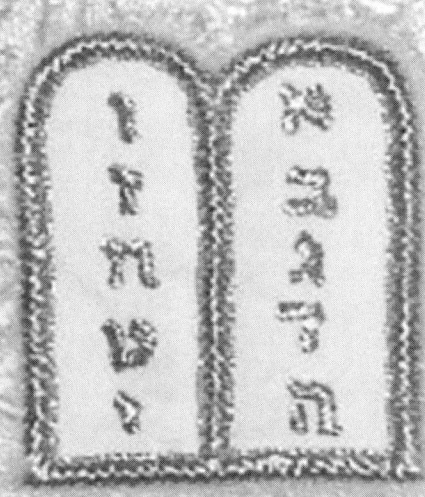

תפילה
PRAYER

*R*av Yosef Chaim provided many interesting explanations for various difficult passages in the prayer liturgy. Among them are the following:

✑§ "Bad Times"

אַב הָרַחֲמִים

In the אַב הָרַחֲמִים prayer recited just before reading from the Torah we ask God to "protect our souls from the bad times (or *hours*)." Just what are these "bad hours" that we seek protection from?

The Gemara (*Kiddushin* 40b) teaches, "A person should always see himself as being exactly half meritorious and half guilty. [In such a situation,] if he does even one mitzvah, fortunate is he, for he tilts the scales of justice in his favor; but if he does even one sin, woe to him, for he tilts the scales of justice against him." Rabbi Elazar beRebbi Shimon goes a step further (ibid.): "The entire world is judged according to the majority [of good vs. evil], just as the individual is. Therefore, if a person does even one mitzvah, he tilts the scale of justice for himself *and for the entire world* in their favor; and if he does even one sin, he tilts the scale of justice for himself *and for the entire world* against them."

The meaning of this phrase cited above, Rav Yosef Chaim suggested, is that we pray to God that if, Heaven forbid, we are ensnared into committing a sin, at least let it not be at such times ("the bad times") when the fate of the entire world is hanging in abeyance and is dependent upon our actions to be judged favorably, for in such a case the results of our deeds would be disproportionately disastrous.

After "All" has Ceased to Be

אֲדוֹן עוֹלָם

One of the lines in the אֲדוֹן עוֹלָם poem states וְאַחֲרֵי כִּכְלוֹת הַכֹּל לְבַדּוֹ יִמְלֹךְ נוֹרָא ("and after all has ceased to be, He, the awesome One, will reign Himself"). The question is asked: If everything ceases to exist, over what will God reign? By definition, "reigning" presupposes the existence of subjects over whom one rules!

The Gemara (*Berachos* 11b) discusses the phrase in the morning prayers, "[God] forms light and creates darkness, makes peace and creates everything." This passage is clearly based on the biblical verse, "[God] forms light and creates darkness, makes peace and creates evil" (*Isaiah* 45:7), except that the word "evil" is replaced with "everything." The reason for this substitution, the Gemara explains, is the desire to avoid the use of the pessimistic, negative-sounding word "evil." The word "everything," of course, includes evil along with everything else in the universe, so that God's creation of evil can be insinuated through this word without mentioning it explicitly.

Here too, said Rav Yosef Chaim, when the poet says, "after all has ceased to be," he does not mean "all" literally, but rather uses it as a euphemism for "evil." In the future, when "all evil will cease as smoke [dissipates]" (Rosh Hashanah liturgy), God will reign over the righteous remnant.

The Most Important Possession

שֶׁעָשָׂה לִי כָּל צָרְכִּי

The blessing "Blessed are You, Hashem, Who has provided me with my every need" is supposed to be recited (see *Berachos* 60b) when one puts on his shoes in the morning (though nowadays the blessing is postponed a bit and is recited in the synagogue). Why is the donning of shoes considered to be the fulfillment of "one's every need" more than any other article of clothing?

The Sages of the Talmud advise us, "A person should make sure he has shoes for his feet, even if he has to sell the beams of his house to get them" (*Shabbos* 129a). Such advice is not given concerning any other possession. We see, then, that owning shoes is considered by the Sages to be of primary importance, and it is for this reason that they refer to it as "my every need."

Rav Yosef Chaim provided a homiletical interpretation of *Tehillim* 8:7-8, in explaining the significance of shoes: "Everything You placed under his [man's] feet — all the sheep and cattle, and even the beasts of the field." When the verse speaks of God placing the animals "under man's feet," said Rav Yosef Chaim, it alludes to the wearing of shoes, which are made of leather produced from animal hides. The wearing of shoes is thus a symbol of man's supremacy over beast and, moreover, of his dominion over all of creation.

✑§ Forgiveness and Healing

רְפָאֵנוּ

In the *Shemoneh Esrei*, the prayer for forgiveness (סְלַח לָנוּ) precedes that for good health (רְפָאֵנוּ). This order is based on a biblical verse (*Tehillim* 103:3): "He forgives all your sins; He heals all your ills" (*Megillah* 17b). In the מִי שֶׁבֵּרַךְ prayer for those who dedicate themselves to community needs, recited before *Musaf* on Shabbos, however, we say, "May God pay them their reward and remove from them all disease and heal all their bodies, and forgive them all their sins." Why is the order reversed in this prayer, with forgiveness preceding good health?

Rav Yosef Chaim answered that the *Shemoneh Esrei* prayer is intended for the requests of the individual. It is recited by every member of the Congregation of Israel, the simple folk and the *tzaddikim* alike. The average person cannot expect God to relieve him of all illness without first seeking forgiveness for his sins, for "there is no such thing as suffering that is not brought on by the committing of a sin" (*Shabbos* 55a). First one must repent and seek God's pardon for his sins; only then can he hope to rid himself of physical suffering and disease. The מִי שֶׁבֵּרַךְ prayer, however, is directed towards those who devote themselves to the needs of the community. In order for them to perform their indispensable tasks, they must be healthy and energetic, for otherwise their performance would decline, and the welfare of the entire community would suffer as well. Thus we pray that even if these individuals are not fully deserving to be blessed with good health on their own merit, the merit of the community as a whole should be enough to provide them with the physical well-being that is necessary for their continued functioning in their sacred tasks.

⋖§ Specific or General Request?

רוֹפֵא חוֹלֵי עַמוֹ יִשְׂרָאֵל

In the *Shemoneh Esrei* blessing that beseeches God to heal all our ills, the ending states, "Blessed are You, Who heals the sick of His people Israel." A similar ending is found in the אֲשֶׁר יָצַר blessing recited after attending to the needs of nature: "Blessed are You, Who heals all flesh." Why does the *Shemoneh Esrei* prayer limit its praise of God to being the Healer of "the sick of Israel," while the אֲשֶׁר יָצַר blessing uses the more general formula, "Who heals *all flesh*" — referring to all of mankind, without respect to nationality, creed, etc.?

The Gemara (*Megillah* 17b) discusses the order of the various blessings of *Shemoneh Esrei*: "Why did the Sages see fit to establish the prayer for healing (רְפָאֵנוּ) as the eighth blessing? To correspond to circumcision (which requires healing), which is performed on the eighth day." Since the *Shemoneh Esrei* blessing is patterned after the mitzvah of circumcision, explained Rav Yosef Chaim, it limits itself to addressing only those who are bound by this mitzvah — the people of Israel. The אֲשֶׁר יָצַר blessing, however, which begins with אֲשֶׁר יָצַר אֶת הָאָדָם בְּחָכְמָה "Who fashioned man with wisdom" — discusses God's wisdom in the creation of mankind in general, and thus ends off praising God as the One "Who heals *all* flesh."

⋖§ Reciting the Thirteen Attributes — Problem and Solution

י״ג מדות

A certain rabbi once expressed wonderment (or displeasure) with the widespread custom by which the congregation interrupts the reading of the Torah on fast days and proclaims aloud the "Thirteen Attributes of Mercy" (in *Shemos* 34:6-7) when the reader gets to that point in the Torah. The congregation's interjection concludes with the end of the Thirteen Attributes, right in the middle of verse 7. This practice seems to contradict the rule that one may not split up the verses of the Torah in any manner other than that which was established by Moses when he wrote the

Torah (*Megillah* 22a). Either the congregation should be told to continue their recital to the end of the verse, or the practice should be discontinued altogether, argued the rabbi, but the custom as it stands seems to be in opposition to the halachah.

Rav Yosef Chaim responded to the rabbi that the custom in question is actually an ancient one (mentioned by Rav Yehudah HeChasid, and even earlier sources), and, being moreover a universally practiced custom in Israel, should not be tampered with. He proposed two possible reasons why the halachah that forbids splitting up verses in the middle might not apply here.

First, the Gemara teaches us that God Himself demonstrated to Moses how the Thirteen Attributes should be recited in praying for God's mercy. In the words of the Gemara, "He wrapped Himself up [in a *tallis*] like a leader of the prayers in the synagogue (שְׁלִיחַ צְבּוּר) and showed Moses the procedure" Since God Himself declared the Thirteen Attributes using these exact words, Rav Yosef Chaim argued, this sets the passage off as a separate, independent unit, and, as such, the halachah against subdividing verses into smaller units does not apply to this case.

The second approach he proposed was that since the reader in any event repeats the Thirteen Attributes and carries on reading to the end of the verse and beyond, he is considered to be completing the verse on behalf of the congregants, so that the verse is, in effect, recited in its complete form.

◆§ The Crown of Prayer

קְדוּשַׁת כֶּתֶר

Rav Yosef Chaim prayed according to the Ashkenaz version of the prayers (נוּסַח אַשְׁכְּנַז), but he enjoyed occasionally visiting a synagogue on Shabbos in which the Sephardic version was used, because he liked their version of the *Musaf Kedushah*, which begins with the word כֶּתֶר (*Crown*).

He pointed out an interesting allusion that lies hidden in the word כֶּתֶר itself. There are nineteen blessing in the weekday *Shemoneh Esrei*. Since we recite this prayer three times daily, this means that we recite 57 blessings in our daily prayers. (*Shemoneh Esrei* is the main prayer of the service, and is often referred to in the Talmud as simply, "the prayer.") Adding another two times for the repetition of the *Shemoneh Esrei* by the *chazan* gives us a total of 95 blessings (5 x 19) each day, or 570 (6 x 95) for the entire week (not including Shabbos). On Shabbos there are four "*Shemoneh Esrei*" prayers, consisting of seven blessings each, for a total of 28 blessings for Shabbos prayers. Adding in the three more "*Shemoneh Esreis*" of the "*chazan's* repetition" gives us a grand total of seven "*Shemoneh Esreis*" over the course of Shabbos, making 49 (7 x 7) blessings altogether for Shabbos prayers. Adding the 570 blessings of the weekday sum to the 49 of the Shabbos sum, we get a total of 619. But there is also a "mini-*Shemoneh Esrei*" (מֵעֵין שֶׁבַע) recited by the *chazan* on Friday night, consisting of one blessing, bringing the final total to 620. This is also the numerical value of the word כֶּתֶר. We are thus declaring in *Musaf* that now, at the culmination of the weekly blessing-cycle, we on earth bless God with כת"ר (620 blessings), just as the angels above crown Him (כֶּתֶר יִתְּנוּ לְךָ... מַלְאָכִים) with their praises.

⇜§ The "Tribes of Israel" and Yom Kippur

סָלְחָן לְיִשְׂרָאֵל וּמָחֲלָן לְשִׁבְטֵי יְשֻׁרוּן בְּכָל דּוֹר וָדוֹר

Just before the conclusion of the main blessing of the Yom Kippur "*Shemoneh Esrei*," we praise God as "the Forgiver of Israel and the Pardoner of the tribes of Jeshurun in every generation." The "tribes of Jeshurun (or Israel)" are not mentioned anywhere else in the prayers. What is their particular relevance to Yom Kippur?

It is known that the brothers of Joseph were never fully forgiven for having sold him into slavery. Rather, the forgiveness for this sin comes gradually, and each year on Yom Kippur a bit more of the guilt for this transgression is erased. This is the reason that the prayer אֵלֶּה אֶזְכְּרָה, which describes the "ten martyrs killed by the Romans (עֲשָׂרָה הֲרוּגֵי מַלְכוּת)" as a punishment for the selling of Joseph, is recited specifically on Yom Kippur.

With this in mind, we can readily understand the relevance of the motif of "the tribes of Jeshurun" to Yom Kippur, for on this day every year a bit of the sin of the original progenitors of the twelve tribes is forgiven.

ארץ ישראל
ERETZ YISRAEL

ארץ ישראל
ERETZ YISRAEL

◆§ The Good Land

כִּי ה׳ אֱלֹקֶיךָ מְבִיאֲךָ אֶל־אֶרֶץ טוֹבָה — *For Hashem, your God, is bringing you to a good Land (Devarim 8:7).*

av Yosef Chaim was one of those rabbis who followed in the footsteps of the illustrious Torah giants of the recent past, in whom burned a passionate love for the Land of our forefathers — the Vilna Gaon, the Baal Shem Tov — and the *Chasam Sofer*. The pioneers and builders of Torah Judaism in *Eretz Yisrael* like Rav Yosef Chaim had an emotional attachment for the Land that went far beyond the connection a person feels to his home or property. Their love for *Eretz Yisrael* knew no bounds, and overshadowed all other considerations in their lives. With rigid determination they came to settle the Land, despite the staggering hardships that were associated with such a move in those days — endemic poverty, disease — and, perhaps worst of all, a high rate of child mortality. We have already related that Rav Yosef Chaim himself lost eight of his eleven children, the names and dates of death of each of them tearfully recorded in the back cover of his pocket *Mishnayos*.

A neighbor and student of his once told him about Rav Naftali

Hertz, at that time the rabbi of Yafo, who, before embarking from Europe for Palestine, declared, "I hereby accept upon myself all sorts of hardship that I may encounter in *Eretz Yisrael*. Even if I have to go begging for bread, I will accept this fate with love, just so that I may merit to live in the Holy Land." Rav Yosef Chaim, not impressed by the story, said, "I don't understand what is so unusual about this. I would be prepared to suffer much more than that to live in *Eretz Yisrael!*"

When he arrived in *Eretz Yisrael*, he literally had no place to lodge at first, and spent his first four nights sleeping outdoors, together with his wife, in an enclosed courtyard. It was only on a Friday afternoon that he managed to find a half-built apartment to which he could "move in."

The security situation in those days was perilous. Even in the cities people lived in fear of the robbers and murderers who lurked on the outskirts of the town. It was not unusual for an Arab to force a Jew to carry him on his shoulders to his destination. Whenever an Arab passed a Jew he would spit at him.

In *Tehillim* 37:3 we read, "Trust in Hashem and do good; dwell in the Land and nourish yourself (lit., *graze*) with faith." A prerequisite for living in *Eretz Yisrael*, Rav Yosef Chaim used to say, is trusting in Hashem, "grazing" on faith in Him. One must realize that he will have to content himself with the bare minimum in terms of material comforts. *Eretz Yisrael* is, after all, one of the three precious items that one can enjoy only after much suffering (*Berachos* 5a). (The other two are Torah and entrance to the Next World.)

While Rav Yosef Chaim was full of unbridled enthusiasm over the development and rebuilding of *Eretz Yisrael* from its ruins and the reclamation of its wastelands, he was equally outspoken against the dominant Zionist Organization and its avowed secularist leadership, which sought aggressively to assert its control over all the affairs of the Jewish community — including the Old Orthodox community.

Rav Yosef Chaim would explain his somewhat paradoxical outlook with a parable:

There was once a marriage broker who arranged a wonderful match between an only son and an only daughter, both fine young people from established, wealthy families. The bride was beautiful and graceful, the groom skilled and well mannered. Both sides were delighted with the matchmaker's work, and approached him to discuss the fee for his services. But whatever sum they offered did not seem to satisfy the matchmaker's greedy ears. He dismissed all their suggestions out of hand. Finally, they asked him, "Well, what *do* you want in return for your services?"

"I'm sure you will agree," said the matchmaker, "that the match I have arranged here is priceless. There is no amount of money that can be said to be a fair payment for my work. What I expect for my services, therefore, is the bride herself!"

The moral of the parable, Rav Yosef Chaim explained, is as follows: The Zionists do splendid work. They spare no toil or expense in their supreme efforts to replace desolation with rejuvenation, to establish new settlements and communities efficiently and successfully. But, like the matchmaker in the parable, what they seek in return for their work amounts to the very undermining of their own accomplishments. "What do we need *Eretz Yisrael* for?" he asked. "What's wrong with America, or any other country in the world, where a Jew can go and assimilate and live happily ever after? The answer is given by King David: 'He gave them the lands of nations and they took possession of the toil of peoples, so that they could observe His laws and keep His teachings' (*Tehillim* 105:44-45). The gift of *Eretz Yisrael* is intended for one purpose only: to provide a means through which we might better serve Hashem. The Zionists, however, have taken the means and transformed it into an end in itself. But they have not sufficed with distorting the import and function of *Eretz Yisrael*; they have taken upon themselves the uprooting of all traditional Judaism and the Torah as their ultimate goal in 'modernizing' the Jewish people."

The numerical value of מְשַׂמֵּחַ צִיּוֹן בְּבָנֶיהָ (*He brings joy to Zion through [the return to her] of her children* — a phrase from the liturgy), Rav Yosef Chaim noted, is 613 — the number of mitzvos in the Torah. Zion is comforted by the return of her lost flock only if it is accomplished through the rubric of the 613 mitzvos of the Torah!

⋅⋅§ Rebuilders of Jerusalem

Rav Yosef Chaim was full of joy when he saw a new building going up in Jerusalem. In the last summer of his life, when he was already too weak to get around on foot, he would often travel by automobile to see the new neighborhoods of Jerusalem firsthand. There was practically no neighborhood that he did not visit at least once.

Whenever he passed through the new city, his face would radiate delight. "The Builder of Jerusalem is Hashem!" (*Tehillim* 147:2)," he would declare.

One time, he expressed his excitement over a certain beautiful new building while taking a walk in the Talbiyeh neighborhood. One of those accompanying him said to him, "Rebbe, that building belongs to non-Jews!"

"So what?" responded the Rav. "Their forefathers participated in the destruction of this land; should they not be obliged to participate in its rebuilding as well?!" He then added, "Don't worry. All these beautiful, luxurious houses will one day be ours."

He waved his hand towards the new part of Jerusalem that was undergoing extensive construction at the time, and declared with great pleasure and satisfaction, "I remember when all this land was complete wasteland, a place where only wolves would tread. And now I have merited to see all this land built up and blossoming!"

⋅⋅§ Aliyah's Importance —
Especially for the Religious

Rav Yosef Chaim's position on the settlement of *Eretz Yisrael* was sometimes misunderstood, or misrepresented. A Hungarian Jew by the name of Professor Pattai, on a visit to Palestine, recorded the following interview with Rav Yosef Chaim in the Hungarian-language weekly magazine of which he was editor:

Professor: "In Hungary, people say that you are the enemy and opponent of the new Jewish settlement in *Eretz Yisrael*."

Rav Yosef Chaim: "Heaven forbid! Do you think that I forgot the words of the *Sifrei* that 'dwelling in *Eretz Yisrael* is equal to all the other mitzvos'? Or the fact that the Sages said, 'I prefer a small group of Jews living in *Eretz Yisrael* to a Sanhedrin in *Chutzah La'aretz* (outside of *Eretz Yisrael*)'? Time and time again I have issued requests and instructions to emissaries to tell the Orthodox Jews abroad that whoever is capable of moving to *Eretz Yisrael* and does not do so will one day have to give an account for his laxity in this matter! I am opposed only to the antireligious spirit of the new settlement movement, for the Holy Land must be built with holiness. I once told Dr. Weizmann, 'If "because of our sins we were exiled from our land" (*Siddur*), how do you expect a return and redemption of our land anew without Torah and without faith?'"

Professor: "But there are those who say in your name that a religious Jew must *not* go to live in *Eretz Yisrael*!"

Rav Yosef Chaim: "Heaven forbid! It is specifically the religious Jews who must move to *Eretz Yisrael* and participate in its rebuilding in purity and holiness, for the Land is waiting for them to redeem it from its ruins! As for the others (nonreligious Jews) — it is written, 'There will come to Zion a redeemer, and for those who repent from sin in Jacob.' First there will be a redemption of Zion, and then the sinners will repent. I believe that for every pioneer who participates in the building of the Land, the merit of *Eretz Yisrael* will provide him with the privilege of eventually repenting. The people who came with Ezra and Nehemiah to resettle *Eretz Yisrael* thousands of years ago were also not the greatest *tzaddikim*, as the Bible makes clear. They did not keep Shabbos or the holidays properly, they intermarried with the non-Jewish residents, etc. Yet, despite this, the Temple was built through the efforts of these people, and they eventually repented and mended their ways. It was from these people that the Maccabis and the Tannaim and Amoraim descended!"

✒ Who is a Native of *Eretz Yisrael*?

Rav Yosef Chaim was very strict — for himself and for others —

about following government regulations, filling out documents, declarations, etc. with the utmost honesty, no matter how urgent the need might be to "stretch the truth" a bit to the authorities. Nevertheless, when someone came to ask him if it was permissible to testify in court that a certain person was born in *Eretz Yisrael*, so that he could be issued automatic permission to enter Palestine (for only native-born Jews were exempted from the "Jewish immigration quota" and were allowed automatic entrance to Palestine by the British), Rav Yosef Chaim answered, "Not only *may* you, but you *must* do so!"

Rav Yosef Chaim explained his position. "This is not really a lie at all. The verse says (*Tehillim* 87:5): 'To Zion will be said: A man and a man were born in her.' The Talmud (*Yevamos* 75a) explains: '[The two times it says *man*] refer to those who were born in her and those who look forward to seeing it [rebuilt].' Thus, we see that for any Jew who desires to come to live in *Eretz Yisrael*, it is as if he actually was born there!"

⋞§ Clear the Path

In Iyar 5689 (1929), a groundbreaking ceremony was held for the new neighborhood of Neveh Shaanan, with the participation of the rabbis of Jerusalem, headed by Rav Yosef Chaim. Some of Rav Yosef Chaim's remarks, as recalled by one of those present at the occasion, were:

The Gemara (*Sanhedrin* 102b) teaches, "Why is it that Omri (an evil king of Israel) merited kingship? Because he added on one city to *Eretz Yisrael*, as it says, 'He bought the mountain Shomron from Shemer for two talents of silver, and he called the name of the city that he built there "Shomron," after Shemer, the [previous] owner of the mountain.'"

From this we can learn how great is the merit of those who involve themselves in settling *Eretz Yisrael* — sufficient merit to be granted dominion on its account! In our days we see that the Zionists are adding on cities and settlements in *Eretz Yisrael*, and this certainly provides them with points of merit in their favor, which have earned them the right to governance and dominion. It is possible that by this merit indeed they will one day, even before the Messiah, attain such dominion in *Eretz Yisrael.*

If this is indeed going to happen, it is of the utmost importance for us to build and establish neighborhoods and settlements that are based on pure Torah values, which can serve as a counterbalance to their work. For it is only through the building up of *Eretz Yisrael* by religious Jews that we will be able to counteract the actions of those who seek to empty the Land of all its holiness

After finishing his address, he turned to the audience and declared, "*Pave, pave the path; clear it from stones* (Isaiah 62:10)! Let every person now remove 53 stones, according to the numerical value of אֶבֶן (*stone*)!"

With the energy and verve of a young man, the elderly rabbi hopped off the speaker's platform onto the site, bent down and began clearing away stones. The entire assembly soon joined in with enthusiasm, all the while chanting, "Pave, pave the path; clear it from stones." Before long an entire path through the site had been cleared.

◄§ See No Evil

There were very few tourists from abroad visiting Jerusalem who did not take advantage of the opportunity to stop in to visit the famed rabbi in his Battei Machaseh home. Each visitor discussed his impressions of the great Holy City, etched into the imagination of every Jew from earliest childhood. Whenever someone would express a negative opinion about some facet of the city that disappointed him, Rav Yosef Chaim would interrupt and say, "Please, take note only of the good things in Jerusalem, for it says, 'See the good of Jerusalem' (*Tehillim* 128:5)!"

He provided a *gematria* to go along with this verse as well: טוב יְרוּשָׁלָיִם (*the good of Jerusalem*) has the numerical value of 613. This indicates that it is only in Jerusalem that one has the capability of fulfilling all 613 mitzvos of the Torah, many of which deal with sacrifices and related matters, which can be observed only in the Temple.

⋙ Protection from Peril

On Friday, the 17th of Av, 5689 (1929), the Arabs of *Eretz Yisrael* began the infamous "riots of 1929 (תרפ״ט)," which culminated the next day, Shabbos, with the murder of 59 Jews — including 29 yeshivah students — in Hebron. After the Friday prayers at the Al-Aqsa mosque on the Temple Mount ended, thousands of frenzied Moslems — incited by the Mufti's inflammatory, hate-filled sermon — marched through the Old City, exiting through *Sha'ar Shechem* (Damascus Gate), heading towards the Meah Shearim and Beis Yisrael quarters, and chanting "Itbah al-Yahud" (*"Kill the Jews!"*). Fright, bordering on hysteria, seized the women and children of these neighborhoods, as word was received of the approaching mob. The men grabbed whatever instruments they could get their hands on — poles, axes, pipes, etc. — to defend themselves and their homes from the marauders. The few Haganah men posted at the entrance of the neighborhood were at a loss as to how to deal with the huge, bloodthirsty mob, which was making its way down St. George Street (now named *Shivtei Yisrael*), headed by a sword-wielding sheikh who egged them on with shouts of "Jihad!" and "No mercy on women and children! Kill all the Jews!"

Suddenly a young Charedi fellow by the name of Alperstein (not his real name; see *Ha'ish Al Hachomah of Jerusalem*, vol. 3, for the fascinating details) emerged from the flour mill at the entrance of Meah Shearim (which served as the Haganah's guard station) and, accompanied by just one other man, confronted the approaching mass of seething rioters. He took out a pistol, aimed it at the sheikh, and fired one shot at his head, killing him instantly. The mob was suddenly seized with panic when they saw that their leader had been slain, and turned on their heels, running back towards *Sha'ar Shechem*. Several of them were trampled to death in the ensuing stampede.

The next day, Shabbos, Rav Yosef Chaim had been scheduled to perform a circumcision in Meah Shearim. Everyone, including the Rav's family, took it for granted that he would not dare to undertake the perilous walk from the Old City to Meah Shearim; it was so obvious that no one even discussed it. How surprised they were, then, when Rav Yosef Chaim put on his frock after *Kiddush* on Shabbos morning and announced that he was going to the *bris*! They shouted and protested, but to no avail. Rav Yosef Chaim had made up his mind. The mitzvah of circumcision would protect him from harm for, as the Sages taught, "Those who travel on a mission to do a mitzvah will experience no harm, neither on their way there nor on their way back" (*Pesachim* 8b).

Since the Rav was already 80 years old, some of his acquaintances decided to accompany him. When they arrived at Street of the Jews, at the end of the Jewish quarter, Rav Yosef Chaim turned to them and told them to go back, for he saw that they were gripped with terror. As they turned to walk back home, they were shocked to see Rav Yosef Chaim head down the street leading to *Sha'ar Shechem* — *which was considered "treacherous terrain" even in the best of days* — *rather than the safer "Bazaar Street" route, which led to Sha'ar Yafo (Jaffa Gate)*. And so, following the very same path that the bloodthirsty rioters had trodden less than twenty-four hours previously, the Rav made his way toward Meah Shearim, confidently and proudly, buoyed by the happy thought that he would soon be bringing "another Jew into God's legion," as he liked to put it.

The first residents of Meah Shearim who noticed the distant black-clad figure walking down St. George Street stared in amazement and fear as the old Jew confidently strode along. As soon as they realized who it was that was coming, they burst out in shouts of joy. Within minutes hundreds of residents assembled to greet Rav Yosef Chaim as he safely entered the neighborhood. Among them were his grandchildren, who promptly invited him to spend the rest of Shabbos with them, so that he would not have to retrace his steps through "enemy territory."

After the *bris*, Rav Yosef Chaim stopped by his grandchild's house to visit for a while, and then bid farewell, as he put on his hat and prepared to head home. The scene of the early morning replayed itself. The family members vehemently protested, arguing that coming to the *bris* was bad enough, but now there was certainly no longer any reason to undertake such a perilous journey. Once again, however, Rav Yosef Chaim's persistence won out in the end. "Those who travel on a mission to do a mitzvah experience no harm, even on their way back," he reminded them. As he began walking down the street toward the edge of Meah Shearim, thousands of residents poured out of their houses to accompany him to the "border." When they reached the Italian hospital (now the Education Ministry, on the corner of Shivtei Yisrael and Nevi'im Streets), the crowd took their leave of the beloved rabbi and watched him as he began to walk, briskly and proudly toward *Sha'ar Yafo!*

Why did he insist on going to the *bris* through *Sha'ar Shechem*? he was later asked. "So that the Arabs should not think that they succeeded in driving out Jewish passersby from even one corner or street of Jerusalem!" he explained. And why did he return through *Sha'ar Yafo*? "This has always been my custom, to leave the Old City through *Sha'ar Shechem* and to return through *Sha'ar Yafo*, to fulfill the verse, 'Walk about Zion and encircle it' (*Tehillim* 48:13)!"

◂§ The Greatest Praise

Rav Yosef Chaim once wrote, "I have no Torah or wisdom to my credit. The only distinction I can apply to myself is that I had the merit, by God's grace, of living my life in the Holy City of Jerusalem."

In his will, he left instructions that no one should eulogize him, and that no one should say anything more than, "Pity the loss of an old *Eretz Yisrael* Jew." For Rav Yosef Chaim that was the ultimate praise!

This volume is part of
THE ARTSCROLL SERIES®
an ongoing project of
translations, commentaries and expositions
on Scripture, Mishnah, Talmud, Halachah,
liturgy, history, the classic Rabbinic writings,
biographies and thought.

For a brochure of current publications
visit your local Hebrew bookseller
or contact the publisher:

Mesorah Publications, ltd

4401 Second Avenue
Brooklyn, New York 11232
(718) 921-9000
www.artscroll.com